THE FILMS OF
RON HOWARD

BY: MICHAEL JOLLS

Praise for Michael Jolls'

THE FILMS OF
STEVEN SPIELBERG

"The book examines in great detail the filmography of one of the most prolific filmmakers that has ever lived."
- Adam C. Better, *Amblin Road*

"An interesting introduction to Spielberg's background, interests, motivations, and collaborations."
- Heather L. Barksdale, *Heather's Bookshelf*

"*The Films of Steven Spielberg* is packed so full of information in such a quick read, that unlike *Jaws*, you won't need a bigger boat… or a longer book."
- Kris Galvan, *@parkedinfrontofthescreen*

"Michael Jolls really displays his love for film, as well as his love for the great and unforgettable directors that we've had over the years."
- *The Awesome Pardon Show*

"Highly recommended for film buffs, students and those who are just fascinated by a man that shaped cinema."
- Luke Andrews, *The Media Diorama*

"A fantastic and interesting read!"
- Alex Fernandes, *@Movie_Geek98*

"Once you start reading it, it is hard to put it down. 5/5!"
- Aakanksha Jain, *Books Charming*

"I was impressed with the depth of the research into this man, his life, and the films he produced."
- Storeybook Reviews

Praise for Michael Jolls'

MAKE HOLLYWOOD GREAT AGAIN

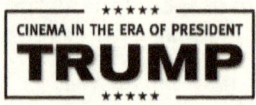

"A smart and in-depth analysis of cinema in the modern political age, demonstrating the extent of Jolls' passion for, and understanding of, cinema as a vehicle for politics."

- **Kate Taylor,** *Kate Reviews Films*

"Michael Jolls' knowledge on cinema and politics extends far and wide in his deeply analytical guide to the importance of filmmaking at the highest level. If there was ever a manuscript which needed to be adhered to when creating films with thoughtful principles, *Make Hollywood Great Again* is most definitely one. Whether for the fans that are fond of cinema or just casual moviegoers, Jolls' latest book will most certainly shed a light on several striking issues in the industry."

- **Sach Harshan,** *The Films Critic*

"Very insightful read. I couldn't put the book down! Brilliant job by Michael Jolls."

- **Anna Brigitta,** *@conservativegirly*

"A fascinating, well-researched, and balanced examination of the ever-evolving relationship between the rhetoric of modern cinema and modern politics."

- **Will Jones,** *Film Fanatic 44*

THE FILMS OF
RON HOWARD

BY: MICHAEL JOLLS

Released: August 2024

ISBN-13: 9798327235731

TABLE OF CONTENTS

Preface..13
Directing Credits..21
Chapter 1: Before the Debut..39
Chapter 2: Authorship: Themes in Ron Howard's Films......49
Chapter 3: Never Making the Same Film Twice................63
Chapter 4: Against All Odds..77
Chapter 5: The Common Individual................................89
Chapter 6: Romance..101
Chapter 7: Strong Feminine Characters........................111
Chapter 8: Partnership/Duality: Opposites Attract........133
Chapter 9: Family...155
Chapter 10: The Ensemble Cast....................................167
Chapter 11: Automotive, Music & Religion..................183
Chapter 12: Authenticity...213
Acknowledgements..241
Producing Credits: Produced by Ron Howard...............245
Imagine Entertainment..249
Endnotes..253
Index..265

PREFACE

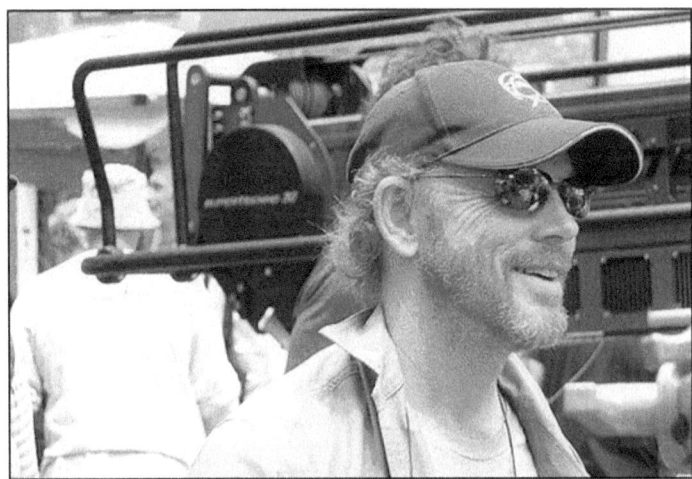

Ron Howard in 2008 on the set of *Angels & Demons* in Rome, Italy.

On account of my own personal penchant of knowing what lead an author to write a book before getting into the thick of it, I'm going to speak in the first person, but only for this segment. Apologizes in advance for my own self-indulgent recap of how and why *The Films of Ron Howard* came to fruition.

Without a doubt, this book does not do justice for what Howard has given us in over forty years of filmmaking. Added to this, Howard is not some sort of niche director whose avant-garde films are only watched by the beau monde class in art-house theatres. Rather, Howard has remained a figure in American pop-culture since the 1960s thanks to his acting career, yet his directing compatriots have been the subject of multiple academic studies. In the timespan it took me to complete this book, Ron Howard was in his late-60s and moved into the septuagenarian club, placing him in the same age range as other mainstream filmmakers who continue to pump out movie after movie at approximately the same level of consistency. The Coen Brothers, Spike Lee, Steven Spielberg and Quentin Tarantino — each have been the subject of *a few* books devoted to their cinema. Even the younger Darren Aronofsky, David Fincher, Christopher Nolan and M. Night Shyamalan have garnished more than one volume of academic attention, yet Howard remains with little commentary from high-brow cinephiles and professors. Meanwhile, Sean Baker, Kathryn Bigelow, Sofia Coppola or Terrence Malick are easier to examine movie-to-movie as there are stretches of time between the various releases, whereas the likes of Woody Allen, Clint Eastwood or Ridley Scott take longer because of how fast their work flow has been. Ron Howard belongs in the latter category as he's constantly working and regularly makes unexpected shifts in the subjects he covers. I'm old enough to remember when Ron Howard wasn't affiliated with documentaries. There are those who at one time only associated him with comedies before the heavy-handed dramas came along. There are fewer who only remember him hanging out with Fonzie on *Happy Days* before they associated the title of "director" with him. And, there are still those that remember little Opie from *The Andy Griffith Show* — long before Richie Cunningham's happy days, the comedies, the dramas and the documentaries.

The process of researching a mainstream Hollywood director takes an exorbitant amount of time, and while I enjoy reading and collecting materials (border-line hoarding if we're being honest), the scope required for a filmography the size of Howard's would take years. Although I consider *The Films of Ron Howard* a watered-down version of what could (and should) be done for Howard's résumé, this concise version still took much longer than I desired.

Technically this all began in April of 2009 before the release of *Angels & Demons*. An assignment for a college class led me to embark on a little directorial authorship research of Mr. Howard's cinema for a presentation, which is where I came up with my own analysis of his motifs and themes. Although my fixation has always been on filmmaking, I loved soaking up whatever I could on the topics of authorship and film theory, making the prospect of writing about film in an academic medium a really cool idea, but not something I was ever going to pursue. And a chance to do something about Ron Howard akin to the authorship books I was reading was a mere pipe dream.

Several term papers later, plus an occasional film academia project here and there, not to mention editing and then knocking out a few books of my own that fell under the genre of directorial authorship was all just enough to keep that silly little Ron Howard book idea alive for nine years… and then…

In early of May 2018, a website hired me to do an article on Ron Howard in anticipation of *Solo: A Star Wars Story*. I had a narrow window of time to complete the article, possibly overextending myself, but I couldn't resist taking the job, so I crammed the task into an already tight schedule. Luckily, I had just gotten hired for a very simple part-time job to make a little extra cash, and this quiet job allowed me to toss movies on while I "worked" (i.e. sat on my butt) and filled up a notebook with observations. I was able to speed watch and revisit each of Howard's directorial studio features in the three-week time frame I had to write this article. By the time I was finished, submitted in the article, I placed that notebook next to my little Ron Howard collection of BluRays and DVDs thinking: *This actually might work for book, but I need a break. Maybe I'll revisit this idea later in the summer.*

So… two and a half years later… I'm in the middle of doing something and I see that notebook on the shelf. It's not like I lost it — haven't you ever not registered what was right in front of you, or became blind to it? I had caught *Pavarotti* in its brief theatrical run in the summer of 2019, but that was over a year ago. It was November 2020, I see this notebook and it hit me: *Wow, Opie's got another movie coming out in a week,* [*Hillbilly Elegy*], *and yet, still,* **no one** *has done something on him???* (And yes, I already had pre-purchased a ticket for opening night. No, of course I didn't care that *Hillbilly Elegy* was going to be available via streaming a few weeks later. Ron Howard is one of several filmmakers I'm adamant about seeing the new releases on the big screen if and whenever possible).

    I had read Beverly Gray's excellent book, *Ron Howard: From Mayberry to the Moon… and Beyond*, a couple years prior and as of 2024, her book is the only other serious work of academia out there. A hybrid of biography and film studies, Gray's book remains the best commentary on the director thus far, but I'm surprised that there hasn't been more. In the Fall of 2021, Ron and Clint Howard's memoir *The Boys* released, but that was focused on their growing up in a successful show business family. *The Boys* doesn't offer much by way of Howard's directorial authorship – or even answered my own curiosity of why Howard gravitates to the themes seen repeatedly in his canon. Although there are films that are inspired by Howard's family history, particularly *Parenthood*, and later *Far and Away*, he is not an autobiographical filmmaker to the extent Scorsese or Spielberg have been.

    Flipping through my notebook, I was struck by how direct my own verbiage was. Although brazenly and hastily written, it read like an abridged film course. When I wrote that article over two years ago, I had re-watched the films in order of release, which meant that this notebook told a story: the development of a director honing his craft movie to movie, thereby rendering a full retrospective about the development of artist. The production backstories, the box-office numbers and the critical reception of each title was not needed; this pseudo-narrative I inadvertently wrote didn't warrant that information. I decided to use the notebook as the base and began to expand on my observations to finally do *this* book. (If I could put the "eye-roll" emoji here, I would.)

    By the end of November 2020, I had already begun the process of purging the BluRays & DVD special features, as well as the audio commentaries to ensure I didn't write something factually incorrect and help fine-tine my analysis with any worthwhile anecdotes. I spent six months researching and writing *this* book, but inevitably life got in the way, and by Spring 2021 I was regulated to the "chipping away" method. The infamous "chipping away" approach successfully made the prospect of getting *this* book finished a new year's resolution for 2022, 2023 and, yes, 2024. Three years in a row of waking up on January 1st thinking: *This is gonna be the year!*

Originally envisioned to be a collection of short essays on each of Howard's films in order of release, the book got progressively more laborious to write. There was some cross-pollination in discussing the films, and the book did flow well until… well, until it didn't. I could sense *this* book was hardening into cement. I got to the halfway point on Howard's directorial resume, which is the beginning of the 2000s decade, and had a strange desire to stop altogether... which was weird because I didn't want to stop. This wasn't writer's block, rather the book simply stopped being fun to write. It felt like a chore. Laborious. Cumbersome. A labor of love is one thing, (and I love Ron Howard's films, and I love film academia), but something was wrong. Unbalanced. I don't think it took me longer than two days, three at most, to realize and accept that I was essentially doing *this* book incorrectly. I needed to pull out the chain saw and reconstruct around the themes. This wasn't discouragement or a reckless emotionally charged decision. Reaffixing *this* book around the motifs simply clicked. It instantly made a lot more sense. Why? Well… a short chapter on the comedy of *Gung Ho*, followed by a short chapter about fantasy via *Willow*, followed by a short chapter on a hybrid of family, comedy and drama in *Parenthood*, followed by a short chapter on heavy handed drama in *Backdraft*… that's a lot of topic changing. Mental whiplash.

It was long after I made the decision to restructure *this* book that I was reviewing the behind-the-scenes of *Inferno* and there was a remark Howard made with regards to the three Robert Langdon films: that he never wants to make the same film twice. (If you would kindly imagine the "ding, ding, ding" of a boxing bell going off when I heard Howard say that). All three of the Robert Langdon movies have a different tone: *The Da Vinci Code* dabbles in the historical folklore; the aesthetic of *Angels and Demons* is a high-octane thriller; and *Inferno* wants to be a horror film. Therein lied what the crux of the problem with trying to do *this* book in a movie-to-movie narrative structure.

As Howard has continued to direct into the 1990s, the subjects he tackles got increasingly complex. In the mid-2000s, he gradually gets more geopolitical – all the while constantly reinventing himself. As of this writing in summer 2024, Howard is reportedly in post-production on his first animated film and his most recent documentary, *Jim Henson: Idea Man*, seems like a dress rehearsal for an animated film. Despite his exploration of different genres, the easiest way to unlock Ron Howard's films is by examining the motifs we see him return to again and again. We can take a silly comedy from the 1980s, and then turn to a drama from the 2000s, and instantly recognize Howard's authorship.

To be clear, I am such a big Ron Howard fan that I hope someone comes along and does a thorough examination of his work. Maybe it's being worked on now? I'm waiting for the *Conversations with Filmmakers Series* to announce an "interviews" volume. Or maybe *BFI Classics* or *Director's Cuts* are working on something? (Hint, hint, to those publishing houses.) Until that happens, I decided to take a crack at it. Again, I will be the first to say that *The Films of Ron Howard* lacks some of the finite detail I believe Howard's work is worthy of, but hopefully you will complete this "film course" with a richer appreciation for his movies and any future releases.

This book was written by a filmmaker who understands the production process and will not go out of his way to brandish flaws. Yes, of course out of 33 movies there are ones I prefer more than others, but I've downplayed my own criticisms. Technically there are 36 titles if we count the made-for-tv movies which are occasionally referenced. The intention of *The Films of Ron Howard* is to extract themes and enrich the reader with an appreciation of Howard's cinema. This book examines the films "directed by" Ron Howard, not his entire résumé. Therefore, the "produced by" credits and the acting years are not critically assessed. The way in which we'll ebb and flow through this "film course" is in no way intended to suggest favoritism of the various titles. Howard's biography was researched in preparation for, and throughout the writing of this book. Many additional sources were consulted throughout the assembly of this book. Aside from the first chapter, we won't be making any deep dives into behind-the-scenes production details.

I've gone out of my way to differentiate between "actor" and "character," defaulting for the actor or actresses' name as much as possible. For example, with regards to *Willow*, I use "Val Kilmer" instead of "Madmartigan," as the reader tends to recall the Hollywood performer's face rather than the character's name. Do not feel obliged to watch all of Howard's directorial features before continuing to read this book. I'll strive to be articulate as possible, although potential spoilers are openly discussed. Sometimes pre-reading about a film before you watch can enhance the viewing experience.

Finally, this book was not presented to Ron Howard or Imagine Entertainment in advance, although should a copy of this book ever come into his possession, I sincerely hope Mr. Howard enjoys my interpretation of his excellent cinema.

DIRECTING CREDITS

GRAND THEFT AUTO
New World Pictures
Released: June 16th, 1977 (U.S.A.)
Directed by: **Ron Howard**
Written by: Rance Howard & **Ron Howard**
Produced by: Roger Corman, Laurence Cruickshank, Jon Davison, Rance Howard
Director of Photography: Gary Graver
Edited by: Joe Dante
Art Direction and Production Management: Keith Michl, Mike Finnell and Harry Wowchuk
Music by: Peter Ivers
Starring: **Ron Howard**, Nancy Morgan, Elizabeth Rogers, Barry Cahill, Paul Linke, Rance Howard, Marion Ross, Peter Isacksen, Hoke Hawell, James Ritz, Jack Perkins and Clint Howard
Production Budget: $602,000
Box Office: $15 million worldwide (approximate)
Running Time: 1 hour and 24 minutes
MPAA Rating: PG

COTTON CANDY
Major H Productions and National Broadcasting Company
Released: October 26th, 1978 (television U.S.A.)
Directed by: **Ron Howard**
Written by: Clint Howard & **Ron Howard**
Produced by: John Thomas Lenox and Rance Howard
Casting: Barbara Hanley and Cathy Henderson
Director of Photography: Robert Jessup
Edited by: Robert James Kern
Art Direction & Production Designer: Cyndy Sverson and Norm Gray
Music by: Joe Renzetti
Starring: Charles Martin Smith, Clint Howard, Leslie King, Kevin Lee Miller, Manuel Padilla Jr., Dean Scofield, Mark Wheeler, Alvy Moore and Joan Crosby
Production Budget: $1.1 million
Running Time: 1 hour and 37 minutes
MPAA Rating: Not Rated

SKYWARD
Anson Productions and National Broadcasting Company
Released: November 20th, 1980 (television U.S.A.)

Directed by: **Ron Howard**
Written by: Nancy Sackett, Anson Williams (story)
Produced by: **Ron Howard**, John A. Kuri and Anson Williams
Casting: Bobby Hoffman
Director of Photography: Robert Jessup
Edited by: Robert James Kern
Art Direction: Jack Marty
Music by: Lee Holdridge
Starring: Suzy Gilstrap, Bette Davis, Howard Hesseman, Marion Ross, Clu Gulager, Ben Marley, Lisa Shelchel, Irma P. Hall and Mark Wheeler
Running Time: 1 hour and 40 minutes
MPAA Rating: Not Rated

THROUGH THE MAGIC PYRAMID

Alternate Titles: "*The Time Crystal*" | "*Tut and Tuttle*"
Major H Productions and Time-Life Video
Released: December 6th, 1981 (television U.S.A.)
Directed by: **Ron Howard**
Written by: Rance Howard and Herbert Wright
Produced by: Rance Howard, **Ron Howard**, John A. Kuri, Russell Vreeland and Herbert Wright
Director of Photography: Gary Graver
Edited by: Robert James Kern
Art Direction and Set Decoration: Bryan Thetford and John A. Kuri
Music by: Joe Renzetti
Starring: Chris Barnes, Hans Zonried, Vic Tayback, Olivia Barash, Betty Beaird, Gino Conforti, Elaine Giftos, Eric Greene, James Hampton, Robbie Rist, Kario Salem and Joe Anne Worley
Production Budget: $1 million
Emmy: Outstanding Children's Program (nomination)
Running Time: 1 hour and 37 minutes
MPAA Rating: Not Rated

NIGHT SHIFT

The Ladd Company, Major Studio Partners, Warner Bros.
Released: July 30th, 1982 (U.S.A.)
Directed by: **Ron Howard**
Written by: Lowell Ganz & Babaloo Mandel
Produced by: Brain Grazer & Don Kranze
Casting: Jane Jenkins
Director of Photography: James Crabe
Edited by: Daniel P. Hanley, Mike Hill and Robert Kern Jr.
Production Design, Art Direction and Set Decoration: Jack T. Collis, Peter Landsdown Smith and Richard C. Goddard
Music by: Burt Bacharach
Starring: Henry Winkler, Michael Keaton, Shelley Long, Gina Hecht, Pat Corley, Bobby DiCicco, Nita Talbot, Basil Hoffman, Tim Rossovich, Clint Howard and Joe Spinell

Production Budget: $8.1 million
Golden Globe: Best Actor (nomination)
Box Office: $21.0 million U.S.A.
Running Time: 1 hour and 46 minutes
MPAA Rating: R

SPLASH

Touchstone Pictures
Released: March 9th, 1984 (U.S.A.)
Directed by: **Ron Howard**
Written by: Brian Grazer (story); Bruce Jay Friedman, Lowell Ganz and Babaloo Mandel
Produced by: Brain Grazer & John Thomas Lenoz
Casting: Bill Shepard
Director of Photography: Donald Peterman
Edited by: Daniel P. Hanley & Mike Hill
Production Design, Art Direction and Set Decoration: Jack T. Collis, John B. Mansbridge, Norman Rockett and Philip Smith
Music by: Lee Holdridge
Starring: Tom Hanks, Daryl Hannah, John Candy, Eugene Levy, Dody Goodman, Shecky Greene, Richard B, Shull and Bobby Di Cicco
Production Budget: $8 million
Academy Awards: Best Original Screenplay (nomination)
Golden Globe: Best Picture (nomination)
Box Office: $69.8 million U.S.A.
Running Time: 1 hour and 51 minutes
MPAA Rating: PG

COCOON

20th Century Fox, Zanuck/Brown
Released: June 21st, 1985 (U.S.A.)
Directed by: **Ron Howard**
Written by: David Saperstein (story); Tom Benedek
Produced by: David Brown, Robert Doudell, Lili Fini Zanuck and Richard D. Zanuck
Casting: Penny Perry
Director of Photography: Donald Peterman
Edited by: Daniel P. Hanley & Mike Hill
Production Design and Set Decoration: Jack T. Collis and Jim Duffy
Music by: James Horner
Starring: Wilford Brimley, Don Ameche, Hume Cronyn, Brain Dennehy, Jack Gilford, Jessica Tandy, Maureen Stapleton, Steve Guttenberg, Tahnee Welch, Herta Ware, Linda Harrison, Barret Oliver, Tyone Power Jr. and Gwen Verdon
Production Budget: $17.5 million
Box Office: $76.1 million U.S.A. | $85.3 million worldwide total
Academy Awards: Best Supporting Actor and Best Visual Effects (won)
Golden Globe: Best Picture (nomination)

Running Time: 1 hour and 57 minutes
MPAA Rating: PG-13

GUNG HO

Paramount Pictures
Released: March 14th, 1986 (U.S.A.)
Directed by: **Ron Howard**
Written by: Edwin Blume (story); Lowell Ganz and Babaloo Mandel
Produced by: Deborah Blum, Lowell Ganz, Tony Ganz, **Ron Howard**, Jan R. Lloyd and Babaloo Mandel
Casting: Karen Rea
Director of Photography: Donald Peterman
Edited by: Daniel P. Hanley & Mike Hill
Production Design, Art Direction and Set Decoration: James L. Schoppe, Jack G. Taylor Jr. and John H. Anderson
Music by: Thomas Newman
Starring: Michael Keaton, Gedde Watanabe, George Wendt, Mimi Rogers, John Turturro and Dennis Sakamoto
Production Budget: $18 million
Box Office: $36.5 million U.S.A.
Running Time: 1 hour and 53 minutes
MPAA Rating: PG-13

WILLOW

Metro-Goldwyn-Metro, Lucasfilm, Imagine Entertainment
Released: May 20th, 1988 (U.S.A.)
Directed by: **Ron Howard**
Written by: George Lucas (story); Bob Dolman
Produced by: Joe Johnston, George Lucas and Nigel Wooll
Casting: Janet Hirshenson & Jane Jenkins
Director of Photography: Adrian Biddle
Edited by: Daniel P. Hanley, Mike Hill, and Richard Hiscott
Production Design and Art Direction: Allan Cameron, Tim Hutchinson, Jim Pohl, Tony Reading, Kim Sinclair and Malcolm Stone
Music by: James Horner
Starring: Warwick Davis, Val Kilmer, Joanne Whalley, Jean Marsh, Patricia Hayes and Bill Bartly
Production Budget: $35 million
Box Office: $57.2 million U.S.A.
Academy Awards: Visual Effects & Sound Editing (nominations)
Running Time: 2 hours and 6 minutes
MPAA Rating: PG

PARENTHOOD

Universal Pictures & Imagine Entertainment
Released: August 2nd, 1989 (U.S.A.)

Directed by: **Ron Howard**
Written by: **Ron Howard** (story); Lowell Ganz & Babaloo Mandel
Produced by: Joseph M. Caracciolo & Brian Grazer
Casting: Janet Hirshenson & Jane Jenkins
Director of Photography: Donald McAlpine
Edited by: Daniel P. Hanley & Mike Hill
Production Design, Art Direction and Set Decoration: Todd Hallowell, Christopher Nowak and Nina Ramsey
Music by: Randy Newman
Starring: Steve Martin, Mary Steenburgen, Dianne Wiest, Jason Robards, Rick Moranis, Harley Kozak, Tom Hulce, Martha Plimpton, Keanu Reeves, Joaquin Phoenix and Helen Shaw
Production Budget: $20 million
Box Office: $100 million U.S.A. | $126.2 million worldwide total
Academy Awards: Best Supporting Actress & Best Original Song (nominations)
Golden Globes: Best Actor, Best Supporting Actress and Best Original Song (nominations)
Running Time: 2 hours and 4 minutes
MPAA Rating: PG-13

BACKDRAFT

Imagine Entertainment, Trilogy Entertainment Group, and Universal Pictures
Released: May 24th, 1991 (U.S.A.)
Directed by: **Ron Howard**
Written by: Gregory Widen
Produced by: Raffaella DeLaurentiis, Pen Densham, Larry DeWaay, Brian Grazer, Todd Hallowell, Richard B. Lewis, and John Watson
Casting: Janet Hirshenson & Jane Jenkins
Director of Photography: Mikael Saloman
Edited by: Daniel P. Hanley & Mike Hill
Production Design, Art Direction and Set Decoration: Albert Brenner, Carol Winstead Wood, Garrett Lewis
Music by: Hans Zimmer
Starring: Kurt Russell, William Baldwin, Robert De Niro, Jennifer Jason Leigh, Scott Glenn and T.J. Walsh
Production Budget: $40 million
Box Office: $77.8 million U.S.A. | $152.3 million worldwide total
Academy Awards: Best Visual Effects, Best Sound and Best Sound Editing (nominations)
BAFTA: Best Visual Effects (nominations)
Running Time: 2 hours and 17 minutes
MPAA Rating: R

FAR AND AWAY

Imagine Entertainment and Universal Pictures
Released: May 22nd, 1992 (U.S.A.)

Directed by: **Ron Howard**
Written by: **Ron Howard** (story); Bob Dolman (also story)
Produced by: Larry DeWaay, Bob Dolman, Brian Grazer, Todd Hallowell, **Ron Howard**, and Louisa Velis
Casting: John Hubbard, Ros Hubbard, and Karen Rea
Director of Photography: Mikael Saloman
Edited by: Daniel P. Hanley & Mike Hill
Production Design, Art Direction and Set Decoration: Allan Cameron, Jack T. Collis, Jack Senter and Richard C. Goddard
Music by: John Williams
Starring: Tom Cruise, Nicole Kidman, Thomas Gibson, Robert Prosky, Barbara Babcock and Cyril Cusack
Production Budget: $60 million
Box Office: $58.8 million U.S.A. | $137.7 million worldwide total
Running Time: 2 hours and 20 minutes
MPAA Rating: PG-13 for some violence and sensuality

THE PAPER

Imagine Entertainment and Universal Pictures
Released: March 25th, 1994 (U.S.A.)
Directed by: **Ron Howard**
Written by: David Koepp & Stephen Koepp
Produced by: Brain Grazer, Todd Hallowell, David Koepp, Aldric La'auli Porter, Dylan Sellers, Louisa Velis and Frederick Zollo
Casting: Janet Hirshenson & Jane Jenkins
Director of Photography: John Seale
Edited by: Daniel P. Hanley & Mike Hill
Production Design, Art Direction and Set Decoration: Todd Hallowell, Maher Ahmad, and Debra Schutt
Music by: Randy Newman
Starring: Michael Keaton, Robert Duvall, Glenn Close, Marisa Tomei, Randy Quaid, Jason Robards, Jason Alexander, Catherine O'Hara, Roma Maffia and Geoffrey Owens
Production Budget: $6 million
Box Office: $38.8 million U.S.A. | $48.4 million worldwide total
Academy Awards: Best Original Song (nomination)
Running Time: 1 hour and 52 minutes
MPAA Rating: R for strong language

APOLLO 13

Imagine Entertainment and Universal Pictures
Released: June 30th, 1995 (U.S.A.)
Directed by: **Ron Howard**
Written by: William Broyles Jr. & Al Reinert, based off the book *Lost Moon* by Jim Lovell & Jeffrey Kluger
Produced by: Michael Bostick, Brain Grazer, Todd Hallowell, Aldric La'auli Porter, Louisa Velis and Lorne Orleans
Casting: Janet Hirshenson & Jane Jenkins

Director of Photography: Dean Cundey
Edited by: Daniel P. Hanley & Mike Hill
Production Design, Art Direction and Set Decoration: Michael Corenblith, David J. Bomba, Bruce Alan Miller and Merideth Boswell
Music by: James Horner
Starring: Tom Hanks, Bill Paxton, Kevin Bacon, Gary Sinise, Ed Harris, Clint Howard and Kathleen Quinlan
Production Budget: $52 million
Box Office: $173.8 million U.S.A. | $355.2 million worldwide total
Academy Awards: Best Editing, Best Sound (won); Best Picture, Best Supporting Actor, Best Supporting Actress, Best Adapted Screenplay, Best Art Direction, Best Score and Best Visual Effects (nomination)
Golden Globe: Best Picture, Best Director, Best Supporting Actor and Best Supporting Actress (nomination)
BAFTA: Best Production Design, Best Visual Effects (won); Best Cinematography, Best Editing and Best Sound (nomination).
Running Time: 2 hours and 20 minutes
MPAA Rating: PG for language and emotional intensity

RANSOM

Touchstone Pictures & Imagine Entertainment
Released: November 8th, 1996 (U.S.A.)
Directed by: **Ron Howard**
Written by: Richard Price & Alexander Ignon; story by Cyril Hume & Richard Maibaum
Produced by: Brian Grazer, Kip Hagopain, Todd Hallowell, Reba Merrill, Susan Merzbach, Aldric La'auli Porter, Scott Rudin, Adam Schroeder and Louisa Velis
Casting: Janet Hirshenson & Jane Jenkins
Director of Photography: Piotr Sobocinski
Edited by: Daniel P. Hanley & Mike Hill
Production Design, Art Direction and Set Decoration: Michael Corenblith, John Kasarda, Susan Bode
Music by: James Horner
Starring: Mel Gibson, Rene Russo, Barwley Nolte, Gary Sinise, Delroy Lindo, Liv Schreiber, Donnie Wahlberg and Lili Taylor
Production Budget: $80 million
Box Office: $136.4 million U.S.A. | $309.4 million worldwide total
Golden Globe: Best Actor (nomination)
Running Time: 2 hours and 1 minute
MPAA Rating: R for graphic bloody violence and strong language

EDTV

Universal Pictures & Imagine Entertainment
Released: March 26th, 1999 (U.S.A.)
Directed by: **Ron Howard**
Written by: Émile Gaudreault, Sylvie Bouchard, Lowell Ganz, and Babaloo Mandel

Produced by: Jeffrey T. Barabe, Brian Grazer, Todd Hallowell, **Ron Howard**, Aldric La'aulo Porter, Michel Roy, Richard Sadler and Louisa Velis
Casting: Janet Hirshenson & Jane Jenkins
Director of Photography: John Schwartzman
Edited by: Daniel P. Hanley & Mike Hill
Production Design, Art Direction and Set Decoration: Michael Corenblith, Dan Webster and Merideth Boswell
Music by: Randy Edelman
Starring: Matthew McConaughey, Jenna Elfman, Woody Harrelson, Ellen DeGeneres, Sally Kirkland, Martin Landau, Rob Reiner, Dennis Hopper and Elizabeth Hurley
Production Budget: $80 million
Box Office: $22.4 million U.S.A. | $35.2 million worldwide total
Running Time: 2 hours and 2 minutes
MPAA Rating: PG-13 for sex-related situations, partial nudity, and crude language

HOW THE GRINCH STOLE CHRISTMAS

Universal Pictures & Imagine Entertainment
Released: November 17th, 2000 (U.S.A.)
Directed by: **Ron Howard**
Written by: Jeffrey Price & Peter S. Seaman, based off the book by Dr. Seuss
Produced by: Linda Fields, Brian Grazer, Todd Hallowell, **Ron Howard**, Aldric La'auli Porter, Louisa Velis and David Womark
Casting: Janet Hirshenson & Jane Jenkins
Director of Photography: Donald Peterman
Edited by: Daniel P. Hanley & Mike Hill
Production Design, Art Direction and Set Decoration: Michael Corenblith, Lauren E. Polizzi, Dan Webster and Merideth Boswell
Music by: James Horner
Starring: Jim Carrey, Taylor Momsen, Jeffrey Tambor, Christine Baranski, Bill Irwin, Molly Shannon, Clint Howard, Josh Ryan Evans and Anthony Hopkins
Production Budget: $123 million
Box Office: $260 million U.S.A. | $345.1 million worldwide total
Academy Awards: Best Make-up (won); Best Art Direction and Best Costume (nomination)
Golden Globe: Best Actor (nomination)
BAFTA: Best Make-Up/Hair (won)
Running Time: 1 hour and 44 minutes
MPAA Rating: PG for some crude humor

A BEAUTIFUL MIND

Universal Pictures, DreamWorks Pictures, and Imagine Entertainment
Released: December 21st, 2001 (limited) | January 4th, 2002 (wide, U.S.A.)

Directed by: **Ron Howard**
Written by: Akiva Goldsman, based off the book by Sylvia Nasar
Produced by: Brian Grazer, Todd Hallowell, **Ron Howard**, Karen
 Kehela Sherwood, Kathleen McGill, Maureen Peyrot,
 Aldric La'auli Porter, and Louisa Velis
Casting: Janet Hirshenson & Jane Jenkins
Director of Photography: Roger Deakins
Edited by: Daniel P. Hanley & Mike Hill
Production Design, Art Direction and Set Decoration: Wynn Thomas,
 Robert Guerra and Leslie E. Rollins
Music by: James Horner
Starring: Russell Crowe, Ed Harris, Jennifer Connelly, Paul Bettany,
 Christopher Plummer, Josh Lucas, Adam Goldberg, Anthony
 Rapp, Vivien Cardone and Judd Hirsch
Production Budget: $58 million
Box Office: $170.7 million U.S.A. | $313.5 million worldwide total
Academy Awards: Best Picture, Best Director, Best Supporting
 Actress, and Best Adapted Screenplay (won); Best Actor,
 Best Editing, Best Score and Best Make-Up (nomination)
Golden Globe: Best Picture, Best Actor, Best Supporting Actress and
 Best Screenplay (won); Best Director and Best Score
 (nomination)
BAFTA: Best Actor and Best Supporting Actress (won); Best Film,
 Best Director and Best Adapted Screenplay (nomination)
Running Time: 2 hours and 15 minutes
MPAA Rating: PG-13 for intense thematic material, sexual content and
 a scene of violence

THE MISSING

Revolution Studios, Imagine Entertainment in association with Daniel
 Ostroff Productions
Released: November 26th, 2002 (U.S.A.)
Directed by: **Ron Howard**
Written by: Ken Kaufman, based off the novel by Thomas Eidson
Produced by: Sue Berger, Steve Crystal, Thomas Eidson, Brian Grazer,
 Todd Hallowell, **Ron Howard**, Kathleen McGill, Daniel
 Ostroff, Aldric La'auli Porter and Louisa Velis
Casting: Janet Hirshenson, Jane Jenkins and Jo Edna Boldin
Director of Photography: Salvatore Totino
Edited by: Daniel P. Hanley & Mike Hill; extended cut by Ron
 Vignone
Art Direction and Set Decoration: Guy Barnes & Wendy Ozols-Barnes
Music by: James Horner
Starring: Tommy Lee Jones, Cate Blanchett, Evan Rachel Wood, Jenna
 Boyd, Aaron Eckhart, Val Kilmer, Sergio Calderón, Eric
 Schweig, Steve Reevis and Jay Tavare
Production Budget: $60 million
Box Office: $27 million U.S.A. | $38.3 million worldwide total
Running Time: 2 hours and 17 minutes (extended edition 2 hours and
 34 minutes)
MPAA Rating: R for violence

CINDERELLA MAN
Universal Pictures, Miramax, Imagine Entertainment in association with Parkway Productions
Released: June 3rd, 2005 (U.S.A.)
Directed by: **Ron Howard**
Written by: Cliff Hollingsworth & Akiva Goldsman; story by Cliff Hollingsworth
Produced by: Brian Grazer, Todd Hallowell, **Ron Howard**, Penny Marshall, Kathleen McGill, Louisa Velis and Jamesm Whitaker
Casting: Janet Hirshenson & Jane Jenkins
Director of Photography: Salvatore Totino
Edited by: Daniel P. Hanley & Mike Hill
Production Design, Art Direction and Set Decoration: Wynn Thomas, Peter Grundy, Dan Yarhi and Gordon Sim
Music by: Thomas Newman
Starring: Russell Crowe, Renée Zellweger, Paul Giamatti, Craig Bierko, Paddy Considine, Bruce McGill, Rosemarie DeWitt, David Huband, Connor Price, Ariel Waller and Patrick Louis
Production Budget: $88 million
Box Office: $61.6 million U.S.A. | $108.5 million worldwide total
Academy Awards: Best Supporting Actor, Best Editing and Best Make-Up (nomination)
Golden Globe: Best Actor & Best Supporting Actor (nomination)
BAFTA: Best Original Screenplay (nomination)
Running Time: 2 hours and 24 minutes
MPAA Rating: PG-13 for intense boxing violence and some language

THE DA VINCI CODE
Columbia Pictures and Imagine Entertainment, Skylark Productions, with the support of the government of Malta
Released: May 16th, 2006 (Cannes Film Festival) | May 19th, 2006 (U.S.A.)
Directed by: **Ron Howard**
Written by: Akiva Goldsman, based off the novel by Dan Brown
Produced by: Dan Brown, John Calley, Brian Grazer, Todd Hallowell, **Ron Howard**, Kathleen McGill and Louisa Velis
Casting: Janet Hirshenson & Jane Jenkins
Director of Photography: Salvatore Totino
Edited by: Daniel P. Hanley & Mike Hill
Art Direction and Set Decoration: Allan Cameron, Giles Masters, Tony Reading and Richard Roberts
Music by: Hans Zimmer
Starring: Tom Hanks, Audrey Tautou, Ian McKellen, Jean Reno, Paul Bettany, Alfred Molina, Jürgen Prochnow, Jean-Yves Berteloot, Etienne Chicot and Jean-Pierre Marielle
Production Budget: $125 million
Box Office: $217.5 million U.S.A. | $760 million worldwide total
Golden Globe: Best Original Score (nomination)

Running Time: 2 hours and 29 minutes (extended edition 2 hours and 54 minutes)
MPAA Rating: PG-13 for disturbing images, violence, some nudity, thematic material, brief drug references and sexual content

FROST/NIXON
Universal Pictures, Imagine Entertainment, Working Title Films, Studio Canal and Relativity Media
Released: December 5th, 2008 (limited) | January 23rd, 2009 (wide, U.S.A.)
Directed by: **Ron Howard**
Written by: Peter Morgan, based on the stage play by him
Produced by: David Bernardi, Tim Bevan, Liza Chasin, William M. Connor, Eric Fellner, Brian Grazer, Todd Hallowell, Debra Hayward, **Ron Howard**, Karen Kehela Sherwood, Kathleen McGill, Peter Morgan, Matthew Byam Shaw and Louisa Velis
Casting: Janet Hirshenson & Jane Jenkins
Director of Photography: Salvatore Totino
Edited by: Daniel P. Hanley, Mike Hill and Robert Komatsu
Production Design, Art Direction, and Set Decoration: Susan Benjamin, Michael Coreblith, Brain O'Hara and Gregory Van Horn
Music by: Hans Zimmer
Starring: Frank Langella, Michael Sheen, Kevin Bacon, Rebecca Hall, Toby Jones, Matthew MacFadyen, Oliver Platt and Sam Rockwell
Production Budget: $25 million
Box Office: $18.6 million U.S.A. | $27.4 million worldwide total
Academy Awards: Best Picture, Best Director, Best Actor, Best Adapted Screenplay and Best Editing (nomination)
Golden Globe: Best Picture, Best Director, Best Actor and Best Screenplay (nomination)
BAFTA: Best Film, Best Director, Best Actor, Best Adapted Screenplay, Best Editing and Best Hair & Make-up (nomination)
Running Time: 2 hours and 3 minutes
MPAA Rating: R for some language

ANGELS & DEMONS
Columbia Pictures, Imagine Entertainment, Skylark Productions and Panorama Films
Released: May 15th, 2009 (U.S.A.)
Directed by: **Ron Howard**
Written by: David Koepp & Akiva Goldsman, based off the novel by Dan Brown
Produced by: Dan Brown, John Calley, William M. Connor, Anna Culp, Brain Grazer, Todd Hallowell, **Ron Howard**, Ute Leonhardt, Kathleen McGill, Marco Valerio Pugini and Louisa Velis

Casting: Janet Hirshenson, Jane Jenkins, Michelle Lewitt and Lene Seested
Director of Photography: Salvatore Totino
Edited by: Daniel P. Hanley & Mike Hall
Production Design, Art Direction, and Set Decoration: Larry Bellantoni, Allan Cameron, Alex Cameron, Keith P. Cunningham, Luke Freeborn, Robert Gould, Marc Homes, Giles Masters and Dawn Swiderski
Music by: Hans Zimmer
Starring: Tom Hanks, Ewan McGregor, Ayelet Zurer, Stellan Skarsgård, Pierfrancesco Favino and Nikolaj Lie Kaas
Production Budget: $150 million
Box Office: $133.3 million U.S.A. | $485.9 million worldwide total
Running Time: 2 hours and 18 minutes (extended edition 2 hours and 26 minutes)
MPAA Rating: PG-13 for sequences of violence, disturbing images and thematic material

THE DILEMMA

Universal Pictures, Imagine Entertainment, Spyglass Entertainment and Wild West Picture Show
Released: January 14th, 2011 (U.S.A.)
Directed by: **Ron Howard**
Written by: Allan Loeb
Produced by: William M. Connor, Brian Grazer, Todd Hallowell, **Ron Howard**, Kathleen McGill, Kim Roth and Victoria Vaughn, Vince Vaughn and Louisa Velis
Casting: Janet Hirshenson & Jane Jenkins
Director of Photography: Salvatore Totino
Edited by: Daniel P. Hanley & Mike Hall
Production Design, Art Direction, and Set Decoration: Daniel B. Clancy, Kathy Lucas, R.J. Mangone and Dawn Swiderski
Music by: Lorne Balfe & Hans Zimmer
Starring: Vince Vaughn, Kevin James, Jennifer Connelly, Winona Ryder, Channing Tatum, Queen Latifah, Amy Morton and Chelcie Ross
Production Budget: $70 million
Box Office: $48.4 million U.S.A. | $69.7 million worldwide total
Running Time: 1 hour and 51 minutes
MPAA Rating: PG-13 for mature thematic elements involving sexual content

MADE IN AMERICA

Imagine Entertainment, Marcy Media, Participant, RadicalMedia and Translation
Released: September 5th, 2013 (Toronto International Film Festival)
Directed by: **Ron Howard**
Produced by: Sidney Beaumont, Jacqueline Brewster-Farquhar, Dave Chamberlain, Paul Chibe, Sara Enright, Brian Grazer, **Ron Howard**, Erica Huggins, Jay-Z, Kristin Jones, Jon Kamen,

Meredith Kaulfers, Anthony Lappé, Maura Mandt, Michael
Richard Martin, Walter Matteson, Sarah Namias, Gina
Paradiso, Allison Roithinger, Jed Rothstein, Alec Sash,
Jonathan Silberberg, Jeff Skoll, Steve Stoute, Diane
Weyermann and Justin Wilkes
Director of Photography: Salvatore Totino
Edited by: Joshua L. Pearson
Music by: Drazen Bosnjak
Starring: Jay-Z, Janelle Monáe, Jill Scott, Rita Ora, Kanye West, Eddie
Vedder, Tyler the Creator, Joseph Simmons, Gary Clark Jr.,
Skrillex, Santigold and Andrew Wyatt
Running Time: 1 hour and 33 minutes

RUSH

Exclusive Media Group, Cross Creek Pictures, Imagine Entertainment,
Revolution Films, Working Title Films, Double Negative
Released: September 12th, 2013 (limited, international markets) |
September 20th, 2013 (limited, U.S.A.)
Directed by: **Ron Howard**
Written by: Peter Morgan
Produced by: Tobin Armbrust, Tim Bevan, Ralph Brosche, Guy East,
Andrew Eaton, Eric Fellner, Brain Grazer, Jim Hajicosta,
Todd Hallowell, Daneil Hetzer, **Ron Howard**, Mark
Mallouk, Peter Mallouk, Jens Meurer, Peter Morgan, Kay
Niessen, Brian Oliver, Anita Overland, Gernot Schaffler,
Nigel Sinclair, Tyler Thompson and Louisa Velis
Casting: Nina Gold
Director of Photography: Anthony Dod Mantle
Edited by: Daniel P. Hanley & Mike Hill
Production Design, Art Direction, and Set Decoration: Michael Day,
Mark Digby, Katrina Mackay, Patrick Rolfe and Chris Wyatt
Music by: Hans Zimmer
Starring: Chris Hemsworth, Daniel Brühl, Olivia Wilde, Alexandra
Maria Lara, Pierfrancesco Favino, Natalie Dormer and
Christian McKay
Production Budget: $38 million
Box Office: $26.9 million U.S.A. | $96.9 million worldwide total
Golden Globe: Best Picture & Best Supporting Actor (nomination)
BAFTA: Best Editing (won); Best British Film, Best Supporting Actor
and Best Sound (nomination)
Running Time: 2 hours and 3 minutes
MPAA Rating: R for sexual content, nudity, language, some disturbing
images and brief drug use

IN THE HEART OF THE SEA

Warner Bros., Village Roadshow Pictures, RatPac-Dune Entertainment
Released: December 3rd, 2015 (Europe) | December 11th, 2015 (U.S.A.)
Directed by: **Ron Howard**
Written by: Charles Leavitt, Rick Jaffa, and Amanda Silver, based off

the book by Nathaniel Philbrick
Produced by: David Bergstein, Bruce Berman, Sarah Bradshaw,
William M. Connor, Brain Grazer, **Ron Howard**, Erica
Huggins, Steven Mnuchin, Palak Patel, Joe Roth, Will Ward
and Paula Weinstein
Casting: Nina Gold
Director of Photography: Anthony Dod Mantle
Edited by: Daniel P. Hanley & Mike Hill
Production Design, Art Direction, and Set Decoration: Mark Tildestey,
Neal Callow, Dean Clegg, Arwel Evans, Nick Gottschalk,
Christian Husband, Niall Moroney and Dominic Capon
Music by: Roque Baños
Starring: Chris Hemsworth, Benjamin Walker, Cillian Murphy, Ben
Whishaw, Charlotte Riley, Tom Holland, Michelle Fairley
and Brendan Gleeson
Production Budget: $100 million
Box Office: $25 million U.S.A. | $68.9 million worldwide
Running Time: 2 hours and 1 minute
MPAA Rating: PG-13 for intense sequences of action and peril, brief
startling violence and thematic material

THE BEATLES: EIGHT DAYS A WEEK – THE TOURING YEARS

Apple Corps, Diamond Docs, Imagine Entertainment, OVOW
Productions, Universal Music Group International, White
Horse Pictures
Released: September 16th, 2016 (limited, U.S.A.)
Directed by: **Ron Howard**
Written by: Mark Monroe
Produced by: MBruce Highman, **Ron Howard**, Jeff Jones, Scott
Pascucci, John Rita, Michael Rosenberg, Stuart Samuels,
Nigel Sinclair, Matthew White
Director of Photography: Caleb Deschanel, Paul Lang, Tim Suhrstedt,
Michael Wood, Jessica Young
Edited by: Paul Crowder
Music by: Ric Markmann, Dan Pinnella, Chris Wagner
Starring: John Lennon, George Harrison, Paul McCartney, Ringo Starr,
Richard Curtis, Ed Sullivan, Whoopi Goldberg, Neil
Aspinall, Brian Epstein, Elvis Costello and Richard Lester
Production Budget: $5 million
Box Office: $1.6 million U.S.A. | $12.2 million worldwide
BAFTA: Best Documentary (nomination)
Emmy: Outstanding Sound Mixing & Outstanding Sound Editing
(won); Outstanding Documentary, Outstanding Writing for
and Outstanding Editing (nomination)
Running Time: 1 hour and 46 minutes
MPAA Rating: Not Rated

INFERNO
    Columbia Pictures, Double Negative, Imagine Entertainment, LSG Productions, LStar Capital, Mid Atlantic Films
    Released: October 12th, 2016 (Europe) | October 28th, 2016 (U.S.A.)
    Directed by: **Ron Howard**
    Written by: David Koepp, (based in part on the novel by Dan Brown)
    Produced by: Dan Brown, William M. Connor, Anna Culp, Brain Grazer, David B. Householter, **Ron Howard**, Jody Johnson, Ute Leonhardt, Ben Waisbren
    Casting: Zsolt Csutak & Nina Gold
    Director of Photography: Salvatore Totino
    Edited by: Tom Elkins & Daniel P. Hanley
    Production Design, Art Direction, and Set Decoration: Jille Azis, Bence Erdelyi, Zsuzsa-Lechner, Phil Sims, Marton Voros and Peter Wenham,
    Music by: Hans Zimmer
    Starring: Tom Hanks, Felicity Jones, Omar Sy, Irrfan Khan, Sidse Babett Knudsen, Ben Foster, Ana Ularu and Ida Darvish
    Production Budget: $75 million
    Box Office: $34.3 million U.S.A. & Canada | $220 million worldwide
    Running Time: 2 hours and 1 minute
    MPAA Rating: PG-13 for sequences of action and violence, disturbing images, some language, thematic elements and brief sensuality

SOLO: A STAR WARS STORY
    Lucasfilm, Walt Disney Pictures, Allison Shearmur Productions and Imagine Entertainment
    Released: May 25th, 2018 (U.S.A.)
    Directed by: **Ron Howard**
    Written by: Jonathan Kasdan & Lawrence Kasdan; based on the characters created by George Lucas
    Produced by: Will Allegra, Rob Bredow, Simon Emanuel, Toby Hefferman, Jonathan Kasdan, Lawrence Kasdan, Kathleen Kennedy, Phil Lord, Jason D. McGatlin, Christopher Miller, Marco Valerio Pugini, Allison Shearmur, John Swartz, Susan Towner and Adreas Wentz
    Casting: Nicole Abellera, Nina Gold and Jeanne McCarthy
    Director of Photography: Bradford Young
    Edited by: Pietro Scalia
    Production Design, Art Direction, and Set Decoration: Neil Lamont, Alex Baily, Oliver Carroll, Peter Drome, Ashley Lamont, Andrew Palmer, Oliver Roberts, Stephen Swain, Gary Tomkins, Tom Weaving, Tom Whitehead and Lee Sandales
    Music by: John Powell
    Starring: Alden Ehrenreich, Joonas Suotoamo, Woody Harrelson, Emila Clark, Donald Glover, Thandie Newton, Phoebe Waller-Bridge, Paul Bettany and Jon Favreau
    Production Budget: $300 million
    Box Office: $213.7 million U.S.A. | $392.9 million worldwide

Academy Awards: Best Visual Effects (nomination)
Running Time: 2 hour and 15 minutes
MPAA Rating: PG-13 for sequences of sci-fi action/violence

PAVAROTTI

White Horse Pictures, Diamond Docs, Imagine Entertainment, Polygram Entertainment, StudioCanal and Wildside
Released: June 4th, 2019 (limited, U.S.A.)
Directed by: **Ron Howard**
Written by: Mark Monroe
Produced by: Mark Ambrose, David Blackman, Paul Crowder, Guy East, Nicholas Ferrall, Jeanne Elfant Festa, Lorenzo Gangarossa, Mario Gianani, Brian Grazer, Cassidy Hartman, **Ron Howard**, Mark McCuno, Lorenzo Mieli, Mark Monroe, Michael Rosenberg, Nigel Sinclair and Dickon Stainer
Director of Photography: Axel Baumann, Luca Ciuti, Michael Dwyer, Alan Gwizdowski, Tom Hurwitz, Patrizio Saccó and Michael Wood
Edited by: Paul Crowder
Music by: Ric Markmann, Dan Pinnella, Chris Wagner
Starring: Luciano Pavarotti, Plácido Domingo, Angela Gheorghiu, Andrea Griminelli and Nicoletta Mantovani
Box Office: $4.6 million U.S.A. | $8.1 million worldwide
Running Time: 1 hour and 54 minute
MPAA Rating: PG-13 for brief strong language and a war related image

REBUILDING PARADISE

National Geographic Documentary Films, Imagine Documentaries
Released: January 24th, 2020 (Sundance Film Festival) | September 8th, 2020 (internet)
Directed by: **Ron Howard**
Produced by: Carolyn Bernstein, Sara Bernstein, Kelsey Field, Brain Grazer, Kristen Roy Hansen, Ryan Harrington, Emily L. Harrold, **Ron Howard**, Lizz Morhaim, Xan Parker, Michael Rosenberg, Christopher Allan Smith, Matthew Patrick Smith, Louisa Velis, Justin Wilkes and Jeremy Zerechak
Director of Photography: Lincoln Else
Edited by: W. Watanabe Milmore & Gladys Murphy
Music by: Lorne Balfe & Hans Zimmer
Starring: Erin Brockovich-Ellis, Michelle John, Matt Gates and Woody Culleton
Running Time: 1 hour and 35 minutes
MPAA Rating: PG-13 for intense sequences of action and peril, brief startling violence and thematic material

HILLBILLY ELEGY

Imagine Entertainment & Netflix
Released: November 11th, 2020 (limited, U.S.A.) | November 24th, 2020 (internet)

Directed by: **Ron Howard**
Written by: Vanessa Taylor, based off the book by J.D. Vance
Produced by: William M. Connor, Brian Grazer, **Ron Howard**, Karen Lunder, Julie Oh, Diana Pokorny, J.D. Vance
Casting: Carmen Cuba
Director of Photography: Maryse Alberti
Edited by: James Wilcox
Production Design, Art Direction, and Set Decoration: Laura Belle, Shawn D. Bronson, Molly Hughes, Merissa Lombardo, Gregory A. Weimerskirch
Music by: David Fleming & Hans Zimmer
Starring: Gabriel Basso, Amy Adams, Haley Bennett, Glenn Close, Owen Asztalos, Freida Pinto and Bo Hopkins
Production Budget: $45 million
Box Office: $38,852
Academy Awards: Best Supporting Actress, Best Makeup & Hairstyling (nomination)
Golden Globe: Best Supporting Actress (nomination)
BAFTA: Best Make Up & Hair (nomination)
Running Time: 1 hour and 56 minutes
MPAA Rating: R for language throughout, drug content and some violence

WE FEED PEOPLE

National Geographic Documentary Films, Imagine Documentaries
Released: March 19th, 2022 (South By Southwest Film Festival) | May 26th, 2022 (internet)
Directed by: **Ron Howard**
Produced by: Carolyn Bernstein, Sara Bernstein, Tracey Cole, Cara Fitts, Brain Grazer, **Ron Howard**, Meredith Kaulfers, Adnelly Marichal, Dan Martensen, Wellington Martinez, Walter Matteson, Nata Mook, Sam Pollard, David Regos, Michael Rosenberg, Matthew Patrick Smith, Louisa Velis, Dora Weekley, Justin Wilkes, Richard Wolffe, Jeremy Zerechak
Director of Photography: Kris Kaczor, Sebastian Lindstrom, Alicia Sully
Edited by: Andrew Morreale and Gladys Murphy
Music by: Sami Jano
Starring: José Andrés, Carlota Andrés, Inés Andrés
Emmy Awards: Outstanding Documentary, Outstanding Cinematography (nomination)
Running Time: 1 hour and 29 minutes
MPAA Rating: Not Rated

THIRTEEN LIVES

Storyteller Productions, Magnolia Mae Films, Imagine Entertainment, BROM Studios, Metro-Goldwyn-Mayer
Released: July 29th, 2022 (limited, U.S.A.) | August 5th, 2022 (internet)
Directed by: **Ron Howard**

Written by: William Nicholson, story by Don MacPherson, William Nicholson
Produced by: Carolyn Marks Blackwood, Jason Cloth, William M. Connor, Aaron L. Gilbert, Brain Grazer, **Ron Howard**, Jon Kuyper, Michael Lesslie, Chris Lowenstein, Karen Lunder, Sharon Miller, Raymond Phathanavirangoon, Jesse Ross, Vorakorn Ruetaivanichkul, Marie Savare, Gabrielle Tana and P.J. van Sandwijk
Director of Photography: Sayombhu Mukdeeprom
Edited by: James Wilcox
Casting by: Nikki Barrett
Production Design, Art Direction, and Set Decoration: Molly Hughes, Sarawut Chincharoen, Lek Chaiyan Chunsuttiwat, Carlo Crescini, Mara Garanzini, Brandt Gordon, Tarnia Nicol, Boontawee Thor Taweepasas, Arnon Pattamarron and Emma Rudkin
Music by: Benjamin Wallfisch
Starring: Viggo Mortensen, Colin Farrell, Joel Edgerton, Sukollawat Kanarot, Tom Bateman, Pattrakorn Tungsupakul, Sahajak Boonthanakit and Theerapat Sajakul
Production Budget: $55 million
Running Time: 2 hours and 30 minutes
MPAA Rating: PG-13 for some strong language and unsettling images

JIM HENSON: IDEA MAN

Released: May 31st, 2024 (internet)
Directed by: **Ron Howard**
Written by: Mark Monroe
Produced by: Kelsey Arlington, Sara Bernstein, Margaret Bodde, Dane Charbeneau, Paul Crowder, Travis Eilerson, Brian Grazer, **Ron Howard**, Meredith Kaulfers, Malia Kobara, Vanessa Maruskin, Jonna McLaughlin, Mark Monroe, Michael Rosenberg, Christopher St. John, Leila Wikel, Justin Wilkes and Jeremy Zerechak
Director of Photography: Vanja Cernjul, John Chater, Igor Martinovic, Jenni Morello
Edited by: Paul Crowder & Sierra Neil
Art Department: Henrique Cirilo, Dezzi Durazo, Brian Henson, Nicholas Kozmin, Emma Magidson and Neil Steinberg
Music by: David Fleming
Starring: Jim Henson, Frank Oz, Alex Rockwell, Heather Henson, Dave Goelz, Lisa Henson, Brian Henson, Cheryl Henson, Fran Brill, Bonnie Eickson, Michael K. Frith, Rita Morino, Jennifer Connelly
Emmy: Outstanding Documentary, Outstanding Directing, Outstanding Writing, Outstanding Cinematography, Outstanding Editing, Outstanding Music, Outstanding Sound Editing, Outstanding Sound Mixing (nomination)
Running Time: 1 hour and 51 minutes
MPAA Rating: Not rated

CHAPTER 1
BEFORE THE DEBUT

For the most part we are dispensing with the production backstories and the cultural reception to Howard's movies, however understanding the set-up of a filmmaker's debut is important because it often sets the tone for how the career will unfold. Every director's path to his or her break is unique, and one might be surprised to learn that Ron Howard was in his early twenties when directing his debut feature, *Grand Theft Auto*. On the one hand, rarely are filmmakers in that young of an age bracket tasked with directing a production with a budget over six-hundred thousand dollars (by forty-year inflation, the $602,000 production budget of *Grand Theft Auto* in the mid-1970s would be around the $3-million-dollar range in the early-to-mid-2020s). On the other hand, we must consider the substantial experience Howard had catalogued as an actor since he was a toddler, particularly with television via *The Andy Griffin Show* (1960–1968), and *The Smith Family* (1971–1972), including a wide range of other acting credits, including the movies, *The Music Man* (1962) and *American Graffiti* (1973). This meant that for two decades Howard had clocked in a radically high number of hours on a film or television set. For perspective, the amount of time Howard spent on a set with exposure to the craft of filmmaking in his first two decades was probably the same amount of time, if not more than what part-time actors are able to obtain within double that time.

It was on the production of *The Wild Country* (1970), where Howard would get the encouragement to follow his directing dream more aggressively:

> I acted for a young director doing a movie for Disney when I was fifteen, it was called *The Wild Country* - a

very formulaic Disney kind of movie, but I got this guy, Robert Totten and he was great. He was only thirty-one years old, I think, and had directed his first feature at twenty-one. I mentioned that I was interested in directing and his attitude was, "What are you waiting for?" whereas everyone else had always been patronizing about it. He gave me the belief that I could still direct a feature film when I was still a teenager![1]

Years after that interview, the influence of Robert Totten is brought up again by both Ron and Clint Howard repeatedly in their memoir, *The Boys*. Although they depict Totten in the vain of a hard-knocks, no nonsense director (occasionally indulging in a shot of whisky on set), it seems that Totten's ideological perspectives on filmmaking had the greatest influence over them; directing for Ron and acting for Clint.[2]

Howard's desire to get behind the camera came during the era when American cinema began moving off of the movie studio lots. Films like *Easy Rider* (1969) and *The Last Picture Show* (1971) were not shot at a studio in Hollywood and were successful enough to establish themselves in American pop-culture. Yes, Ron Howard was certainly part of the 1970's "car on the open road" trend as he was one of the faces of it, but he wasn't at the forefront of creating it.

Furthermore, given Howard's tenure in show business and the length of time he's been known to the American public, this can lead many to falsely assume he was always a bankable name. Consider whatever the current popular television shows or movies are: we can easily assume that any of the teenage screen talent from those shows and/or movies are not going to be given a multi-million-dollar budget for a feature length film. Ron Howard in the early-1970s was no different, therefore he still had to resort to finding ways to fundraise an independent movie. Both Beverly Gray's book and Howard's own memoir detail some of his strange ideas for fundraising including a door-to-door campaign, and even contemplating if a brief excursion into the adult film industry would result in getting the attention of studio executives.(3)(4) Howard later admitted he seriously contemplated the idea for a grand total of three seconds, however the concept of the unmade *Opie Gets Laid* has been a running joke for decades.(5) Additionally, *Happy Days* did not reach its zenith of wild popularity in the United States until it's later seasons in the late-1970s,(6) therefore Howard did not have the pull of that sitcom (yet), to get him gigs in Hollywood for making inroads as a director.

Around the mid-1970s, Howard's agent sent him the script for *Eat My Dust!*, which came by way of Roger Corman's company, New World Pictures. Howard claims there were many screenplays like *Eat My Dust!* being sent his way, however the fact it came from Corman made the offer particularly intriguing. In the mid-1970s, Corman was responsible for launching the careers of filmmakers Peter Bogdanovich and Francis Ford Coppola – both directors that Howard would have been familiar with on account of their popularity at the time.* Furthermore, Beverly Gray notes in her book that Howard getting cast in a Roger Corman movie was not likely going to enhance his prestige as an actor.(7) Corman describes the beginning of his and Howard's relationship as such:

> I first met Ron when he did a picture called *Eat My Dust!* He'd been the star of *Happy Days* and I had a teenage-comedy-car-crash picture I wanted to make, and he was the logical person to play the lead. I couldn't afford his salary, so I gave him a [smaller] salary and a percentage of the profits on *Eat My Dust!* It opened to really huge figures on a Friday night, and I called him mid-morning on Monday to say "Ron, we got a giant winner here. You're going to really do well on your percentage!" And he [Howard] said, "I already checked, I know, I've been waiting for your call and I

---

*Other directors that credit Roger Corman as being the man who gave them a break into the industry include James Cameron, Joe Dante, Jonathan Demme and Martin Scorsese. Corman has also been credited with influencing small budgeted, yet pivotal films that helped excel the careers of Sandra Bullock, Robert De Niro, Pam Grier, Jack Nicholson and William Shatner.

assume you want to do a sequel?" and I said "Of course." and he said "Wait right there, I'm coming in!"

So I waited, he came into the office and he did all the talking! Howard said, "I know it's customary when somebody stars in a hit picture to come back and get more money for the sequel. I will not ask for that. I'll come back and do the sequel for exactly the same money and I'll do another job for nothing!"

And I said, "What's that, Ron?" He said, "I'll direct the picture." And I said, "Ron, you always looked like a director to me."

That's exactly the way it went, and it went that fast – there were no hesitations on the part of either one of us. He had given us a big hit, and he could of said he wanted my job, and I would have probably said, "Ron, you look like a producer to me!"

I knew he had studied at the SC [Southern California] film school and I had done several short subjects, and he was an intelligent, very hard working young man, and I felt all of those things together it was worth the gamble.[8]

In *The Boys*, Howard claims that he went to Corman with the directing trade offer before agreeing to be in *Eat My Dust!*, having written a screenplay with his father, Rance, that he was trying to get funding for. Howard indicates that Corman said the script they penned was something that New World Pictures didn't do. After the release and box office success of *Eat My Dust!*, Howard pitched several other concepts to Corman which were turned down. Instead, Corman told Howard that New World Pictures had been testing titles with audiences, and one that scored well was, "Grand Theft Auto." Corman asked Howard to come up with something appropriate for the New World Picture's brand using that title which brought about Howard's first directorial feature.(9)

Foreshadowing what would come:
Grand Theft Auto

Despite the formulaic, and relative obscurity of *Grand Theft Auto* in the modern era, the film did foreshadow many of the themes that would become recurrent throughout Howard's cinema, particularly the high number of supporting characters, the cars themselves, and the axis of the storyline hinging off a romance between leading characters.

Inspired by the likes of *It's a Mad Mad Mad Mad World* (1963) and *What's Up Doc?* (1972), Howard's directorial debut is something he used to cut his teeth on. The film is unapologetically a product of the 1970s; one would never say that *Grand Theft Auto* is a "classic" of American 70s cinema — yet the film completely embraces a 70s milieu. Viewing *Grand Theft Auto* forty years after its release, the movie looks like a mockery of the times, less we forget that the majority of Roger Corman's New World Pictures were nonsensical fun. Therefore, it's obvious that Ron Howard is playing around in his *Happy Days* comfort zone with a no questions asked, over the top scenarios.

As quickly as the film starts, the audience begins getting introduced to one zany stereotype after the next, each tagging along in this nonsensical car chase between Los Angeles to Las Vegas. To analyze the characters of *Grand Theft Auto* for insight to Ron Howard's philosophy or perspective on American culture is a waste of time; the wealthy characters are just as goofy as the middle class characters – and the cops, politicians and gangsters are all bumbling around the picture for comedic value. The over-zealous southern Christian preacher is the *only* character that prefigures Howard's critical eye in his depiction of religion in later years (and even that observation is a stretch).

What's really interesting about *Grand Theft Auto* is that the film devotes screen time to the romance. The love story is the "gasoline" for the narrative – it's the inciting incident and the key component that the avalanche of characters get fixated on. What particularly stands out is that the film allows for one quiet scene in the middle of all the noise to address a discrepancy in the romance between Ron Howard and Nancy Morgan's characters. *Grand Theft Auto* displays a momentary break-up between the two leads, where the convictions of the characters are accosted. This motif of lovers challenging each other would become go-to material that Howard uses repeatedly throughout his career. For all the love affairs Howard will put on screen in his subsequent career, it has its birth with a short argument and resolve in *Grand Theft Auto*. In the film, Ron Howard's character becomes irritated that Nancy Morgan has made all the decisions leading them into the mess they're currently in, sparking a rift between them. Although both aim for the same goal (running away from controlling people and eloping in Las Vegas), they fail to listen to each other and develop a misunderstanding. This is not unlike the division that we'll see in *Splash*; *Parenthood*; *Backdraft*; *Ransom*; *Cinderella Man* and *Solo*, where two people who clearly love each other are placed in circumstances that force a strain on them.

What's slightly deceptive about *Grand Theft Auto* as Howard's first movie is the aesthetic completely betrays what's coming. The first theatrical releases of Terrence Malick (*Badlands*) Steven Spielberg (*The Sugarland Express*) and Quentin Tarantino (*Reservoir Dogs*) all hint at a visual style and tone that those respective directors will embrace in their future work. The editing of *Grand Theft Auto* is not as polished as Howard's future films, in that we see superfluous shots of cars zooming in and out of frame during chase sequences just for the visual sensation of movement. We see repeated cuts of car crashes, an editing technique where an action is shown three times repeatedly in rapid succession from different angles – a technique Howard has never re-used in forty years of filmmaking. In hindsight, the fact that *Grand Theft Auto* both anticipates and betrays what Howard's filmography would become confirms that he does rework himself project to project.

Although Howard was catering to what Roger Corman wanted via Howard's own celebrity stature in the mid-1970s, his television directing endeavors are the first to indicate his intentional departure from a set style.

The Made-for-TV Movies:
Cotton Candy, Skyward **and** *Through the Magic Pyramid*

The five-year gap between the releases of *Grand Theft Auto* and *Night Shift* (1977 to 1982) may initially appear unusual in a director's early career, less we forget Howard's commitment to *Happy Days*, which had by then reached extreme levels of popularity. Howard had repeatedly expressed interest to ABC, the network that broadcast *Happy Days*, that he wanted to take on directing jobs, but nothing worthwhile ever materialized. Rival television network NBC however did make Howard directing offers, albeit for less money, but he leapt at the opportunities which resulted in three made-for-tv movies that he directed during the hiatus when *Happy Days* wasn't shooting.

We need to be mindful that Howard was still a "director for hire" on these films, as he was for Roger Corman on *Grand Theft Auto*. They should be viewed as "jobs," which doesn't lessen their artistic integrity, however the movies themselves are of a different caliber than one might expect to see from a director's early work. We wouldn't see the breakout films of contemporary filmmakers Spike Lee (*She's Gotta Have It*); Steven Soderbergh (*sex, lies, and videotape*); Darren Aronofsky (*Pi*); or Christopher Nolan (*Following*) blowing their miniscule production budgets on doing a kiddie Egyptian time travel movie. There is a level of ingenuity seen when young filmmakers have limited access to resources to compose their narratives. This should not be taken as a discredit of integrity for Howard's television movies. *Skyward* in particular took the bold step of casting Suzy Gilstrap, who was an actual paraplegic, in the title role. With the made-for-tv movies, Howard was given the opportunity to tackle large scale endeavors such as access to a shopping mall for a battle-of-the-bands concert in

Cotton Candy; an airfield for *Skyward*; or the collection of Egyptian costumes and sets for *Through the Magic Pyramid* – not to mention chariots on loan from Paramount Pictures. What's important to note with these three films is that Howard is managing multifaceted productions, which included a pseudo tv-pilot in *Through the Magic Pyramid*, which was shot in 1979, but didn't release until 1981. (In some places it's listed as "*The Time Crystal*" or mistakenly as it's working title: "*Tut and Tuttle*".) The likes of Darren Aronofsky, Spike Lee, Christopher Nolan and Steven Soderbergh all debuted with independent films that had to play the festival circuit, get noticed by a distributor who would then purchase the movie, get it shown and hopefully recoup some money. Ron Howard had the benefit of directing for NBC, complete with a nationwide audience already in attendance, and was paid for his work. To be clear, Howard has never disparaged any of his television movies or shied away from talking about them – in fact in *The Boys*, Howard notes that the made-for-tv movies helped "hone" his confidence as a director.*[10]

Although he would make cameos from time to time, Ron Howard's final season of *Happy Days* was the seventh, which he was contractually obligated to do. He was offered a doubling of his salary for Season 8, but turned it down to pursue his directing ambitions.

***

The three made-for-tv movies include a number of themes that we see present throughout Howard's body of work, particularly family dynamics. What's most poignant is that all three are of different genres (*Cotton Candy* is a comedy; *Skyward* is a drama; and *Through the Magic Pyramid* is for children), which mirrors the mixture that Howard embraces throughout his directing choices.

---

*As of this writing, all three films seem only to be available on YouTube via digital archiving, presumably from a VHS tape. This has resulted in a pixelated image with poor sound quality, but they are watchable. *Through the Magic Pyramid* in particular is difficult to actually see what's happening in lower lit interior scenes. Even library databases don't seem to have copies of them. If VHS or DVD copies of the three films do exist, they are probably only available through resellers or off-brand independent retailers.

His films only occasionally "talk to each other" in sequential order, but the common pattern is that Howard addresses a topic and circles back to it years later. Both *Ransom* and *The Missing* complement each other on account of their many juxtapositions, but there is a seven-year gap between the two heavy dramas. The three music documentaries (*Made in America*; *Eight Days A Week* and *Pavarotti*) are all made in the 2010s, yet they showcase three very distinctive elements of the music industry.

This is why the best approach to Howard's cinema is looking at the motifs and see how they develop throughout the collection of titles.

CHAPTER 2
AUTHORSHIP:
THEMES IN RON HOWARD'S FILMS

The emphasis on the movie director was not always a mainstream concept between the studio's marketing departments and the movie going audience. Obviously the directors from Hollywood's golden years were certainly key players in the studio system, but Frank Capra, Michael Curtiz or Howard Hawks did not have the same panache or carried the same weight with consumers in the 1930s and 1940s that they would have in the following decades. Make no mistake, directors were important and respected people in the industry, but it wasn't until the auteur theory took hold in the 1960s that audiences began to really notice the directors. Prior to the 1960s, the director was not given the same recognition as they are today. Although we can look back and read into any filmmaker's authorship, it was not a major selling point for the consumer. As the emphasis on directors spread in the United States throughout the 1960s, they became a crucial element in attracting ticket buyers.

This was very evident by the 1970s as Francis Ford Coppola, Brian De Palma, Terrence Malick, Martin Scorsese and Steven Spielberg all emerged on the scene with movies that would catapult them into widespread recognition.* As acknowledgement in the role of the director began to rise in the 1960s and 1970s, some

---

*Francis Ford Coppola's *The Godfather* (1972); Brian De Palma's *Carrie* (1975); Terrence Malick's *Badlands* (1973) and *Days of Heaven* (1977); Martin Scorsese's *Mean Streets* (1973) and *Taxi Driver* (1975); Steven Spielberg's *Jaws* (1975) and *Close Encounters of the Third Kind* (1977).

actors began to try their hands at directing, specifically Woody Allen, Clint Eastwood, and Sydney Pollack.

The study of a single director's body of work allows the viewer to read in between the lines and gain a richer subtext of the film(s). Despite how much pull a "name" director has, the size of his or her production, how many theatres the movie gets released in, the rating it received on Rotten Tomatoes, or who's featured in the cast – the intertextuality can always be analyzed throughout the varied films.

Some of the most basic forms of authorship can be by how regularly a director will work with the same actor — examples include Tim Burton & Johnny Depp, or Pedro Almodóvar & Penélope Cruz. Another way of identifying authorship is by examining themes seen over and over in a director's body of work. One might consider the superfluous amount of explosions in Michael Bay's films (*Armageddon*; *Pearl Harbor*; *Transformers*), or the recurring theme of absent fathers in Steven Spielberg's films (*E.T.*; *Hook*; *War of the Worlds*). Another way of examining authorship is how a director may comingle genres, such as Adam McKay's comedies (*Anchorman; Step Brothers; The Other Guys*), and then later intertwining humor into his dramas (*The Big Short*; *Vice*; *Don't Look Up*). Furthermore, this intertextuality remains present in every single project even when breaking from the norm; this means that the authorship of a director is always present even when it doesn't appear to be. *Memento* (2000) is a crime thriller, *Interstellar* (2014) a science-fiction adventure, and *Oppenheimer* (2023) a period drama – yet all three of Christopher Nolan's films use a non-linear structure or manipulate time in some way to tell the story.

These same concepts are very applicable to Ron Howard's body of work despite that he doesn't have a definitive visual style or genre that can be instantly tacked to his cinema. Consider the perfectly symmetrical oblong mise-en-scène of Wes Anderson films, or the black swirls that subliminally invoke Tim Burton films. Ron Howard has not been credited with having his own trademark aesthetic, such as the hyper slow-motion of a Zack Snyder action scene, or a face tilt down, glaring into the lens which has come to be known as the "[Stanley] Kubrick stare." Rather, Howard gravitates to certain narrative themes repeatedly, with a few distinct film production traits. Many of the predominate themes in Howard's body of work can be appreciated on account of his production choices, no different than understanding that the imperfections seen in the acting performances from a Paul Greengrass or a Terrence Malick film come by way of how they manage their sets and shoot their movies.

Never Making the Same Film Twice

Despite how certain titles might appear similar at-a-glance, Howard remains devoted to changing up his game. Although the concept of the impossible conquest is the most recurrent theme in each narrative, Howard's constant switching of genres are what dominate his directorial resume. As stated previously, the three Dan Brown adaptations are about deciphering centuries old history while Tom Hanks tries not to get killed, yet the tone of the three changes: *The Da Vinci Code* has a significant amount of walking & talking; *Angels & Demons* they're running & talking; and *Inferno* has them doing it again, but inside of a horror film.

One of the genres we see pop up a couple of times is the "rescue mission," although to make the argument that it's a recurring theme throughout all his movies is a stretch. A compare and contrast between the divers saving the Thai soccer team in *Thirteen Lives*, and saying how Michael Keaton "saved" Henry Winkler in *Night Shift* is a bit excessive. Yet what we do see is the conceptualization of survival presented in different ways throughout the body of work. The ending of *Apollo 13* is meant to make the audience stand up and cheer, whereas the return of the surviving crew of the Essex from *In the Heart of the Sea* is drastically different. The lost seamen are not met with jubilation or a celebratory soundtrack; rather we are told that they were looked at as if they were "apparitions, phantoms" as they slowly walk on deck and the villagers stare at them.

There are a couple tonal shifts within Howard's cinema over the course of the decades, yet movie to movie, especially when reviewing the titles in release date order, Howard alters a lot of the ingredients. This doesn't mean that each film is automatically better than the previous — rather, there are distinctions in all of them which is largely in credit to the way he avoids repeating himself.

Against All Odds

In the countless hours of Ron Howard interviews and audio-commentaries, there is one quote with respects to *Cinderella Man* that nearly sum up Howard's entire filmography:

> The stories that I wanna tell, they generally are about tests. A period of time in a set of characters, or a single character's life, where they're challenged in a way they never expected they would be challenged. The story of the Braddock's, Jim and Mae [Russell Crowe and Renèe Zellweger] and their children, is one of those examples of survival stories. Those are my favorite kinds of stories.(1)

On face value, Howard's earlier comedies are pure science-fiction: a love affair with a mermaid (*Splash*), and aliens hiding their brethren near a Tampa Bay retirement home (*Cocoon*). Yet neither of those situations hold the gravitas of the film: the plight of the characters is the emotional heart of the respective stories. The mermaid is a plot device for the indecisive Tom Hanks to allow himself to fall in love with someone. The energy radiating from the cocoons in the swimming pool is a plot device that forces the elderly Hume Cronyn and Jessica Tandy to re-evaluate their marriage in their twilight years.

Should we remove the humor from *Night Shift*, you have two men attempting to operate an illegal escorting service under the disguise of a city morgue. There is a suspension of disbelief that audiences naturally give comedies, especially with a frantic Michael Keaton running all over the place, which pulls the viewer's interest into the scheme, so that when things begin to go wrong, (despite how ridiculous the original concept sounded), the difficult logistics become rather unique. Remove the humor from *Gung Ho* and you have a factory town depending on the production of 15,000 cars in a month's time. Remove the humor from *EDtv* and you have the story of a man who signed away his right to privacy.

The cinema of Ron Howard is the cinema of the impossible conquest. The implausible situation. The overcoming of an incredible challenge. Succeeding when everything is stacked against you. The main character(s) in all his films never escape without undergoing a severe flogging of some kind. The stakes are always raised at some point in the narrative, making the challenge more difficult, increasing the severity of the task at hand. In some cases, achieving success present a whole new set of obstacles, and because Howard is a character driven filmmaker, who has repeatedly stated that the lead character(s) are the one(s) whom he wants the audience invested in, that in turn accents the pressure for the viewer. This is not exclusive to the dramatizations – all six of the documentaries exhibit this narrative structure as well.

It's not enough for the astronauts in *Apollo 13* to get stuck in space, lose the moon and have poisonous CO_2 being pumped into their small space craft — in their final stretch towards Earth, Bill Paxton gets very sick and dangerously close to death. The invasion of privacy that Matthew McConaughey suffers from in *EDtv* eventually comprises his whole family's to the point where all of them are being trailed by a camera crew. In *Cinderella Man* and *Rush*, the protagonists are not just participating in a dangerous sport, but are also rattled by the death of someone else in the line of work. There is sudden betrayal in *Inferno* and *Solo*, leaving the hero seemingly defeated. Despite all of Luciano Pavarotti's fame and monetary value he acquired, he still suffers ridicule for trying to bridge opera with rock & pop in *Pavarotti*. In *Hillbilly Elegy*, the son is not just dealing with his drug addicted mother and the problems she's caused, but he also needs to undertake a 10-hour drive back to school for a prominent job interview.

The Common Individual

An element that often goes hand-in-hand with the idea of the impossible conquest is that the main character(s) are not people destined for greatness. There is an everyman simplicity about them. They are not remarkable people, but rather people thrown into remarkable circumstances. With this in mind, even the real-life characters in the live-action dramatizations* are all individuals that achieved a level of notoriety, but they were gifted with a talent, or were plucked from obscurity. David Frost, played by Michael Sheen in *Frost/Nixon* was a successful television personality in his own right, but struggles to move into the realm of political journalism and is painted to seem particularly out of his element when confronting the former president.

Romance

We often see a love story, or a romantic relationship positioned in the center of Howard's films. Most of the time the romance fuels the narrative; the "love interest" is not simply a disposable character or a sub-plot that's casually given a scene or two. In the case of *Grand Theft Auto*, *Splash* and *Solo*, the romance is the inciting incident for the film's events. In most other cases, it directly impacts the objectives of the characters; remove the wife/girlfriend from *Apollo 13*; *Cinderella Man*; *Hillbilly Elegy* or *We Feed People* and a major tenant of the movie is gone. Yes, another director or screenwriter could still tell those stories and/or make those films without the love interest — yet the end product would have an entirely different feel with the feminine perspective omitted.

---

*Jim Lovell (*Apollo 13*); John Nash (*A Beautiful Mind*); James J. Braddock (*Cinderella Man*); Richard Nixon & David Frost (*Frost/Nixon*); James Hunt & Niki Lauda (*Rush*); J.D. Vance (*Hillbilly Elegy*); Rick Stanton, John Volanthen & Harry Harris (*Thirteen Lives*).

In some cases the romance is a juxtapose of each other: *Far and Away* would be pure grandeur of cinematography and music, if not for the antagonist relationship between Tom Cruise and Nicole Kidman for which the movie really invests screen time into showing. The premise of *EDtv* is the marvel of actually broadcasting a single person 24/7, but all of the drama from that concept comes by way of the budding romance Matthew McConaughey has for Jenna Elfman and creating a love triangle with Woody Harrelson. The biographies of Luciano Pavarotti (*Pavarotti*), José Andrés (*We Feed People*) and Jim Henson (*Jim Henson: Idea Man*) cannot be told without ample commentary from their significant others.

Strong Feminine Characters

In the hectic multi-story plot that is *The Paper*, the concept of women not having a career after childbirth becomes something that Marisa Tomei gets fixated on. For a fast-paced film which is about the morality and the responsibilities of promulgating a false narrative that would fuel racial tensions – Tomei's concerns are not something you would expect a male director to dive into. Yet Ron Howard makes it a crucial element of the film. There is no successful resolution to the news-team solving the cover up without Tomei getting into the action, and Howard makes Tomei's practical concerns part of what drives her actions.

We see powerful female roles throughout Howard's full directorial roster, but it's not until later in his résumé that it becomes distinctly prevalent. For all of the male leads in each of Howard's films, where romance is a factor, that leading man's significant other is equally strong willed. The women are always crucial to the leading men, and but as we get to the end of the 1980s and into the 1990s, Howard really begins to dabble with the gender roles. By the time of *The Missing* in the 2000s, there is a quote worth pondering:

> When I read the draft of *The Missing*, I was so taken by the characters – its very strong female characters.

I've never really had a chance to do that in a film and yet I live in a family with a wife and three daughters and one son. I got a lot of strong women around me.(2)

It's a unique perspective on Howard's part considering the strong female roles that he had presented by 2003, however this quote accents his admiration for women that we see him continue well into the 2010s and 2020s.

In conjunction with the motif a strong union presented in the love story, it underscores a theme of a successful partnership. There is no triumph for the male leads without the support of a strong woman: Nicole Kidman is arguably the true instigator of bringing Tom Cruise to the United States in *Far and Away*. Russell Crowe would be vanquished to a mental institution without the persistence of his wife, Jennifer Connelly, in *A Beautiful Mind*. Gabriel Basso's determination for a better life away from the chaos of his hometown is encouraged by the love and support of Freida Pinto in *Hillbilly Elegy*.

Partnership, Duality and Opposites

The theme of the partnership extends beyond romantic interests into the areas of friendship, culture and rivalry. In many ways there is a case to be made that *Solo: A Star Wars Story* is one of the most quintessential "Ron Howard films" because he completely takes ownership of the source material in a franchise that has stupendously operated in its own universe (no pun intended) for decades prior to his involvement. In the development process of the voluminous amount of *Star Wars* sequels following its debut in 1977, in no way was the large hairy Chewbacca ever to be subservient to the character of Han Solo. Therefore, when telling their origin story nearly forty years later, their relationship begins on an antagonistic level by way of the monstrous Chewbacca trying to eat Han Solo. The two characters maintain a buddy-comedy vibe throughout the entire *Star Wars* lore, so it's presented in a traditional jocular sense of having them at odds with each other right from the get go.

The concept of opposites is something that we see Howard play with almost obsessively as the theme fluctuates between something prominently established between characters, to being something buried in the milieu of a film's narrative. The contrast of two leading characters generally implies the "opposites attract" concept, which we see on full display in something farcical like *Night Shift* and *Gung Ho*, or in a romance such as *Far and Away*. Another version of this comes by way of how characters are positioned against each other with the audience caught in the middle. *Frost/Nixon* and *Rush* remain Howard's greatest example of this as both films really don't try and push the viewer in who to root for. Furthermore, consider the difference in tone between a political drama about a high profile interview, and the life threatening Formula 1 racing – here we see that desire of never making the same thing twice. This duality gets extended to the mindsets in the way the respective "teams" of the various parties think and operate in *Frost/Nixon* and *Rush*. There is a reason why Howard showcases the support staff of the duo leads in both films: to contrast the views and work ethics. The differences in mindsets seen in both films originates from Howard's contrasting of cultures in his earlier work.

Family

Due to the inner connectivity of all the players, we see "family" at the nucleus in so many of the films. *Parenthood*; *The Missing* and *Hillbilly Elegy* are obvious examples because the whole drama arises out of family dysfunction. Although *Cocoon* showcases four elderly men, their families are a factor in the choices the retirees make. Even the two climate change documentaries, *Rebuilding Paradise* and *We Feed People* are not so much focused on the cause of the natural disasters as they are the human-interest stories seen by way of the various families showcased throughout.

The mission of *Apollo 13* is for the astronauts to return home safely, yet consider the screen time prior to lift off that the film devotes to Tom Hanks and his family. Compare *Apollo 13* to other "Tom Hanks gets stranded" dramas: *Cast Away* (2000); *The Terminal* (2004) and *Captain Phillips* (2013) where his family is off-camera, especially throughout the duration of Hanks being deserted or detained – yet in *Apollo 13*, the audience is regularly shown Hanks' family back on Earth.

The Ensemble Cast

It's no surprise that a filmmaker who examines families, familial structured relationships and culture clashes, is going to gravitate towards large cast ensembles. Howard is repeatedly quoted as stating that characters are the most important aspect of any movie as they are who the audience is going to relate to.

Never in Howard's films are the supporting characters *not* vital to the narrative. More often than not, the side characters overshadow the leads because the collective behavior of the whole cast is intriguing. Howard incorporates multiple perspectives, presenting many points of view. Look at the number of "names above the title" in the posters or the DVD box of Howard's movies. These all-star casts are not simply to get "asses into seats," although that is certainly part of Hollywood marketing – but rather, Howard uses a large throng of characters to support the narrative.

Automotive, Deception, Music & Religion

While the impossible challenges, romances and families are the nexus of his movies, we see a couple of topics that periodically show up within the body of work. These are not the highest governing priorities for Howard, yet they often become crucial elements. Ron Howard's love of cars is, at the very least, a trivial motif within his films. They are given a special place of honor and often are extensions of the characters themselves. Is it really a surprise that *Rush*, (which is set in 1976, the same year that *Grand Theft Auto* was in production), was directed by the same man who at twenty-three-year-old was racing and smashing cars across the desert at the time? Looking at *Apollo 13*; *In the Heart of the Sea* and *Solo*, the "car" is substituted for something else, be it the lunar module, the Essex, or the Millennium Falcon.

Few would classify Ron Howard under the category of conspiratorial or mystery, yet Howard's execution of misdirecting the audience is borderline habitual. Obviously the sight-gags peppered throughout the movies is the clearest example of this, especially considering that Howard seems to favor physical humor over verbal. Tom Hanks yelling is probably one of the most distinguishable sounds in American pop-culture, but when he cries out `"The little boat?!"` in *Splash*, the beat is emphasized on account of the tiny boat he's already sitting in. Yet it's used as a narrative device regularly; sometimes the audience is in on the deception such as seeing Hume Cronyn cheat on his wife, or witnessing Michael Keaton lift a news tip off the desk of a rival paper. In later years the deception is used to throw the viewer off course such as Matthew McConaughey's confusion about Martin Landau's death in *EDtv*, or switching out boxers on Russell Crowe through one hectic panning shot between bouts in *Cinderella Man*. More poignantly however there are a handful of turncoat villains in Howard's films, which isn't all that surprising on account of how much Howard uses deception to tell the stories. The documentaries are difficult to do this with, however had Howard chosen to do more live action movies, there is no doubt that there would be more examples of this.

Music is a big element of Howard's films on account of how gratuitous the scores are in the majority of his films – say nothing with regards to him directing three feature length documentaries about musicians. While some filmmakers can be pegged on account of the type of music in their films, Howard doesn't get audibly typecast like that. The versatility of the films results in a variety of music, and since composers themselves also share a form of authorship, we get a blend of music from different musicians. Howard himself has disclosed:

> Music is an area that I take very seriously and put a lot of thought into. At the end of the day, my films rely on the imagination and talent of the composers.
>
> Of all the jobs in the filmmaking process, I know that composing the score is the one that I can't do. And yet, it remains my responsibility to work with the composer. I've learned that they're very creative people who can interpret direction the same way an actor can. If you talk about a dramatic or emotional objective, the composer is remarkably capable of delivering on it. And then we make the connection that will bring the scene to life.(3)

While music has undoubtedly been a key element of Howard's career, the topic of religion and spirituality is something he doesn't seem all that concerned with, until the mid-2000s. The popularity of *The Da Vinci Code*, a film where the "noise" of the controversy, which was drummed up for nearly two years before the film released, was louder than the movie itself – gives us a reason to go back and reexamine the subject. If and when Christianity is a subject in Howard's films, it's simply matter-of-fact; an aspect of the story that really doesn't contribute to the film (i.e. John Candy and Tom Hanks being ushers at a church for a wedding in *Splash* doesn't offer anything to the conversation). What is unique is that the controversial material from *The Da Vinci Code* itself, Howard really didn't dive deeply into, except the concept of the "sacred feminine". Given Howard's emphasis on strong women, does this surprise us? He goes from being somewhat ambivalent to religious devotions, to then incorporating it into his films. A brief conversation between the two leads, Chris Hemsworth and Benjamin Walker from *In the Heart of the Sea* questioning if they offended God on account of being stranded by the whale. This is a debate we don't see in other dramas, but starts to show up in the latter half of Howard's films, albeit never with great depth. Hemsworth and Walker arguing about human dominion over the planet and being make in "God's own likeness" only gets one scene, and then never revisited.

Authenticity

If you did an internet search for the top-ten most historically accurate movies, there are a few titles that will likely grace the various listings. *Tora! Tora! Tora!* (1970); *Das Boot* (1981); and *Lincoln* (2012) come up with regularity, but *Apollo 13* is almost always guaranteed to appear.

The topic of accurate biopics and the recreation of real events on film is a fascinating subject, but wildly complicated due to the mountain of history one needs to unpack, particularly when it's about a conflict. Of Howard's directorial features, fourteen of them are non-fiction, and of those fourteen, six are documentaries. This means that to date, there are currently more fantasy than historical on his résumé. Howard's desire to make the emotional struggle of his characters accessible for viewers results in accurate performances. There is an intention to bring a level of authenticity into films, despite being fiction (i.e. firefighters in *Backdraft*), and tell stories that are rooted in reality. The fictional titles have a believability laced into them because of the emphasis placed on character driven stories. On the other hand, there is a fine line screenwriters, directors and producers walk to compress a narrative into a 2 or 3 hour-long window. In the case of Ron Howard's cinema, each of the non-fiction films are a lesson in conveying the emotions tied to the histories. Make no mistake, the practicality of Steve Martin in *Parenthood* donning a homemade cowboy outfit for a birthday party is entirely for a soft shoe comedy. At the same time, it's the frustrations Martin has throughout the film that push him to do something as ridiculous as put on a kiddie cowboy act, because those concerns are taken seriously by the movie itself. In other words, there's a side of *Parenthood* that isn't just about laughs which is the legitimacy Howard looks for in all his films

CHAPTER 3
NEVER MAKING THE SAME FILM TWICE

The vast majority of people will identify Jane Austin and Stephen King as novelists. One doesn't have to have read any of Austin's or King's books to know what genres they write in. Kobe Bryant will always be affiliated with basketball and a tragic death, regardless of other noteworthy events and achievements in his life. Those unfamiliar with fashion will easily deduce that Mauizio Gucci was affiliated with the high-end Italian brand. Despite other biological information about these figures, they are easy to categorize – no different than associating Ron Howard with Hollywood.

Digging a little deeper into this categorization process, people who don't follow movies are not going to be able to rattle off four or five Alfred Hitchcock titles, but they know that he is associated with suspense mysteries. The name Clint Eastwood tends to evoke one of three images: a cowboy, dirty Harry Callahan holding a gun (often directly at the camera), or an old man behind a movie camera. We are able to mentally categorize Eastwood into different departments because he's been affiliated with them for so long. With the exception of Eastwood fans, the average person will not likely bring up that he composes music, writes and plays jazz, directed a film in Japanese (*Letters from Iwo Jima*), a rugby movie (*Invictus*), a spiritual sci-fi (*Hereafter*), and a musical (*Jersey Boys*). How many will recall that he was a one-term mayor of a small California town, let alone his speech at the Republican convention in summer 2012?

Ron Howard is uniquely different. Throughout the 1960s, when billed as Ronny Howard playing Opie on *The Andy Griffith Show*, he was timestamped in an era that is now considered wholesome television. In the late-70s and early-80s, he's gets reimagined in the American conscious as Richie Cunningham on *Happy Days*. It's worth pointing out that *Happy Days* is set in the 1950s and 1960s, despite having been broadcast in the 1970s, thereby subconsciously aging Ron Howard indirectly in the mainstream. The 1980s is also when he starts directing movies which are marketed as comedies. The comedies don't star him, but there are several in the 1980s that were successful enough at the box office to allow him to keep directing. It's in the 1990s Howard starts to rebrand himself as a director of dramas, swinging for blockbusters, yet he still committed himself to a comedy periodically. By the late-1990s and certainly into the 2000s, Howard's acting days are long behind him and his acting career starts to become the stuff of "fun-fact" trivia. Not that Howard needed a Golden Globe or an Oscar to solidify the shift, but earning acolytes for dramas certainly branded him a serious filmmaker – enough to the point that *The Da Vinci Code* was buzzed-up with serious anticipation months before its release. In the mid-2020s, the vast majority of people do not quite think of Howard as a documentarian since documentaries don't have the commercial impact – yet should he continue in that vain, another mediation could take place in pop-culture, as Howard was able to "chameleon" himself from Opie, to Richie, to comedy director, to power house director.

With all that in mind, one of the reasons why Howard is so hard to pigeonhole is because of his constant exploration within the movies he takes on. When Eastwood was in his seventies (the age Howard is at now), his iconography was emblazoned on the American subconscious on account of his celebrity imagery from the late-1960s. Eastwood's continuation of this, via directing and starring in cop dramas and westerns, only solidified the image further – but Howard does not fit nicely into a similar pop culture box. Generally speaking, Howard transitioned from comedies in the 1980s to dramas in the 1990s, but the various ways in which he continued to expand into new territory throughout the collected body of work is not able to be arranged by decades. There's a lot of alterations between categories of comedy and drama, and Howard blends the two in his films.

This also extends to the visual aesthetic in Howard's body of work. The influence of cinematographer Anthony Dod Mantle is very present in both *Rush* and *In the Heart of the Sea*, giving the two dramas a visual style that that rings similar to Mantle's work with director Danny Boyle in *Slumdog Millionaire* (2008); *127 Hours* (2010) or *Trance* (2013). Although Boyle has a strikingly distinct look in all of his films – which is in a large measure credited to the editing – Mantle's abundant usage of camera coverage, particularly in the extreme close-ups of props, creates very dynamic shots. Being on the front of a hydraulic pneumatic wrench going into a bolt being changed on a car tire in *Rush*, or the extreme close up of a pen scratching paper in *In the Heart of the Sea* all contribute to a new style that we see Howard fully embrace for two films in the mid-2010s, but doesn't return back to. Or rather, we hardly see any shots like those with respects to later films.

In his memoir, *The Boys*, this diversity is something Howard acknowledges and traces back to – of all things – coaching a children's basketball in his teenage years. There are two brief passages from the book that are worth keeping in mind:

> There was nothing subliminal about why I was so driven to do this [coach children's basketball]: it was to prepare myself to become a film director. I actually said the words aloud: *If I can learn about to handle a bunch of unruly eight-year-olds, I could one day probably figure out how to cope with a temperamental actor.*

> It's extraordinary, how well my stint coaching these kids prepared me for my directing career. I have found that I work best and achieve the most by tailoring a plan to the strengths of the people with whom I am collaborating, rather than rigidly adhering to some preconceived Ron Howard Method. There is no such method. In fact, that's one of the reasons that I don't have what you'd call an authorial signature, and why my films have been so varied in tone and subject matter.(1)

Alterations and combinations:
Splash and *Cocoon*

There's an old adage, particularly in the film industry that's commonly referred to as, "one for them, one for you," with regards to the content that mainstream directors get to make. Ideally the filmmaker who gets successful enough doing studio work, will be offered to direct something more personal. Upon the completion of *Night Shift*, Howard, producer Brian Grazer, and the screenwriters Lowell Ganz & Babaloo Mandel set out to make another movie together, (*Night Shift* was greenlit on account of Henry Winkler's involvement). The next film they developed adheres closer to what Howard's comedies often embody: a combination of humor with heartfelt. Reflecting on the production of *Splash* decades later Howard says:

> No one wanted to make it [*Splash*] for two reasons. When they read the script they said, "This is too many different tones. What is it? Is it a slapstick comedy? Is it a romantic comedy?" And I kept saying "It's all of those blended in a way that's gonna be really organic."(2)

When getting the green light for *Splash*, the four advanced to a higher tier of production budget with a major studio overseeing the project* and although *Splash* is categorized alongside Howard's comedies, the heart of the movie is a love story.

There are aspects of *Splash* that compliment *Night Shift*: the setting of New York City, the upper-middle class characters, the gimmick presented to the audience at the 30-minute mark (i.e. the decision to use the city morgue for escorting; Hanks meeting a mermaid) – thus giving the audience a rather significant length of time to get familiar with the characters, as well as another goofy, girl-obsessed screwball duo with Tom Hanks and John Candy†, akin to Henry Winkler and Michael Keaton in *Night Shift*. However, one of the key differences is that *Splash* indulges in the romance beginning with the prologue where the young mermaid is left teary-eyed at not being able to have a human friend (the 8-year-old boy). In *Grand Theft Auto* and *Night Shift*, the romance is present, staged at the very beginning and slowly massaged throughout, yet the entanglement between Tom Hanks and Daryl Hannah becomes the dominate subject by the finale. The affection and/or struggles of lovers is essentially reserved for one or two scenes in *Grand Theft Auto* and *Night Shift*, whereas that is the central focus of *Splash*.

A little over year later, Howard's *Cocoon* would release, and while going from a mermaid in one movie to a group of aliens in the next doesn't sound like a big stretch – the transitioning from an on-screen romance between Tom Hanks and Daryl Hannah, to the relationship between the retired elders and their families is a mature refined development. Displaying love between a heterosexual couple in *Splash* is one thing — displaying love between a grandfather and his grandson in *Cocoon* requires different types of emotional cues.

---

*Walt Disney Pictures agreed to produce *Splash*, however it was known in advance that the end product was going to be a tad too "adult" for Disney's flair. They decided to create a separate branch inside Disney for more mature movies, which became Touchstone Pictures, thereby making *Splash* the first Touch Stone release.(3)

†Although this will seem wildly unthinkable by modern standards: at the time of *Splash*'s production, John Candy was the biggest star in the film and the most expensive actor on set. Tom Hanks was not someone Disney relied on to bring in audiences.

Cocoon embodies a more subdued tone; the retirement community is somewhat charming and the three men have a friendly repertoire with each other – yet there is a somber tone in the opening 15-to-20 minutes of the film. *Cocoon* reminds the audience that these folks don't have much time left, which holds a sullen mood over the narrative. *Cocoon* hits the audience with the implied death of a cohabitant at the retirement home and showcases medical issues with some of the main characters. All of the issues with the characters such as Hume Cronyn's declining health, Herta Ware's memory lapse, and Wilford Brimley's bad eye sight are plot devices that the film circles back to, as well as helping to keep the theme of mortality at the forefront. It's a perfect example of Howard's use of a big cast and multiple subplots in a comprehensive narrative. The conversations between Wilford Brimley and his grandson offers dialogue that actually gives gravitas to the decision for the seniors to leave Earth.[4] On the other hand, *Cocoon* is perfectly balanced out with just enough light hearted humor, such as Don Ameche giving a $100-dollar bill to the bank teller and proceeding to give cash away to nearby strangers. Unlike *Splash*, which begins with comedy and moves towards drama, *Cocoon* warms up to its humor. Make no mistake, *Cocoon* is still a part of Howard's 1980s comedy collection, with jokes, innuendo and sight gags, yet the film remains predominantly a drama.

A key indicator of Howard's intention for change between *Splash* and *Cocoon* is seen in the cinematography. Despite having a larger production budget (*Splash* was $8-million; *Cocoon* was $17.5-million), there is an acute sense about the mise-en-scene in *Cocoon* and better lighting. The camera moves a lot throughout the picture, as was Howard's and cinematographer Don Peterman's intention to give *Cocoon* a lyrical feel as the film contemplates a pseudo afterlife.[5]

Descent into the Dramatic

As noted though the process of getting *Splash* greenlit, Howard's films throughout the 1980s continued to be a combination of comedy and drama – yet the humor was progressively paired more and more with adult subjects as the decade continued. A quizzical looking Steve Martin on the poster or BluRay case of *Parenthood* suggests comedy and humor, whereas the image of a firefighter silhouetted against flames on the *Backdraft* marketing material indicates something rather different from what Ron Howard was offering audiences previously in just the timespan of two years.

In chronicling Ron Howard's development as a filmmaker, it's not until we arrive at the *Willow*; *Parenthood* and *Backdraft* juncture that his whole tone changes. Prior to 1991, all of the films "feel" like they are by the same author; even *Willow* which is the most different due to the costumes, fantasy, special effects and darker imagery still consists of a similar tone that preceding films had (the "buddy-adventure" and comedic moments in particular). Since *Parenthood* was conceptualized by the same four key filmmakers of previous films – Howard, Grazer, Ganz and Mandel – it can be viewed with a profound level of authorship, especially since Howard personally drew on his own experiences to conceptualize *Parenthood*. The humor and comedy are so tightly fused in *Parenthood* that it's arguably semi-uncomfortable to watch because you're never too sure if it's "okay" to laugh at something. While *Backdraft* looked like the beginning of new movement in Howard's career, it's *Parenthood* that's actually far more mature than it appears. As Howard moves into the dramas, and the comedies become intermittent, his ambitions get bolder on account of the subject matter he's addressing: *Far and Away* looks at immigration in America's Gilded Age. A major portion of *Apollo 13* takes place in outer space. *Ransom* is a grizzly crime drama about kidnapping a kid. Meanwhile, the comedies also do not revisit the same subject matter: *The Paper* takes place in a newsroom over the course of 24-hours, whereas *EDtv* is about the television industry and spanned over the course of several weeks.

When Howard revisits topics, it's always done in a new framework. The kidnapping of Mel Gibson's son in *Ransom* takes place in the modern era, whereas the kidnapping of Cate Blanchett's daughter in *The Missing* takes place a hundred years in the past. *Far and Away* showcases a fictional Irish couple in a big sweeping drama where Tom Cruise boxes for money. *Cinderella Man* showcases a real couple, descendants of Irish immigrants, with children, all within the confines of a big metropolitan city during the Great Depression... and yes, Russell Crowe also boxes for money. The similarities between the collection of films are easy to spot, but there are core differences that allow the various movies to stand on their own. That said, Ron Howard has yet to make a companion piece set – two films that are linked as opposites, meant to be contemplated as one, but still can be watched individually as they are not direct sequels.* His résumé doesn't really share a consistent agenda or message. Occasionally some titles will "talk to each other", or Howard will re-evaluate a premise such as a person or group relating to something foreign, be it a mermaid in *Splash*, aliens in *Cocoon*, or the Japanese in *Gung Ho*. The most intertextuality offered are the narrative motifs. That said, we would be remiss to fail to acknowledge the recurrence of Howard's family in different roles (specifically his brother, Clint, and father, Rance) as they are little trademarks, or a pseudo artist signature in the corner of a paintings that fans come to expect.

Shifting perspectives:
Made in America, *Eight Days A Week* and *Pavarotti*

The documentaries don't come up until the 2010s, however in the lead up to 2013's *Made in America*, we see Howard slowly move towards a documentarian approach. His collaboration with Salvatore Totino on *The Missing* in 2003 has proven to be a crucial moment. Howard said that he was comfortable with storyboards and pre-planning exactly what he would shoot, yet Totino's approach was picking up the camera and shooting, ergo spontaneity and trying new ways of filming, (Totino first came to Howard's

---

*Examples include Clint Eastwood's *Flags of Our Fathers* & *Letters from Iwo Jima* (both 2006); Sam Mendes' *Revolutionary Road* (2008) & *Away We Go* (2009); and Darren Aronofsky's *The Wrestler* (2008) & *Black Swan* (2010).

attention for his work on 1999's *Any Given Sunday* and 2002's *Changing Lanes*). To date, Howard has worked with Totino more times than any other cinematographer on a total of eight movies together.(6)

***

The documentaries were not a one-off experimental departure for Howard, but rather something he's devoted himself to, which is a different kind of filmmaking altogether, yet he crafts narratives that still conform to his authorship. The temptation to refer to his first three documentaries as an ad hoc music trilogy is appealing being that they're each an examination of a musical celebrity, however every single one of the films operates differently (not unlike the three Robert Langdon/Dan Brown adaptations). Buoyed from Howard's constant experimentation in ways to tell a story and the type of story he wants to tell, is what brought him to documentaries in the first place. It's no surprise that Howard's first three have intrinsic variations in their assembly, yet we see the same motifs present in all three of the documentaries.

Made in America uses a culmination of people to tell the story of a music festival; famous headliners such as Jay Z and Pearl Jam, to the younger up-and-coming artists. Yet the substance that comprises *Made in America* comes from the people on the lower spectrum of the totem poll of the festival's production. The intermixing of big names with the workers and the citizenry make a contrast, yet unified message about the greatness of American prosperity. Howard actually allows himself to be a presence in the film, albeit just off to the side or only his voice, which he doesn't do in any of the other documentaries. There's a sense of Howard getting knee deep into the production by physically being in the atmosphere of the EDM, hip-hop, rap and rock artists – but at the same time, giving attention to the food trucks and the neighborhood residents. One could say that the first-time documentarian director himself is physically pulling all of these perspectives together to tell the "story" of Philadelphia's Labor Day weekend *Made in America* concert. The back n' forth editing delivers a lot of information to the audience simply by loitering on the assembly, technicalities and scope of the music festival. The "behind-the-scenes" ambiance seen in *The Paper*, *Apollo 13* and *EDtv* is flushed out more in this documentary with the bank of video monitors and operations being managed.

In all three of Howard's music documentaries, the performances aren't presented in the traditional concert film style. Contrasted to Martin Scorsese's *The Last Waltz* (1978) and *Shine A Light* (2008) where the vast majority of the film is transfixed on the performances, Howard gives the viewer snippets of the concerts, although he uses them differently. For *Made in America*, the performances are a moment of triumph for the performers; with *Eight Days A Week* there's the technical achievement of bringing modern audiences as close to a Beatles concert as possible; and *Pavarotti*'s editing and structure is intended to create a link between song and performer.

Made in America is the one film in Howard's directorial features that lacks a looming "threat." Although the documentary showcases some of the complexities involved in putting on a music fest, it's primarily centered on the success of the performers and the circumstances they had to overcome, (whereas in *Eight Days A Week* and *Pavarotti*, there are concrete elements that could harm the performers). Yes, *Made in America* includes a scene showcasing disappointment, yet it's countered with Jay Z explaining how failure is part of the creative process. Without any pinpoint antagonist, *Made in America* is a "feel good" piece focused on fulfilling destiny.

Both *Made in America* and *Eight Days A Week* look at what those concerts say about American culture – yet the big contrast is that one takes place over the course of one weekend in the 2010s, and the other over the course of a few years in the 1960s. Both films are authentic, yet the fifty-year gap is a unique hurdle because *Made in America* is able to pick up all the little nuances with so many cameras covering a single event – whereas *Eight Days A Week* needed to be assembled with archival footage, recorded interviews and modern perspectives. The goal for *Eight Days A Week* was to bring audiences to something they were not present for and Howard notes this saying:

> It stretches me as a filmmaker to start to delve into the documentary world, and so that's something myself, my partner Brian Grazer at Imagine, have been doing more of. I think it's broadening me creatively – and it's also thrilling to get to interview Paul McCartney and interview Ringo Starr.(7)

Released three years after *Made in America*, *Eight Days A Week* is an evolution of the issues addressed in the first documentary and plays closer to the tropes that Howard loves so much. Although the film focuses on just one aspect of The Beatles long and enticing history, multiple perspectives are presented throughout, including looking at the role of managers Brian Epstein and George Martin. Where *Made in America* detailed how just one music festival affected just one city – *Eight Days A Week* pulls the scope back to look at a four year window of time (1962-1966), and what the culture of the United States was in that era. A lot of voices are brought in to reflect on the atmosphere of the country in the 1960s, just as Jay Z pontificates about the state of America in the early 2010s.

The logistics are the antagonists in *Made in America*, but the complications presented are peanuts compared to the threats to the wellbeing of The Beatles in their tours of the United States. A riot in Cleveland, a bomb scare in Memphis, rain in another city and as their final tour progresses, the darker the situation becomes. There is a legitimate form of fear and intimidation in the footage we're shown of the massive crowds. The culmination of the San Francisco show and the uncontainable crowd resulting in the four being taken away in an armored truck for protection is poignantly somber. Ringo points out that to cope with the nightmare they had to go back into the studio to aid in their recovery from the intensity of the Beatlemania that endangered them repeatedly. Paul and

Ringo discuss how The Beatles expressed themselves through their records and since they decided against playing in public again, they did their music strictly in studio, which brought about a change in their music – going from the upbeat pop of "I Wanna Hold Your Hand" to the psychedelic rock of "Lucy in the Sky with Diamonds." There is no question that Howard's *Eight Days A Week* celebrates this creative change with The Beatles by packaging the development as the key achievement and success from the touring years. It's a reflection of an occasional Howard theme: bad things happen for good reasons. By Jim Carrey stealing the decorations and presents, the citizens of Whoville realize they over-commercialized the holiday in *How the Grinch Stole Christmas*. Russell Crowe breaking his hand in a fight lead him to strengthening his other arm on the docks in *Cinderella Man*. Although it's not explicitly said, *Eight Days A Week* strongly implies the Beatles' bestselling album, "Sgt. Pepper's Lonely Hearts Club Band" was on account of them withdrawing from touring.

If the contrast between rap and British rock weren't different enough, Howard elects for opera in his third musical venture. *Pavarotti* maintains its own identity separate from the previous two, yet the tropes of "a Ron Howard film" are there: Luciano Pavarotti comes from humble beginnings, his love life is messy, his children get interviewed giving the film a family perspective, and with his family being predominantly women, we have the feminine perspective giving witness to the biography.

Made in America is centered in one location (Philadelphia), and *Eight Days A Week* is specifically about touring for a limited number of years. With *Pavarotti*, the concept of worldwide touring is brought out as it went on for longer, and segues into Luciano's desire to collaborate with other artists to bring opera mainstream. With the stock footage available of The Beatles, *Eight Days A Week* is able to showcase something that the majority of modern audiences weren't able to witness. The development of technology and the accessibility of cameras thirty years later would allow for more lenses to capture additional content and get close-ups of Luciano during performances. On account of this, *Pavarotti* gets a little more into the mechanics of opera singing to underscore the explanation of the arias, thereby showcasing more live performances than the other two, the irony being that Luciano isn't doing as much physical running around on stage as Jay Z or The Beatles. Howard found that the face-to-face observation that the viewer got from watching close-ups on Luciano's face was a more emotional experience.[8] *Made in America*'s emotional heart is through the story of the vendors and the young artists. *Eight Days A Week*'s emotional heart comes from watching the hype of the "fab four" presence in the United States reach a dangerous crescendo. *Pavarotti*'s emotional heart comes from the artist's personal journey reflected in the passion he sings the songs with. This is uniquely telling as *Pavarotti* released just before Howard gets more retrospective in his work. Prior to the 2020s, Howard only occasionally put "himself" into his work, as opposed to how Luciano pours his own emotions into the arias according to *Pavarotti*. Make no mistake, every artist does this to some extent in his or her work, but this concept is emphasized in *Pavarotti* more than the previous two music documentaries. It's telling that Howard zones in on this concept just before the release of material that he opines having a closer connection with.

CHAPTER 4
AGAINST ALL ODDS

There isn't an exact science to this, but the rhythm of Howard's films seems to follow as such: something goes wrong around the 30-minute mark, the protagonist works really hard to overcome the obstacle and seems successful, but then stuff gets worse.

A lot of movies have the "all hope is lost" plot twist in the latter half, and those moments are really emphasized in Howard's films. This is something Howard doesn't reflect on very much in his interviews and audio commentaries – rather Howard repeatedly brings up how character driven his vision is. Regardless if it's a comedy or a drama, Howard is frequently on the record saying that he wants the audience to connect with the characters. Therefore, since striving to mold an intimate portrait of the main character(s) is the objective, any increase in peril or any level of defeat becomes accentuated as the viewer's interest is intended to be surrogated through the main character(s).

There are scores of movies, both fiction and non-fiction, that try to penetrate the inside mind of its characters, although more commonly tried with biographical pictures such as *Raging Bull* (1980); *The Aviator* (2004) and *Capone* (2020). Consider the portrayals of Richard M. Nixon in Olivier Stone's *Nixon* (1995) and Howard's in *Frost/Nixon*. While both films address different elements of the president's life, Oliver Stone's film periodically descends into President Nixon's mental thoughts. The tone of the various scenes in *Nixon* change accordingly to reflect the main character's own feelings, whereas *Frost/Nixon* isn't trying to place the audience inside the mind of the former president. *Frost/Nixon* allows for a semi-private revelation of Nixon/Frank Langella through a drunken rant, but it's shared with the films other title character, David Frost/Michael Sheen. The usage of staged interviews with the other characters from *Frost/Nixon* gives the viewer commentary on the story. The supporting cast doesn't offer too much on what the two main characters are thinking, as they are there to underscore what Richard Nixon and/or David Frost are trying to accomplish.

Movies that dabble with an inward mental plot structure are generally psychological thrillers such as *Memento* (2000); *Black Swan* (2010) or *Nightcrawler* (2014). We can point to Howard's *A Beautiful Mind* and *Inferno* as two that categorically belong in this genre, however Howard doesn't leave the audience uninformed from start to near-finish; the viewer is told what the deception is by the halfway point. At the risk of listing titles that the reader hasn't seen, thereby spoiling them, there are a number of popular films where the plot-twist is revealed in the final act; to date Howard has yet to make a film where the ruse is disclosed at the tail end. In the case of *A Beautiful Mind* and *Inferno*, the impending danger overrides the internal mental anguish of the lead characters, *after* the deception is told to us. We are put on the edge of our seats by the near-drowning of Russell Crowe's baby in the bathtub, or the possibility of a bioweapon's explosion underneath Istanbul *after* knowing what the plot hoax was.

At the risk of oversimplifying Howard's films, nearly all of the storylines are structured around a series of objectives that stand in the way of the protagonist(s) achieving their goal. How many trials is it going to take for Henry Winkler to not be such a push over in *Night Shift*? How much family drama does Steve Martin need to navigate through to finally chill and believe he can be a competent father in *Parenthood*? How does Russell Crowe get his family out of poverty in *Cinderella Man*? The three "real world" documentaries even function off of this principal: *Made in America* is about the process of putting together a successful music festival. *Rebuilding Paradise* and *We Feed People* are a series of objectives that need to be accomplished to help bring people back to some form of normalcy.

These factors are why the most recurrent motif in every single one of Ron Howard's films are the leading character(s) being up against all odds to achieve success. Stories of seemingly impossible conquests have been done multiple times, but on account of Howard giving the audience ample screen time to warm up to the characters, it allows there to be an edge to his films when elements go awry. The patience for allowing the audiences a significant window of time to get familiar with the character increases the entertainment value later in the film. There is little doubt that whatever future films Howard releases that this premise will be absent, lest he willingly chooses to direct a film where characters freely meander on screen without some form of impending conflict such as *Nomadland* (2020) or *Perfect Days* (2023).

The first quintessential "Ron Howard film":
Gung Ho

Following the critical and financial success of *Splash*, Howard said he felt his directing career advance via *Cocoon*. He claims that the first time going into David Brown & Richard Zanuck's office and seeing the Oscar statuette for *The Sting* (1973) and the poster for *Jaws* (1975) was an indication that he was stepping into the big leagues.[1] This notion was accurate: although *Cocoon* has multiple comical moments, the film had a higher production value and an emotional maturity stronger than what Howard had done previously (or, at least on par with NBC's *Skyward*). *Cocoon* achieved a critical and commercial success that would position Howard with more leverage in Hollywood. According to Beverly Gray's biography:

> After *Cocoon*, Howard found himself in the comfortable position of no longer needing to be a director for hire. Surveys established that his name in the credits could bring audiences into theatres. Clout

of this sort is priceless in Hollywood, and industry watchers began to wonder what Howard would do next.(2)

Yet, Howard's next step was to return to the comedic genre with *Gung Ho*, and it's truly the first of his films to have all the authorship troupes attached: a big cast with duo leading characters, both of whom are seemingly average people. This duality seeps into administrative and work ethic differences between the two cultures. There's a love story that affects Michael Keaton's actions. Domesticated family life is present in the story, but it's in the background as the American workers all treat each other like one big family. *Gung Ho* is set in a location that Howard hadn't yet made a film in prior, industrial Pennsylvania where cars and the appreciation of the automobile is the lifeblood of the characters, and it's the first movie where Howard comfortably utilizes a handheld camera aesthetic. Yet, what's arguably the most noteworthy element of *Gung Ho* is the presentation of a seemingly impossible conquest that the narrative will hinge itself on, lest the venture be all for not.

As a comedy, *Gung Ho* is filled with sight-gags, innuendo and wily Michael Keaton taking center stage. Up until 1986, the straight man in Howard's films had always been the main character with a comic relief in a supporting role. While there is no mistaking that *Gung Ho* is Keaton's "story" (the marketing of the film also implies this), the film is rooted in a duality between Keaton and Gedde Watanabe. The opening sequence of the film is edited to display the contrast between Keaton and Watanabe; the clueless foreigner roaming through Japan, all while Watanabe is brutally over-extending himself for a job that will ultimately treat him poorly. This contrast extends to the American and Japanese workers in the auto factory, thereby being the first film in Howard's canon to showcase two contrasting characters – hence, two contrasting ideologies battling it out. There's a healthy amount of humor in this dichotomy, yet as the narrative progresses, Howard diminishes the humor a little bit, and favors the dramatic. *Gung Ho* never reaches for the severe dramatic tones akin to *Splash* (a breakup) and *Cocoon* (families saying goodbye) – rather the film is more focused on exploring a cultural conflict. The baseline ingredient for a good story is conflict, a protagonist and an antagonist pitted against each other. In Howard's films, this quandary is stressed because the paired leads are often flawed characters: the duo of *Night Shift* and *Splash* as well as the three men of *Cocoon*, all have flaws they need to overcome, and *Gung Ho* is no different through showcasing Keaton and Watanabe's inadequacies. Michael Keaton is overtly cocky and treats a big lie akin to a small fib, whereas Watanabe sets unrealistic expectations for himself and refuses to amend.

Despite this duality of cultures being boxed inside of a comedy, we get the arrival of a fundamental aspect of Howard's authorship: the production of 15,000 cars. The seemingly impossible conquest. An objective thrust upon the protagonist(s) that demands victory lest complete failure. Regardless of all the supporting characters in the film or the juxtaposition of Keaton and Watanabe, once the task of completing 15,000 cars presents itself in *Gung Ho*, the livelihood of the industrial town and the credibility of the Japanese is what the narrative hinges on. It's positioned in the movie as a giant hurdle for the workers to overcome. The viewer may anticipate that the goal will be achieved in the end, but watching the drama unfold is the thrill of "a Ron Howard film."

It's safe to assume that the audience knew the astronauts would return home alive in *Apollo 13*, that Jim Carrey wasn't actually going to steal a holiday in *How the Grinch Stole Christmas*, and that St. Peter's Basilica wasn't going be blown to smithereens in *Angels & Demons* – yet how was that going to be accomplished? When the task of producing 15,000 cars is presented to Keaton, and he's unable to negotiate a compromise, it's reasonable to presume that the audience would still innocuously expect a happy ending on account of *Gung Ho*'s predisposed charm. Nevertheless, the question of how Keaton and company are going to pull off this Herculean task draws the viewer into the story.

The reason why the production of 15,000 cars in *Gung Ho* is significant in Howard's filmography is the United States patriotism that the film is centered on. The usage of a blue-collar factory town going into remission, the politics of a worker's union, a Fourth of July picnic setting and the "can do" spirit that Keaton presses upon the employees plays into the theme of American ingenuity. After the task of making 15,000 cars becomes engraved into the narrative, it's followed by a scene in which Keaton gives a speech to the worker's union. The lighting, cinematography and editing of the moment is telling because, even though *Gung Ho* billed itself as a comedy, the task of 15,000 cars holds gravitas over the film's story, eventually becoming central to the finale. When Keaton must admit he over-extended himself and lied to the town about fulfilling a portion of the work for a partial raise, it's set in the backdrop of July Fourth.

There is something to consider with this: Ron Howard as an American filmmaker. With the exception of *Far and Away*; *Apollo 13* and *Cinderella Man* — his films aren't necessarily awashed in patriotism. Rather we see a comparison and contrast of the United States from different angles. With *Gung Ho*, the American work ethic is scrutinized; Michael Keaton is placed out of his comfort zone by wandering around Japan in the film's opening, but is this not similar to the European adventures Tom Hanks has in the three Robert Langdon thrillers? There's a constant exploration of the American culture and history in Howard's filmography. *Eight Days A Week* displays foreigners coming to America — not unlike Watanabe and his family trying to accustom to an American lifestyle in *Gung Ho*.

In typical 1980s American cinematic fashion, the rapid assembly of the 15,000 cars is shown in a music montage. One needs only to consider popular titles of the decade such as 1983's *Flashdance*; 1985's *The Breakfast Club* and *Rocky IV*; or 1986's *Top Gun* to grasp how prevalent the "music video" influence was to mainstream American movies. When the Japanize boss is touring the facility and counting the cars, they get to 14,994, being six automobiles short. In typical Howard fashion, the moment of the impending decision is teased to increase suspense. Witnessing the workers rushing to finish the remaining cars, the moment is filled with comedy which only frustrates the Japanese president more and he decides that it's no good. In turn, Michael Keaton's swagger kicks in and his grandstanding dominates the exchange and ultimately convinces the company president to change his mind. Impressed with the pluck of the American workers and their fraternity with their fellow Japanese coworkers, the president changes his mind and all are rewarded with an upbeat happy ending. *Gung Ho* really doesn't abandon its humor in the exchange between Keaton and the president, but the final moments have all the ingredients we see Howard make use of in the conclusions of his future films. In hindsight, *Gung Ho* really looks like a trial run, or the prototype for the sorts of successful and uplifting stories audiences would see in later decades.

Celebrating determination and ingenuity:
Thirteen Lives

Nearly all of Ron Howard's films, including a significant number of Imagine Entertainment's titles, are a case study in will power. Regardless of how nonsensical one considers Howard's comedies, the theme of persistence resonates within the various protagonists. By the start of the 2020s as Howard began to look at natural disaster topics, and *Thirteen Lives* epitomizes the same rhythm of the other impossible conquest narratives: things are bad, and then they get worse.

Howard's aspiration for change remains evident: with *Apollo 13* and *The Missing*, we are shown two accounts of those who are lost and those trying to save them. One is staged in the modern space-age era, and the other in the desolate western frontier. Note that in *The Missing*, Evan Rachel Wood longs to be a part of America's Gilded Age, wanting to be at a nearby fair and see the emerging technology, yet she's resigned to the brutal lifestyle of barren and undeveloped New Mexico. When Howard takes on *In the Heart of the Sea* the audience is left stranded with the shipwrecked crew and doesn't show the viewer what's happening back home. The opposite is at play in *Thirteen Lives*; by the 6-minute mark of the film, the audience doesn't get to see the young kids anymore, and are left uninformed of their circumstances until the 44-minute mark when they are discovered malnourished. The added irony is that the events of *In the Heart of the Sea* are dated to the 1820s, *The Missing* to the 1880s, and *Apollo 13* the 1970s. The technological advances from the ocean, to the western frontier, to traversing outer space are staggering from this historical perspective – and yet the events of *Thirteen Lives* takes place in the late-2010s, and the complications of underwater caving are profoundly difficult.

During the course of the opening 40-odd minute timeframe of *Thirteen Lives* we're shown great struggling on the part of the Thai government and various divers struggling to assess the situation and navigate the cave. There's a lot of problem solving, including trial and error with making sense of the cave's layout, and recurring implications that the boys are dead inside the cavern. In actuality, the two British divers were already convinced the boys and their coach were dead by the time they arrived in Thailand.[3] Once the boys are discovered, (again, at the 44-minute mark of a two-and-a-half-hour long film), a celebration breaks out that Viggo Mortensen believes is premature as he firmly believes there is no way to remove the boys trapped inside the cave. Here the audience is presented with an apparent success of miraculously finding all thirteen of them alive, which is compounded with something more tragic: instead of finding decaying bodies, they will be forced to witness the soccer team slowly starve, or suffocate, or drown should the cave continue to flood.

As the predicament of how to save the boys is contemplated, the possibility of putting them under anesthesia comes up, yet the audience is teased with this recommendation. The conversation between Viggo Mortensen and Colin Farrell implies that bringing in Joel Edgerton's character is, "just a crazy idea" that only *might* work. Once Joel Edgerton, the anesthetist, enters the story he's grateful to be asked, but considers himself below the level of expertise when compared to the other divers. It's implied that putting boys under anesthesia will kill them, but again, it's teased. The viewer innately knows "this" is the direction that *Thirteen Lives* is heading without it being explicitly told.

Instinctively we know Edgerton is the expert that will contrive and supervise the dangerous procedure to save the soccer team. In an effort for emotional accuracy, the proposal for this idea was changed for the movie – the exchange between Viggo Mortensen (Rick Stanton) and Joel Edgerton (Dr. Harry Harris) took place over text message, not in person after his arrival. However, to accurately convey the severity of putting children under anesthesia and then under water, the audience needs to view the exchange between these professionals face to face. The human emotion reigns supreme in Howard's cinema, particularly when danger is on the horizon. The film elusively tells us that this is the option they will ultimately pursue by Edgerton explicitly saying that he will *not* do it. As actually happened, *Thirteen Lives* exacerbates the danger depicting the death of one of the Thai military divers, thereby increasing the desperation to try inoculating children in an unsuitable environment.

Unlike the majority of Howard's dramas, *Thirteen Lives'* musical score is subdued and the dramatic moments are played with relatively matter-of-factness. There's only one "yelling" scene courtesy of Viggo Mortensen, yet he's not unruly or bombastic in voicing his opinion about the danger of the media announcing that the kids were found alive. The usage of sound underwater in the cave adds the greatest threat to the situation. Unlike the august scores of John Williams for *Far and Away*, and James Horner in *Apollo 13*, or the intense cinematography and editing of *Cinderella Man* and *Rush* – the underwater cave dives of *Thirteen Lives* are claustrophobic, murky, slow and audibly orotund. The intensity of being inside a submerged tight cave is uniquely on par with the intensity of *Rush*'s Formula 1 race, or *Cinderella Man*'s boxing match. The death of the Thai diver is alarming on account of the scene's loudness, followed by its silence. His death pushes all the rescuers to reconsider the risks of trying to get as many of the boys out alive, not to mention the sedation, and inability to monitor them.

Thirteen Lives doesn't need to dabble in the science of anesthesia as the audience is given enough baseline facts to comprehend the hazards involved. When formally proposing the idea to the governor and going through the various threats, the tone is set: "So, you are expecting causalities?" - "Yes. I expect casualties." For those who knew the story prior to seeing the film, there is a fascination about how they orchestrated this delicate process. Those who are/were unfamiliar with the story prior to seeing the film witness the agonizing process of getting just two of the boys through the confined caverns – with needing to do it eleven more times.

For a rescue mission that involved so many shifting factors, the film blends all these plots together, creating a narrative yarn that sounds messy, but successfully articulates the power of teamwork. We recognize recurring faces throughout the film; each character has their own plot, although we don't follow each one thoroughly, and nor does *Thirteen Lives* require us to do so. The twelve boys and their coach need to be rescued – that's the baseline. There are several different subplots going on that come to fruition in the finale. We don't exit *Thirteen Lives* with every single subplot recalled down to every detail. Instead we have a sense of the multiple efforts required to pull off the challenge of surviving mother nature.

A recap of all these subplots makes for a heavy load: first there is the threat of the cave flooding above via the monsoon rain. Secondly, the mother of the youngest boy is from a minority group and is concerned he won't be included in any rescue mission. This segues into another subplot about how that boy is physically the smallest and therefore the most difficult to find a mask for. The film accounts for Colin Farrell's emotional difficulties, thinking of his own son in correlation to the plight of the boys. There is a diver (played by Tom Bateman), who is struggling with emotions of the situation when getting lost on the last day. Another compounded emotional difficulty nods to problems outside of the current crisis, through Joel Edgerton's sick father back home. If this wasn't enough there are the politics to consider: this happened during the Governor's final days in office, and he's handed a crisis that quickly turns into an international event within a mere few days. Carefully crafted into the film is another political football showcased through the subtleness of the acting performances: the animosity between the Thai government, the Thai Navy SEAL divers and the volunteer British divers. Last, but not least, throughout all of this is the presence of the "sleeping princess" on account of the mountainous terrain that resembles a pregnant lady laying on her back. For those aware of the religious belief, it's certainly edited into the movie – and for those unfamiliar, it's presented voyeuristically through Viggo Mortensen and his irritation with the prayer beads.[4] For the western audience, attention will be fixated on the British divers and their bravado.

These cumbersome subplots come to fruition in the final act of the film, and although it makes for a loaded screenplay – these different plots keep the audience engaged, while the other boys are taken out. *Thirteen Lives* began as a logistical puzzle, but it slowly shifts to a timed thriller due to the divers needing to extract the boys before the monsoon water floods them. The young mother, played by Pattarakorn Tangsupakul, becomes the focal point for the strife of the families awaiting news outside. Her young son is the smallest and most delicate, yet also the most eager to leave. Balled up into this, we're given a scene were Colin Farrell struggles to make sure the breathing is consistent on one of the boys, reminding us that each body is going to react differently to the drugs. This did in fact happen to John Volanthen; the scene wasn't embellished or altered to increase tension. With that in mind, the scene remains poignant on account of moments we saw previously of Farrell's affection for his son and talking with him over the phone back home. During the final rescue of the remaining boys, the nerves of Tom Bateman's character start to get to him, which puts the audience on edge anticipating another freak accident. Once all are extracted from the cave, we are told about the death of Edgerton's father, which services as a reminder to the audience of the extensive amount of time and effort this rescue took that separated people from their own lives.

The undercurrent in all this is the friction between the foreign UK divers and the Thai government. As the hazards of the situation are understood and the threat to the boy's livelihood is increasing pearled, the groups start working together. *Thirteen Lives* is a long jump from the 1980s slapstick of *Gung Ho*, to the true story of the Thai cave rescue, but we see that bridge between an Asian culture and an Anglo-Saxon culture accomplishing an incredible feat. Nearly thirty years after *Gung Ho*, Howard is still pointing his camera at two cultures figuring out how to work together.

Throughout all this drama are tiny moments of resourcefulness that don't require an explanation. These moments showcase a spirit of creativity in pulling off the rescue. Only a couple seconds of screen time are devoted to Viggo Mortensen realizing the boy's bare feet are getting bruised along the bottom surface of the cave during the swim out. The usage of the half-filled plastic water bottles around the boy's ankles to give buoyancy doesn't require explanation as the audience simply just witnesses the action unfolding. The way in which Joel Edgerton talks to and handles the boys while administering the ketamine is very matter-of-fact because we, the audience, have had the chance to process he's merely a volunteer doctor asked to help in something that's way outside of his limits. The fact that Edgerton is so down to Earth and casual in handling the traumatic events makes the exchange between him and the boys enticing to watch. All of the multiple efforts that went into helping the soccer team survive something that should have killed them comes down to taking a risk. The resourcefulness of the unassuming common person are the ones who conquer the seemingly impossible conquest.

CHAPTER 5
THE COMMON INDIVIDUAL

It's a bit of a mental challenge to not automatically associate the main character(s) in a movie as "leading figure" therefore, a "leader" because we're imagining the face of a celebrity – someone that the vast majority of us have not, and probably will never meet in person. We generally presume that recognizable people are wealthy and influential. The name and face of Russell Crowe surely results in "movie star," and while he portrayed impressive individuals in powerhouse acting performances in both *A Beautiful Mind* and *Cinderella Man*, are not the appearance of both John Nash and Jim Braddock generally simple people? Neither of Crowe's performances evoke that of an imposing military officer (*Master & Commander*; *Les Misérables*); an aggressive law enforcement agent (*L.A. Confidential*; *American Gangster*) or a violent sociopath (*3:10 to Yuma*; *Unhinged*), let alone a roman gladiator. Make no mistake, boxers often strike a posing figure, but the audience sees significantly more of a family man in the first 15-minutes of *Cinderella Man* than a boxer in the square circle. Even *The New York Times* had reported that Braddock was tagged with the nickname "Plain Jim" by friends.[1] The math student turned professor in *A Beautiful Mind* maintains the appearance of a quirky simpleton infatuated with his own projects.

If we consider the variety of characters in Howard's canon of movies, there are few with a grandiose ego, and more often than not, their inflated sense of self ends up leading to their demise or mistakes. The bratty Suzy Gilstrap in *Skyward*; the overzealous Michael Keaton in *Gung Ho*; the lonely Frank Langella in *Frost/Nixon* and the egocentric Chris Hemsworth in *Rush* are each their own worst enemy. While some of the antagonists aren't concrete individuals in Howard's movies (circumstances like rain are the adversary in *Thirteen Lives*), the villains often falter on account of their pride. The poor decisions made by Gary Sinise in *Ransom*, Jeffrey Tambor in *How the Grinch Stole Christmas* and Ewan McGregor in *Angels & Demons* all come from a place of ostentatious self-righteousness. Meanwhile, the majority of the leading characters in Howard's films are content with doing their best in their respective lives and almost reluctantly accept the adulation that comes their way.

Exultation of the smallest:
Willow

Of all Howard's films, none suffer from datedness as badly as *Willow*. Whereas *Grand Theft Auto* remains an unapologetic reflection of the 1970s, and *Gung Ho* is an unapologetic product of the 1980s, *Willow* sits on the rung of the ladder leading to where cinema was developing towards with regards to technology and genre.

It helps to use other blockbusters from around the time to help unpackage *Willow* as it's arguably the most unrelatable movie in Howard's filmography. The year prior to *Willow*'s release gave audiences *The Princess Bride* (1987), a comedy that mocked the medieval genre and never took itself too seriously. *Willow* offers a lot of comedy, but there is an equal amount of dark moments throughout the film. Something as brief as the death of the midwife in the opening, the shot of Warwick Davis' daughter screaming in fear during a dog attack, or the ghastly sight of people turning into pigs — these images and the action scenes that accompany them tilt *Willow* in the direction of a drama. There should be no dissolution that the production was intended to be an adventure fantasy, albeit one that took itself much more seriously than *The Princess Bride*. Two years following *Willow*, Hollywood would deliver another medieval-era epic with *Robin Hood: Prince of Thieves* (1991). Although the film would maintain some comedic flair, *Robin Hood* did without the fantasy (i.e. magic and monsters), and was aiming to cash in on the box-office fortune that Kevin Costner could garnish in the late 1980s and early 1990s. As the medieval genre developed in the 1990s, the humor and visual effects were progressively becoming out of style.

By the time *Braveheart* (1995) arrived, the comedy and the magic/witchcraft were essentially drained from the "medieval" genre. By modern standards, even *Braveheart* looks a tad dated, yet it didn't rely on computer graphics and the production took itself significantly more seriously than the films that came before it in the previous decades. (The "sword and sandals" epics of the 1950s and 1960s are a class of their own). The datedness of *Willow* was an aspect that the production couldn't have avoided at the time, and their shared composer of James Horner emphasizes this. If you played the soundtracks to *Braveheart* and *Willow* side by side, the similarities are obvious, via the usage of instruments and the way Horner inserts "sounds" of fright that periodically blare through a piece of music. Yet, if you screened the movies themselves back to back, specifically the characters of Val Kilmer vs. Mel Gibson, the contrast of *Willow* and *Braveheart* are blatant. George Lucas, *Willow*'s producer and story author, ensured that his previous fictitious creations, (the *Star Wars* and *Indiana Jones* franchises), had a healthy dose of comedy intermixed with the fantasy — yet *Willow* uses humor significantly more than Lucas' other films. With Howard coming from a comedic background, it's no surprise that *Willow* is filled with more sight gags and a significant amount of bickering between characters – banter that fits *The Princess Bride*, yet would be unbefitting towards *Braveheart*.

The films that would truly date *Willow* arrive in the early 2000s with vastly popular *The Lord of the Rings* and the *Pirates of the Caribbean* franchises. The movies owe their success to outstanding visual effects — not that *Willow*'s effects were terrible (in fact, some look very authentic when compared to CGI), yet the formula for adventure/fantasy in mainstream movies had been perfected. Particularly *The Lord of the Rings* ages *Willow* exponentially to the point that one has to assume that if Hollywood attempted to adapt J.R.R. Tolkien's books in the late-1980s, *Willow* is a very good representation of how the trilogy probably would have looked.*

It's worth considering what Dennis Muren, one of the greatest pioneers in movie special effects, and who worked on *Willow*, said over a decade later:

> For me, *Willow* is a unique film because it very much represented the end of the photo chemical era of filmmaking, and the promise, or the beginning of digital. *Willow* was unique because it had a number of wonderful things we could do with it, but it was also very frustrating that we couldn't quite get into the digital and computer graphic world yet. If we just could get this working, it would be that much neater and that much better, but if we do the best we can right now with what we got — and that's how we ended up with morphing and we ended up with a few things that were showing the future. So you've got both types of work in the film: you've got the best that could be done in the late 1980s and you got a preview of what's coming in the 90s.(2)

Although *Willow* often gets categorized into the company of technological breakthroughs of the late 80s and early 90s, the fact that it was "a Ron Howard film" has almost become an afterthought. Nevertheless Howard's authorship is still at work in *Willow*: it was completely different from what he did up until that point, it's a buddy-comedy between Warwick Davis and Val Kilmer, even though there is a considerable delay until this "team-

---

*The parallels between *Willow* and *The Lord of the Rings* seem countless: there is a village of small people who live in burrowed huts with circular entrances almost exactly like the hobbits. A wizard emphasizes self-encouragement to Warwick Davis, not unlike the wizard in *The Lord of the Rings*, who inspires courage in the hobbits. The company that sets out with the baby are transporting something small, but very dangerous — much like the One Ring itself. Val Kilmner is a great warrior renegade, not unlike the king hiding within the traveling company. There is a fairy queen who gives Warwick Davis a special tool of magic, not unlike the elvish queen who bestows powerful weapons to the fellowship. The scary hunting dogs look a lot like the wolf-esque Warg-Riders. Even from a production standpoint a correlation is present, being that a significant portion of *Willow* was shot in New Zealand, the main location used for *The Lord of the Rings* and *The Hobbit* films.

up" happens (at the 48-minute mark of the film). The pressure is on Warwick Davis from the moment he appears on screen with children taking his harvest and a landlord accusing him of stealing seed. Yet more than anything else, *Willow* is a perfect example of Howard's attraction towards the exaltation of the smallest (literally), and most ordinary person, to levels of profound adulation.

In the first act of the film, the wizard discards Warwick Davis' attraction to magic, saying that true "powers" come from within. It's one person's own self-confidence and belief that results in success, which is a fundamental moral we see Howard fixate on. There is no magic behind Russell Crowe's determination in *Cinderella Man*; there's no divine powers that Audrey Tautou possesses in *The Da Vinci Code*; Alden Ehrenreich has no understanding of "the force" in *Solo*. Time and time again, Howard's characters come from a disadvantage and work against a larger system where the odds are stacked against them. We see this very plainly in the way Warwick Davis uses his own personal talents on his conquest, growing as a person upon the completion of his quest. He believes he is a great sorcerer, therefore he allows himself to become one.

Just doing the job:
The Paper

The small Warwick Davis in *Willow* is an unextraordinary person who is hurled into an extraordinary adventure. This is exactly where the audience find Michael Keaton as an editor for one of New York's City's lesser popular newspapers, however that's irrelevant to him because he just wants to do his job and help out the disadvantaged.

***

There is an exchange between Michael Keaton and Marisa Tomei in *The Paper* that is worth reflecting on. As tensions build in an office, Randy Quaid begrudgingly starts stacking newspapers in a corner as the overlapping conversations ensue. Without warning, we hear a loud gunshot, revealing that Randy Quid had just fired a gun into the stack of papers, putting the camped room into deadpan silence. Quaid then slowly insists, "Let Marty [Marisa Tomei] talk to her husband. Please." Everyone files out of the small office in silence, to which Marisa Tomei (Marty) looks to Michael Keaton (Henry) and says, "God, I miss this place!"

Seconds later, the next scene, shows Michael Keaton (Henry) staggering around the press room looking for a working Coca-Cola vending machine, followed by his very pregnant wife who is questioning him about the developing story of the day, his potential job offer at a rival newspaper – but, in actuality, Marisa Tomei (Marty) is all worked up following a lunch date she had with a friend. Briskly walking around the newsroom trying to find a working Coca-Cola machine, the following conversation between Keaton (Henry) and Tomei (Marty) takes place:

```
INT. NEWS FLOOR - DAY.
HENRY power walks through the newsroom with a very
pregnant looking MARTY following a couple steps
behind.

                    MARTY
          Let me give you a hypothetical.

                    HENRY
          (Checking his wrist watch)
          Can it be a short hypothetical?

                    MARTY
          You're a professional tennis player.
          You love tennis, but you wreck your
          knee and you can't play tennis again.

Henry turns into a small office, arriving at a Coca-
Cola machine, and starts depositing change into it.

                    MARTY (cont'd)
          Your doubles partner however goes on
          and wins Wimbledon! How do ya feel?
```

                    HENRY
          Wins Wimbledon? Happy as hell, couldn't be
          happier.

                    MARTY
          Oh bullshit! You hate him.

                    HENRY
          Do not.

Henry bends down to grab a can of Coke from the machine.

                    MARTY
          I don't wanna hate you Henry.

A STAFFER runs through the office.

                    STAFFER
          Henry, they're doing it now.

                    HENRY
          (To STAFFER)
          Yeah, yeah, yeah, yeah. Coming.

Henry returns attention to Marty.

                    HENRY (cont'd)
          I gotta go to this. Okay?

Marty is visibly defeated.

                    MARTY
          Yeah, yeah, I'll see you at dinner
          tonight.

Marty and Henry begin to backtrack out of the small space and back into the larger newsroom.

                    MARTY (cont'd)
          8:30, Gus's Place. Your parents.
          Please, don't be late. Please.

                         HENRY
          Honey, am I ever late?

                         MARTY
          (Letting out a "happy" sigh)
          It's not funny.

                         HENRY
          It's a little bit funny. Hey - see
          you.

                         MARTY
          See you.

                         HENRY
          Hey, give me a kiss.

Marty stands firm in her place, her pregnant belly is pronounced. Henry leans awkwardly over with his lips pursed for a kiss and pecks her on the cheek.

Henry is still looking at her, but begins to walk off in the opposite direction.

                    HENRY (cont'd)
          That's it?

                         MARTY
          See you.

                         HENRY
          K.

Still walking down the long office, Henry kisses the palm of his hand and extends it out towards Marty. He continues to make a goofy "kissy" face at her as he walks in the opposite direction. He

```
finally turns and jogs down towards the EDITOR'S
OFFICE.

Marty cracks a smile watching him leave, and
returns the air kiss in his direction.
```

Less than 30 seconds after this exchange, Michael Keaton (Henry) stares out at Marisa Tomei (Marty) through a large picture window, watching her exit the newsroom. What's evident in this quickly paced exchange is that the romance is totally embedded into both of the character's being and existence despite whatever drama is going on in their lives. The lovey-dovey back n' forth between Keaton & Tomei underscores a healthy romantic status between the couple (which is fundamental for Howard's characters). It's also a perfect exchange showcasing that Keaton would be happy for his hypothetical tennis partner winning a major championship. It reflects a common trait for many of Howard's protagonists: they aren't striving for fame and fortune.

In the first act of *The Paper*, Keaton expresses mixed emotions about potentially receiving a job offer from one of the biggest newspapers in the country (the fictional "*Sentinel*" is clearly meant to be *The New York Times*). Once the drama about the fraudulent arrest of two young men comes into the plot, the opportunity Keaton has about advancing his journalism career becomes an afterthought. Getting caught in lifting a news tip off the desk of the rival *Sentinel* publication during his job interview, costs Keaton the career opportunity.

Similar to *Gung Ho*, Keaton is arguably his own worst enemy. Blowing the job offer from the larger newspaper on account of stealing a news tip from the desk of the head editor, thereby blowing his chances. On the flip side, the intention of getting the story corrected in time to save the lives of the two innocent youths becomes the moral quandary of the second half of the film. Keaton is rewarded by way of his team breaking the story and saving the lives of the falsely accused. When Keaton and Tomei are reunited the next morning in the hospital – Tomei, the workaholic shows him the headline of the paper, `"I guess you kinda kicked everyone's butt today, huh?"` But in a Ron Howard film: Keaton takes the paper, looks at it, and then tosses it on the floor turning his attention to Tomei. Herein lies Keaton's other sin: failing to make time for his wife, skimping out on dinner with her parents and not being at home when she began prematurely hemorrhaging with their newborn.

In the end, what's Keaton's greatest triumph? Altering a fake narrative to save the lives of two innocent kids and making it back into bed with Marisa Tomei. He doesn't need a Pulitzer Prize for the story or a job promotion – he just wants to be a good husband. Recalling Keaton's semi-reluctance to `"cover the world"` with the larger newspaper, despite the pay raise, holds true to that he would rather keep his sleeves rolled up and be in the thick of it with his on-the-ground team.

The outcasts:
How the Grinch Stole Christmas

Of all the comedies, *How the Grinch Stole Christmas* remains the most ostentatious with regards to production value. A dream of Brian Grazer's to adapt Dr. Suess' immensely popular children's books,[3] Howard's version of *The Grinch* does display his authorship, yet ultimately the film is much more attune to the canon of Jim Carry comedies that dominated the 1990s box office, In fact, Howard credits Carrey with the structure and tone of the film due to the amount of improvisation that took place on set with Carrey pushing for multiple takes. Referring to Carrey as a musician, Howard says he was constantly trying out new styles and various rifts.[4] With this in mind, *The Grinch* is closer to Carrey's sense of humor (a la 1994's *The Mask* or *Ace Ventura*), yet still packaged inside of a Ron Howard film, with a majestic James Horner score and the production team that already had the dramas *Backdraft*; *Far and Away*; *Apollo 13* and *Ransom* under their belts.

Although *How the Grinch Stole Christmas* is a callback to Howard's comedies of the 1980s, the *Grinch* has a significantly stronger sense of cinema about it. One aspect that sets it apart from every single one of Howard's other films is the use of Dutch angles throughout the entire picture. Despite the brazen tone of the comedy, this simple tilting of every frame adds a dramatic undertone. In addition, it's very difficult to find a flush 90° angle anywhere in the film, which was done to maintain a Dr. "Suess-ian" aesthetic. Cinematographer Don Peterman wanted all the colors to be aggressive and bold — a concept that extended to the costumes, make-up as well as the supporting cast (a handful of the Who's are Cirque du Soleil performers).[5][6] Although detractors may be turned off by the outlandish humor, this combination of the set design without any right angles, and askew mise-en-scene make for very cinematic shots.

The theme of opposites is particularly present in Howard's films as the Grinch (Jim Carrey) and Cindy Lou Who (Taylor Momsen) fit the bill. The two are the most isolated characters in the film by being the most misunderstood by everyone in Whoville. Composer James Horner suggested linking their discontent and loneliness by way of a song which resulted in the "Where Are You Christmas" which appears towards the end of the first Act. Howard wanted to emphasize that the two were the only characters that recognized that the holiday season was losing its fervor due to overt commercialization.[7] Although Carrey is correct in his ridicule of the Whos cheapening the holiday with materialism, there is no way for him to possibly steal Christmas itself. Meanwhile, Momsen (Cindy Lou) is unsuccessful in convincing Jeffrey Tambor (the Mayor) to have a charitable spirit. Momsen is a young ambitious girl with a strong personality, but she's never snotty in her demeanor while being different from the other Whos.

Anyone familiar with Dr. Suess' original short story knows that the first half of Howard's film is a heavy embellishment. The entire first hour of the film is primarily used to fuel Carrey's acumen to steal Christmas. Again, Carrey is not wrong in his denunciation of the Whobilation, which functions as an allegorical depiction, of what secularism has done to Christmas. Howard refers to Carrey's rant as the "Jimmy Stewart" moment, (a reference to the famous speech in 1939's *Mr. Smith Goes to Washington*).[8]

Although we are supposed to laugh at Jim Carrey's outlandish behavior, the variety of accents that Carrey uses throughout the film could suggests that the Grinch is mentally ill. Therefore, the speech at the Whobilation can be viewed as the outcast miscreant who deserves being listened to. The exultation of the different, sometimes outcast, person is something we see with Michael Keaton in *Night Shift*; Daryl Hannah in *Splash*; Warwick Davis in *Willow*; Tom Cruise in *Far and Away*; Russell Crowe in *A Beautiful Mind*; Daniel Brühl in *Rush* and Alden Ehrenreich in *Solo*.

Although two radically different films, is not Gabriel Basso telling off the Yale elite at the fancy dinner in *Hillbilly Elegy* exactly on par with Jim Carrey's rant? The unexpected person ends up undermining everyone around them. Although Howard's dominating theme is watching these characters overcome incredible resistance, it reflects Howard's favoring of the proverbial "little guy."

Needless to say, the yelling and wild antics of Jim Carrey doesn't necessarily make him the ideal model of someone whose humility would influence the betterment of society. He requires the innocent guidance of a child to realize the errors of his ways – a contrast to Jeffrey Tambor who can't hide his irritation at letting an outsider into the fold. For all of the repugnant things Jim Carrey does throughout the film, none of them register in comparison to Tambor talking down to Momsen Christmas morning after the big heist takes place. Admonishing her in front of the citizens: "Did anyone listen to me? No. You choose to listen to a little not-to-be-taken-seriously girl." with a malicious emphasis placed on the word "girl." Yet it's Momsen's father who comes to her defense, pointing out that her actions reaffixed the spirit of Christmas, which in turn uplifts the other Whos. The supposed influential mayor of Whoville fails to understand the Whos' favorite holiday; the common mailman and her daughter on the other hand figured it out on their own.

CHAPTER 6
ROMANCE

The seemingly impossible conquests are the MacGuffins that Ron Howard's films are built around. The challenges and struggles are the lifeblood of the stories. This was blatant in Howard's early career as seen through *Cotton Candy* and *Skyward*, both which drum up the romantic subplot to the point it becomes integral as to where the leading characters end up by the finale. Dr. Seuss' *How the Grinch Stole Christmas* children's book has no references to any sort of romantic interest, yet in Howard's cinematic adaptation, the kiddie school flirting becomes the inflection point for what turns Jim Carrey into loathing the Christmas holiday. Nathaniel Philbrick's book, *In the Heart of the Sea*, has very few references to Peggy Chase, the wife of Owen Chase, the main character played by Chris Hemsworth in the film. In Howard's adaptation, Owen and Peggy Chase are elevated by having the couple have two scenes together prior to The Essex's departure. Later, Peggy Chase, played by Charlotte Riley, is squarely stationed on the dock when The Essex departs. When the lost crew return home, Hemsworth's focal point is his love interest, once again standing on the dock. As in the true story, Peggy Chase had given birth to a daughter during the time that her husband was lost at sea.[1]

To date, *The Da Vinci Code* and *Eight Days A Week* are the only two films where a love story is entirely omitted, however there is definitely a form of screen chemistry between Hanks and his co-star, Audrey Tautou. Although accurate to the novel, the co-op feels more for marketing purposes (the posters for *The Da Vinci Code* certainly underscore this), as Hanks and Tautou never have romantic implications. By the third film, *Inferno*, Tom Hanks is given a love interest, albeit a former girlfriend, thereby keeping with his bachelor status from the novels. It's also worth noting the same character in the *Inferno* novel had no romantic past with the Robert Langdon character – the subplot was intentionally created for the film to give more background to Langdon's/Hanks' past.[2] With regards to *Eight Days A Week*, there is something to consider about the girls fawning over The Beatles throughout their touring, which does not qualify for a "love story" per say, but exhibits attraction to the opposite sex, which is something that Howard regularly addresses.

The amorous themes in Howard's films are never taken for granted: despite there being several romantic comedies on his résumé, with ample amounts of humor sowed into the rapport, the couples' relationship are always threated seriously. We could almost go as far as saying that romantic interests are given a reverence in Howard's cinematic universe because they're woven so tightly into the crux of the story. Something as zany as *Grand Theft Auto* which never takes a breath… except… when the two leads have a quarrel. It's as if the movie hit the "pause" button on itself and needs the young lovers to work out their differences before continuing on. Once they do settle their differences, what happens? They're resolve to continue their journey and elope in Las Vegas becomes stronger than before. We see the exact same pattern repeat itself in *Cotton Candy*; *Skyward* and *Night Shift* in that a romance appears in the film, strictly for the main characters to express romantic feelings, and then the movie goes right back to the main event.

Complicated romance in a comedy:
Splash

There's a short moment in the beginning of *Splash* when Tom Hanks receives a call from his girlfriend who is breaking up with him. The audience is only privy to his side of the conversation and we hear Hanks repeat a question directed at him: "Do I love you?" to which he stutters for a couple of seconds unable to respond, clearly indicating he doesn't. Or maybe he's hesitant to actually speak those words to another person? It's a short moment, with a comedic beat at the end, courtesy of John Candy listening in on the other phone, but the exchange holds just enough weight to it giving the audience an honest emotional connection to Hanks. The foundation of Tom Hanks' character flaw is his inability to express or acknowledge love for another person.

On the flip side of the coin, Daryl Hannah's secret of being a mermaid, which she won't disclose to Hanks, conjures a romantic irk between the two. Despite *Splash* being a fantasy, the concept of one "lover" hiding a major secret to the other "lover" is something that audiences can understand. It's an intriguing plot point to hook viewers in with given the nonsensical premise: *Splash* is an implausible storyline, yet the narrative is structured around a contrast of emotions. The mermaid in New York City might be what's on the poster and DVD box, but *Splash* is about a contrast of emotions: Tom Hanks' aversion to profess love, then falling in love with Daryl Hannah, and her being cagy around him on account of her damning secret identity.

A consequential moment comes byway of an ice-skating scene at Rockefeller Center, where Hanks asks Hannah to marry him and she turns him down, stating she only have three days left before she has to depart. Considering the level of aversion the audience already knows Hanks has to allowing himself to fall in love with someone makes Hannah's rejection crushing. Furthermore, the audience also comprehends Hannah's innocence to such human emotions causing more relatable vexation to the viewer.

Although Hanks and Hannah are given a reunion the following morning, the truth of the mermaid has yet to be tested, and the film has this disclosed to Hanks in the worst possible way. When Hannah gets sprayed with water, revealing the mermaid in front of media cameras, the two lovers are taken away by government scientists. The lovers are reunited in a large water tank, but with Hannah now in mermaid form. When Hannah goes to swim towards Hanks, he flinches back. It's a subtle moment that speaks volumes as Hannah picks up on this rejection, and it shatters the romance between the two. Ron Howard's "against all odds" barrier has arrived: it's not enough to place lovers in contrasting living environments, have them break up and get back together with a stronger resolve – rather, it's the brutal truth that shatters them.

Being a comedy of course, Hanks will team-up with his friends to rescue and break Daryl Hannah free from the science lab in a whole sequence rooted in humor. The two will live together happily-ever-after in an ocean kingdom but only *after* they both go through serious turmoil that tests the strength of their romantic bond.

Romance embedded into the authorship:
Far and Away

Something to take note of right off the bat in *Far and Away*: "produced by," "story by" and "directed by" credits — which tells us there is a hefty amount of Howard's personal authorship going on here. Howard's Irish heritage and his father's roots from Oklahoma, the location where Cruise and Kidman end up, are the baseline for this very personal film. The immigrant drama anticipates exactly where Howard's career was going in the early 1990s and fits the mold of many future films he would direct.

Far and Away has moments of comedy peppered throughout, but the humor is more tempered as the story is more invested in the plight of the two leads. In the first 20 minutes, Cruise's Father dies, his family home burned down the day of his father's funeral, and his attempt to seek revenge is mocked by the local villagers. Cruise is obviously the weakest character in the Irish providence despite his strength and zeal. His conquest to avenge his father begins as a weak revenge tale, which is a fitting start since the story doesn't really take off until Nicole Kidman is added into the mix. The budding romance between the two becomes the kinetic spark that elevates the film. The fruit bowl over Cruise's crotch in the bedroom is typical of Ron Howard's use of a sexual tease to establish a dynamic of attraction between the characters. As Cruise and Kidman's respective life in Boston progresses, their views of America change, and so too their respective views on class division and labor. The duality between Cruise and Kidman grows as their standings in society continue to juxtapose each other, leading them in further frustration, but at the same time, drawing them into a better understanding of each other.

Far and Away can be seen as a "dress rehearsal" for *Cinderella Man*, specifically the Irish boxer fighting for financial gain and to raise himself out of poverty. The relationship between the male and female leads is a crucial element of both films. When the audience is introduced to Russell Crowe and Renée Zellweger in *Cinderella Man*, their screen-romance is already a few years into their marriage along with three children – whereas the dynamics between Tom Cruise and Nicole Kidman are that of immature youth.

As Cruise rises in the ranks of amateur boxing, Kidman sinks lower in her factory job. Their morale and financial situation reflects this until an opportunity arrives (again, note Howard's motif of life granting extraordinary opportunities). When the match between Cruise and the big Italian fighter comes into play, the bout becomes another hurdle for Cruise to conquer on his long term conquest to go claim land in Oklahoma. Kidman is staged well in the context of the boxing match; this bout is clearly an important fight, and it results in the impending love affair between the two beginning to materialize. The audience gets two important story developments at once: during the fight, one of the Irish bosses gets handsy with Kidman, and Cruise pauses the fight in attempt to break up the behavior, yet upon Cruise's inability to separate Kidman from the Irish mafioso, he gets tossed back into the ring and illegally passes the chalk line which continues the fight. The devastating punch delivered to Cruise's side comes just as things seem on the up and up for the couple, but rather it begins an avalanche of setbacks: Cruise loses the fight, they discover that Kidman's family from Ireland has arrived in Boston looking for them, they are made homeless, and just after the two openly admit their love for each other, Kidman is shot.

It's worth taking a moment to highlight the pretend dinner scene at night in the big fancy house that Cruise and Kidman sneak into after he loses the fight. Silhouetted by snowfall, the romantic exchange between the two was a different caliber from Howard than what he put on screen throughout the 1980s. As Howard progressed as a director, so did the romantic tension in his movies. Obviously there is a maturity in the way the elderly couples interact in *Cocoon*, vs. William Baldwin and Jennifer Jason Leigh being intimate on top of the firetruck in *Backdraft*. Tom Cruise and Nicole Kidman professing their love for each other before getting separated is the hurdle that kicks off the final act of the film, bringing the characters to the Oklahoma territory.

If it weren't enough, *Far and Away* also includes a love-triangle with one of Kidman's love interests from Ireland. Given the amount of attention given to the budding romance between Cruise and Kidman, the audience *knows* they're going to end up together. The set designs, costumes, cinematography and music throughout the film are much more focused on recreating the Oklahoma Land Run of 1893 – yet what draws is it that us into the investing into this story? The lavish romance.

Couples in contrast:
Cinderella Man & The Dilemma

The majority of the time that Howard's screen couples have an argument, they reunite in the aftermath. The arguments are nearly all ideological based; Howard has never directed domestic violence or intentional psychological spousal abuse. To date, we haven't seen something on the level of *Casablanca* (1943); *Annie Hall* (1977); or *La La Land* (2016), where the separation of the leading couple culminates the film's ending. Additionally, since many of the films have male leads, we see Howard's affinity for strong female characters present when looking at the difficult situations. More often than not, the reason the on-screen couples are victorious is on account of the maturity of the woman.

***

In a decision made out of profound concern for the health of their children, Renée Zellweger in *Cinderella Man* sends her three kids away to live with relatives who can at least keep them warm in the winter – without telling her husband, Russell Crowe.* *Cinderella Man* makes perfectly clear within less than 20 minutes of screen time that both Crowe and Zellweger are upstanding people and loving parents – leaving the viewer with no doubt that they both try and want to do what's best for their children. The hardships of the Great Depression bring about the couple's opposing views on how to grapple with their poverty status and it brings them to a breaking point. After the heated exchange between Crowe and Zellweger, realizing that his kids are gone, Crowe leaves the apartment without explaining what he intends to do, which was intentional: for a few minutes even the audience isn't supposed to know where Russel Crowe is going.(5)

We could call Zellweger's decision one of weakness, however her actions indirectly push Crowe to confronting his own self-righteousness: going back to the people and the business that let him go, and begging for desperately needed funds. The circumstances of the Great Depression ruffle a conflict between husband and wife, thereby stresses the relationship between parents & children, as well as former employee & boss(es). It's a profile in courage because the audience is shown building up to this scene that Crowe is trying his best to handle the domestic instability and his lousy financial situation, but he cannot do it alone. He has to accept that he needs to turn to the generosity of others for help.

Although the politics of the 1930s boxing industry are a major feature of the film, *Cinderella Man* is very much invested in examining the family situation. A scene soon following shows an

---

*Whether or not the Braddock children were sent away is up for debate: in researching the film there were illusions to it made by both Mae and her eldest son, Jay, but nothing ever concrete. The book by Jeremy Schaap says that the kids were sent away to grandparents, but doesn't make note of James Braddock protesting that decision.(3) On the contrary, some of the other Braddock children denied ever being sent away – however, they were approximately 2 or 3 years younger than the age they are portrayed in the film. That said, the widow of Jay Braddock, the eldest son of James Braddock, firmly believes that Mae would have never sent the kids away without consulting her husband.(4)

outdoor birthday party where we see Crowe's co-worker from the docks, Paddy Considine in an argument with his wife. Considine's character was created for the film to be a "mirror image" of Russell Crowe; a good-natured person who makes bad decisions and becomes the dark portrait of what *could* happen to Russell Crowe.[6] Knowing this behind-the-scenes fact gives depth to the outdoor party scene: the audience has witnessed Crowe on the brink of tears in the boxing office begging for money, literally hat-in-hand, doing what he had to do to keep his family together. Now, attending a collective birthday party intended for all the neighborhood kids sponsored by the church, Paddy Considine openly struggles that his family has resorted to attending this event instead of being able to provide his kids with their own cake and party. Crowe accepts what the Great Depression has done to him and his family, and finds happiness being with his kids. This is not all that different from Bill Irwin telling the Mayor of Whoville that all he needs for Christmas is his family at the end of *How the Grinch Stole Christmas*, or Colin Farrell's connection with his son while witnessing the suffering parents in *Thirteen Lives*. Paddy Considine as Russell Crowe's metaphorical dark twin remains on the other the street, flask in hand, unaccepting of his circumstances instead of embracing them – which ends up provoking an argument with his wife. Here we see the intentional contrast of how these two fathers dealt with The Great Depression: we never see Crowe result to drinking, let alone drunk and disorderly. Crowe forced himself to do the incredibly difficult task of swallowing his pride to ask for and accept help when needed, whereas Paddy Considine cannot bring himself to do so. Furthermore, any and all conflicts we see between Crowe and Zellweger are private; they never happen in the public forum, whereas Considine embarrasses himself, his wife and his family by his actions. Also, it's Zellweger who asks Crowe to intervene between Considine and his wife. The contrast in *Cinderella Man* is for the audience to decide (not that we need much convincing): who do we want to strive to be in times of conflict?

In many ways, the best romances of Howard's films showcases couples we want to emulate.

***

Paddy Considine in *Cinderella Man* is another Howard character who fits the bill of someone who remains his own worst enemy. Bad decisions lead to Considine's death, but in the comedies it's typically the leading characters, nearly always the men, who are responsible for their self-inflicted wounds. When Howard made his reprieve to some lighthearted flair with *The Dilemma*, Vince Vaughn continued that trend.

Considering how late *The Dilemma* arrived in Howard's canon of movies (early 2010s), and how modest of a production scale it was compared to all the big budgeted movies that came before it, the film certainly "feels" like Howard & company did *The Dilemma* for themselves. We could almost go as far as calling the 2011 feature Howard's most carefree since it released after he had solidified his prestige as a major filmmaker, and especially because he spent the decade following *The Dilemma* continuing to undertake new cinematic challenges. The story is constructed around a lot of complicated emotions coming at Vaughn's character, be it business or personal life. He's somewhat of a continuation of the Michael Keaton characters in *Gung Ho* and *The Paper*: someone who is a tad too energetic and can't leave well enough alone. The people to blame for the problems in *The Dilemma* are Kevin James and Winona Ryder, but everything that gets worse is on account of Vaughn's actions. As Vaughn's life gets messier and messier, it's Jennifer Connelly who does everything in her wisdom to keep him stable. The difficulties that Vaughn & Connelly go through, even though they should be slipping apart, is what brings them closer together. A key plot point in *The Dilemma* that takes a backseat to becoming a subplot as the story unfolds is Vaughn's continual delaying of asking Connelly to marry him. At the end of the traumatic ordeal, Vaughn finally does so in a humble, quiet and simple manner (passing over a paper bag that's supposed to have a meal in it, but instead has an engagement ring). The cute maneuver is perfectly sufficient, and more charming than any of his oversized proposal ideas. It also solidifies Vaughn's love for Connelly, being that she stayed with him throughout the storm.

Oppositely, the relationship between Kevin James and Winona Ryder is the closest Howard has ever come to showcasing a truly toxic couple, and in the end of the film, they aren't together anymore. They both lie to each other, and we notice that Howard doesn't allow his camera to go behind their doors and show us their marital strife. Ryder repeatedly says to Vaughn `"Stay out of my marriage."` and the audience becomes a spectator voyeuristically through Vaughn, trying to leer in. The only closed-door conversations *The Dilemma* gives the viewer are between Vaughn and Connelly. What *The Dilemma* tells us about Kevin James and Winona Ryder is that they are drifting apart, not talking to one another, finding sexual release through cheating, and that James' work frustrations are the underpinning virus that's poisoning their marriage. Again, the contrast seen in *Cinderella Man* is applicable here: which couple do we want to be? What type of relationship with our significant other do we want to have? Make no mistake, both Vince Vaughn and Kevin James have their faults, but who handles it better?

***

The Dilemma cannot be appropriately assessed without discussing the role the women have in the story. There's a distinctive parallel between Vince Vaughn & Jennifer Connelly in *The Dilemma* and Steve Martin & Mary Steenburgen in *Parenthood* twenty years prior. Jennifer Connelly and Mary Steenburgen, specifically as heroines through being stalwarts in the midst of their man's poor decision making requires examination.

CHAPTER 7
STRONG FEMININE CHARACTERS

Both Steve Martin in *Parenthood* and Vince Vaughn in *The Dilemma* are their own worst enemy. For all their good virtues, the most significant mistakes they make are of their own doing, and in their hour of desperation they commit unforgivable sins to their significant other. *Parenthood* is arguably a rather uncomfortable film because almost every funny, positive or upward moment is instantly contrasted with a setback. When Steve Martin and Mary Steenburgen are told that their eldest son has an emotional developmental disorder, he impulsively stands up declares that Steenburgen "`smoked grass`" to the child psychologist and principal. Being that *Parenthood* is in part a comedy, the audience is allowed to laugh at the moment despite how uncomfortable Steenburgen is at her husband's impulsive announcement. Later, when Steve Martin – again, impulsively – quits his job after being treated poorly and failing to "`dazzle`" his boss, the viewer cannot help but agree and cheer for this decision. However, the impracticality of Martin's action is quickly called out in the next scene by Steenburgen. Martin's decision results in a lack of income, needing to go through the process of finding a new job, and then: surprise, Steenburgen informs Martin that she's pregnant with a fourth child. In this exchange, seeing how Martin awkwardly and quietly takes the news, Steenburgen pressures him to voice his opinion about her having an abortion, which Martin never explicitly says, but eventually discloses that an abortion is actually his wish through his behavior. Toward the end of the film, Martin insults his own grandmother over her rollercoaster vs. merry-go-round analogy for life that she offers to settle the nerves of Martin & Steenburgen. Martin's belittling of his grandmother's metaphor evokes a fiery response from Steenburgen, calling out Martin for being too caught up in his own vexations.

If we turn to *The Dilemma* we see similarities in Vince Vaughn: he sees something wrong, has evidence that both individuals are guilty of bad behavior (Winona Ryder having an affair with Channing Tatum; Kevin James frequenting a seedy Asian massage parlor) – and yet, Vaughn cannot leave well enough alone. Vaughn "has to fix it," not unlike the way Martin "has to fix" his son's stunted emotional development. There's an unhealthy ego with both Steve Martin and Vince Vaughn from their respective movies, falsely believing that they alone can solve the problems. What does it get them? An angry wife/girlfriend. In the case of *The Dilemma*, Vaughn gives the impression to those around him that he's relapsing to a gambling addiction from years past. There's a bit of humor to this because we get to watch a false impression grow, however we come to an uncomfortable moment at a dinner party celebrating the 45th wedding anniversary for Jennifer Connelly's parents. Despite *The Dilemma* being a comedy, Vaugh decides to impulsively (again, note impulsively), give a highly inappropriate toast to the couple on the subject of honesty. As with the exchange about abortion in *Parenthood*, the elongated toast is another scene that's uncomfortable to watch. Once again, Howard crafts a comedy that sits on the edge of making the audience unsure if they're allowed to laugh at it. Afterwards, Connelly pulls Vaughn aside and doesn't chew him out or break up with him… but interrogates him. Connelly digs to find out what what's wrong with him. What's the braver thing to do? To say "the hell with it" and be rid of someone who does that, or actually investigate to see what the problem is?

Steve Martin's bravado results in him disrespecting Mary Steenburgen repeatedly. Vince Vaughn's hubris results in him pouring more drama into Connelly's life. Both characters cross a line that should or would ruin the relationship… and what do the women do? Mary Steenburgen and Jennifer Connelly weather the storm, stick by their man, and make them better individuals in the end. Yes, both *Parenthood* and *The Dilemma* are going to be found under the comedy section, but despite the humor, the respective stories are examples of women toughing it out and doing the righteous thing and being rewarded for it.

Heroines

How different would *Apollo 13* be if Tom Hank's wife, Kathleen Quinlan, were removed for the film? What happens to the tone of *Rush* if Daniel Brühl's wife, Alexandra Maria Lara, was omitted? What would *Hillbilly Elegy*'s tone be if the Indian girlfriend, Freida Pinto, were omitted from the story? The presence of the women in Ron Howard's films is a major inflection point in the narratives and directs the emotions of the situations.

The popular meme, "Never travel with Tom Hanks," that has pictures from his various movies is worth contemplating with regards to Ron Howard's partiality to strong female roles. *Cast Away* (2000) and *Captain Phillips* (2013) all establish to the viewer that Tom Hanks has a female companion back home, but the vast majority of the screen time in both films is spent with Hanks trapped in a difficult situation. In *Apollo 13*, Kathleen Quinlan has significant presence because the film uses her character to emphasize the desperate emotions of the situation. In Jim Lovell's book, *Lost Moon: The Perilous Voyage of Apollo 13*, the professionalism of the Mission Control is accented, but the movie's screenplay doesn't have time to emphasize the years of training that went into the mindset of Mission Control team members – that topic would be a film unto itself. In lieu of this, Quinlan's steadfast insistence that her husband comes home is something that an audience member can instantly relate to: the vitality of her husband's safety and being the father of her children is a primal sense. We can more easily relate to Quinlan's resolve than comprehend the logistics going through all the different people behind desks at Mission Control. The determination was the same, but we empathize with Quinlan much faster than we understand the intricacies of rocket science. Biographer and film theorist Beverly Gray observes:

> Through quiet scenes such as the one in which Marilyn (Kathleen Quinlan) is drawn to her husband's videotaped image on her television screen, *Apollo 13* becomes their love story, a take of a husband and wife yearning for each other across the void of outer space.(1)

The strong feminine characters exhibited in Howard's films is something that gets refined with time. It's a motif that's always been there, going back to the lone female member of the high school rock band in *Cotton Candy*, or the strong willed student and teacher in *Skyward*. Shelley Long's character in *Night Shift* is not a dumb blonde or a troubled disturbed streetwalker. There is a confidence about Long's character that's written into the screenplay which buttresses the insecurities of Henry Winkler character. We see this same trope with Maureen Stapleton in *Cocoon* and Mimi Rogers in *Gung Ho* – they all function as catalysts strengthening the plot. Few, if any of the female characters in Howard's films are disposable love interests. Although *Frost/Nixon* could have easily omitted Rebecca Hall's character (Caroline Cushing Graham) from the film, the socialite and journalist was in fact David Frost's girlfriend at the time, and was present for the interviews as portrayed in the film.*

Again, the big shift in Howard's career comes with 1989's *Parenthood* and it's in this film where the women really dominate. The wives and moms are the ones keeping suburbia afloat, and we start to see a version of this idea become a fundamental tenant in the Ron Howard canon. The women are the ones conquering the impossible conquest just as much as the men are. Again, in *Apollo 13*, we see this from a narrative structural perspective, being that Kathleen Quinlan is an emotional frame of reference for the audience. The little girl in *How the Grinch Stole Christmas* is truly the protagonist, (or at least a co-protagonist), as she's trying to pull Jim Carrey out from his self-imposed gloom. Russell Crowe is the one doing the boxing in *Cinderella Man*, yet he tells Renée

---

*In actuality, David Frost and Caroline Cushing met a couple of years prior to the Nixon interviews, rather than how it's depicted in the film of them meeting for the first time.

Zellweger, "But I can't win if you're not behind me." This is carried into the documentaries also: consider how much commentary the wives and daughters of Luciano Pavarotti and José Andrés provide in the films *Pavarotti* and *We Feed People*.

Steadfast mothers:
Parenthood

We could debate if *Parenthood* is subject to classification in the "dumb dad" stereotype since that become a popular trend starting in the late-1980s television, as the film is packed with poor father figures. All of them are victims to Howard's "own worse enemy" trope: Steve Martin cannot control his anxiety; Rick Moranis sets unrealistic high expectations of his daughter; Tom Hulce completely ignores his son; and the dominate father figure played by Jason Robards is an overall grump and disliked (or tolerated) by the collective family. That said, three of the four fathers are given redemption: Moranis acknowledges his error after realizing that his wife wants to leave him on account of his obsessive behavior, asking for forgiveness, and tempers his rigorous academic approach with their daughter. As for Steve Martin, with zero resolve on how to solve the various problems in his life, is given the extraordinary opportunity we see Howard bestow on his lead characters, but in the form of forgiveness. When his father, Jason Robards, wants his "advice" regarding Tom Hulce's, gambling debt, Steve Martin is shocked that he's being asked. Robards gives his son the validation he needs: "Because I know you think I was a shitty father." This exchange doesn't solve all of Steve Martin's various domestic problems but it's a readjustment, bringing a level of equilibrium to his chronic foreboding. Martin's son catching the fly ball in the little league baseball game in the following scene also brings Martin closer to this mental readjustment in having positives in his life. Tom Hulce is the only father in *Parenthood* to depart the movie without a solidified path. Hulce abandons his child repeatedly, and his self-centeredness forbids him from acknowledging his own short comings. Hulce is dishonest to others and therefore is dishonest to himself in thinking he can overcome the financial hole he's in. There's one other crucial factor about Hulce's character that separates him from Steve Martin, Rick Moranis, Jason Robards, and even Keanu Reeves: there is no female presence in Hulce's life to keep him on the straight and narrow.

In *Parenthood*'s presentation of poor paternal leaders, we see the moms correcting errors in the respective families. Harley Kozak convinces Rich Moranis to settle down with the amount of academia he's pouring on their 3-year-old. Dianne Wiest's family might be in perpetual chaos, but she's resolved to hold it together as best she can. Arguably the most irksome character is the bratty and self-assured Martha Plimpton who spends the entirety of *Parenthood* making immature decisions. What is the moment that finally sets her right? Following Reeve's car crash at the race track and being pulled from the crashed vehicle, Plimpton begins to run away from the crash site saying, "I can't! This is too intense!" and it's Diane Wiest, her mother, who has to set Plimpton straight: "This is marriage! Now, let's get in the truck" while Reeves is about to be driven away in a medical van.

In the mayhem that is *Parenthood*, the aged wisdom of Helen Shaw, the elderly grandmother, demands revisiting. Towards the finale of the film, just as circumstances seem to be on an upswing for all the characters, the audience suffers through another Steve Martin (Gil) complaint ridden diatribe at life, worrying about events that haven't even happened with his kids, fixating on superficial "what if's." Worse, Martin (Gill) is pouring out his irrational anxiety onto his ever patient wife, Mary Steenburgen (Karen) who tolerates the neurosis to the point she finally needs to remind him that:

INT. KITCHEN - EVENING
KAREN is at table sowing a plush headband for the school play. She is at wits end listening to GIL get argumentative about potential problems with his kids.

                    KAREN
          Life is messy!

                     GIL
          I hate messy. It's just so... messy.

GRANDMA walks into the dining room from the kitchen and inserts herself into the conversation, walking directly up to Gil.

                   GRANDMA
          You know, when I was 19, Grandpa took
          me on a roller coaster.

An awkward pause. Grandma smiles at Gil, and he smiles back.

                     GIL
          Oh?

                   GRANDMA
          Up, down, up down. Oh, what a ride.

                     GIL
          (Taking a deep breath, with sarcasm)
          What a great story.

Karen looks up at Gil, incredulous.

Grandma begins to walking around the table.

                   GRANDMA
          I always wanted to go again. You
          know, it was just interesting to me
          that a ride could make me so
          frightened...

Reaching the other side, Grandma addresses both of them.

> GRANDMA (cont'd)
> ...so scared, so sick, so... so excited, and so thrilled all together.
> (beat)
> Some didn't like it. They went on the merry-go-ground. That just goes around. Nothing.
> (smiles)
> I like the roller coaster. You get more out of it.

Karen smiles. Gil rolls his eyes.

> GRANDMA (cont'd)
> Well, I'll be seeing you in the car.

Grandma walks out of the room.

> KAREN
> She's a very smart lady.

Karen gets up to the table with the plush headband.

> KAREN (cont'd)
> Come on, Taylor. Your ears are ready.

> GIL
> Yeah, a minute ago I was really confused about life, then Grandma came in with her wonderful and effecting roller coaster story, and now everything is great again!

Karen WHIPS the plush headband at Gil, striking him.

> KAREN
> I happen to like the roller coaster, okay?

Beat. Gil is shocked into silence.

                    KAREN (cont'd)
          As far as I'm concerned your
          Grandmother is brilliant.

Almost on the verge of tears, Karen runs up the
stairs calling for the kids.

                    KAREN (cont'd)
          Come on, Taylor. Come on, hurry up.

Gil stands alone. He looks out in the direction of
where Grandma went, and then yells out.

                        GIL
          Yeah, if she's so brilliant, how come
          she's sitting in our neighbor's car?

The messiness of family life at the heart of *Parenthood* is succinctly presented through Helen Shaw's witticism, and adds evidence to why *Parenthood* is the pivotal maturation in Howard's career. Here we see Steve Martin fulfilling the role of being his own worst enemy because he can't keep his mouth shut, but more interestingly is that his condescension towards his grandmother evokes an aggressive reaction from Mary Steenburgen. Nearly every other scene with Steve Martin is him complaining about hypothetical crises and there's only so much that Steenburgen allows him before finally calling it out. Even the indirect suggestion of the abortion doesn't get the hostile reaction from Steenburgen as compared to his failure to comprehend life's "roller coaster." Since *Parenthood* walks a comedy/drama tightrope, it ends the pivotal exchange on a joke regarding Grandma getting into the wrong car. (Which the audience never sees, Martin only says it. It's left to our imagination if she actually did, or Martin just made it up). There is not a single Ron Howard film that doesn't have at least a few charming moments, regardless how dark the subject matter – but a heated exchange on par with Steve Martin and Mary Steenburgen regarding the roller coaster analogy would never end on a joke in future films.

In the following scene, Martin and Steenburgen are at their children's school play, and Martin physically hears the roller coaster metaphor after his youngest son rushes the stage and creates a literal "mess" out of the kiddie production. It's here that Martin understands what his Grandmother was referring to. Martin's accomplishment is the ability the relinquish trying to control life's every single problem. The disarray of life is literally displayed for Steve Martin on stage for him to sit there and watch – not as torture, but to enjoy. Or rather, *learn* to enjoy. In the school's theatre, who does Martin turn to? The woman who stayed by his side and pushed him through it all.

Parenthood is an examination of practical emotions within a family shown in relatable real-word scenarios, yet packaged as a comedy. There's no doubt that *Cocoon* was as equally emotionally sophisticated, yet it had the usage of the space aliens; *Parenthood* can't hide under a unique MacGuffin like friendly aliens. *Gung Ho* has the smug autoworkers, quizzical Japanese and a cocksure Michael Keaton to keep the tone light. *Parenthood* contains plenty of beats that fit within the pantheon of comedy, but it wants to be more adult. Composer Randy Newman, who's scores are particularly recognizable and brilliantly simplistic makes the observation that:

> I was drawn to *Parenthood* because, shockingly enough, it was one of the very few pictures ever made about the biggest thing that most adults do in their lives, which is raising kids. There hadn't been many serious films made where the parents were portrayed as human beings.(2)

The concept of authentic families becomes something we see Howard contemplate in earnest post-1989. Prior to *Parenthood*, families are a theme, but not to the extent they are in the 1990s and onward. After *Parenthood* there is a great emphasis on families and Howard really rolls up his sleeves and really gets into it. How does he do this? Through the strength of the feminine characters.

Entirely different on second viewing: *A Beautiful Mind*

A disclaimer is required. The difficulty of discussing *A Beautiful Mind* in the context of an authorship study is the trope that hangs on the film (sometimes like an albatross) – its little gold statue. It is best to try and ignore the Oscar, therefore, in attempt to relieve ourselves of this acumen, let us begin by addressing the obvious: Howard was finally nominated for Best Director, would win the Academy Award, and *A Beautiful Mind* would take home Best Picture honors. Although *Apollo 13* was nominated for Best Picture six years prior, to the shock of many, Ron Howard did not receive a Best Directing nomination. As of this writing, the only other film Howard received a Best Director nomination was for was *Frost/Nixon*.

With that said, film critics and historians tend to spill a lot of ink as to why a director's Best Picture winner(s) is/are the keystone to understanding their repertoire. Make no mistake, that can easily be done with Ron Howard and *A Beautiful Mind*, yet we must try and analyze the film without fixating on the laurels it received. It bears repeating that *Gung Ho*, which is a far cry from Oscar-worthy material, still functions as a quintessential "Ron Howard film" in its own right. Yes, *A Beautiful Mind* got the gold, but let us examine the film without being compelled to view it through Oscar's "gold-colored spectacles."

***

The screen romances Howard presented prior to *A Beautiful Mind* were unions of two lovers whose affection and care for one another propelled them to success. Any director could still have made the same movies and have dialed down the love story, yet to remove the romance from any of Howard's movies, the whole film would have embodied a different tone. In the case of *A Beautiful Mind*, Jennifer Connelly's decision to remain with Crowe throughout his trauma is what ultimately saves him. The love story is so profoundly rooted into *A Beautiful Mind* that it does something wholly unique to the film. On first viewing (specifically if the viewer doesn't know the twist), the attention is on Crowe's plight.

On second viewing, after already knowing what's going to happen, the viewer follows Connelly as the leading character. The audience is kept in the dark with regards to how much is actually Crowe's imagination, and how much of it is a government operation orchestrated by Ed Harris; this causes our attention to remain on Russell Crowe. It's "his" story, therefore we focus on him – not that we ignore Jennifer Connelly's role, but rather we are trying to decide what's real and what's fake. Once we are privy to the scheme, the viewer cannot help but fixate on the struggles of Connelly, and thereby voyeuristically watch the drama through her perspective and have a significant amount of empathy with her plight.

A Beautiful Mind was released in a unique timeframe when movies with twists were very much in vogue.[*] Whether this was circumstantial, or a trend that studios were copying off of each other, *A Beautiful Mind* offers more than just seeing how the puzzle was assembled on the second watch. Once Jennifer Connelly comes into the story, she arguably owns the narrative because the story becomes about her struggle. Crowe is handicapped since everything we watch him do is, frankly, just fiction. Conflict is the predominant driving force in all films, and Connelly's struggle inevitably becomes more heightened after Crowe's arc is known to the audience. Yes, Crowe is a brilliant mathematician, and yes, he is the one who "solves" his own schizophrenia (by realizing that the little girl he's known for years never ages), yet there is no way he would have accomplished this in *A Beautiful Mind* without Connelly choosing to stay by his side and help him. Once the audience knows that Crowe's concerns and fixations are all hodgepodge, then our focus is on watching Jennifer Connelly be married to a man who is racked with medical complications. There is also a maternal element to Connelly's struggles by way of the baby whom we see Crowe is emotionally detached from and later almost accidentally drowns.

---

[*]*The Sixth Sense* (1999, M. Night Shyamalan); *Fight Club* (1999, David Fincher) and *Memento* (2001, Christopher Nolan).

The moment Connelly decides to stay with Crowe after his major relapse – we hear the sound effect of a car driving away, leaving Crowe isolated in the bedroom for several devastating seconds. The viewer is misdirected into thinking Connelly drove off, but then she returns saying that it was the doctor who left. The scene calls our attention to the pivotal factor in Crowe's recovery: he needs a woman's compassion, care and support to navigate his illness. Coming into the bedroom and kneeling in front of him, Connelly says, `You wanna know what's real?` touching the side of his head, `This,` taking his hand and placing it on the side of her face, `This,` moving his hand down to her chest, `This, this is real. Maybe the part that knows the waking from the dream, maybe it isn't here,` and finally moving her hand from his face down to his chest over his heart, `maybe it's here.`

***

Sometimes pinpointing the intertextuality between movies can come off as excessive "reading the tea leaves." It's almost too on-the-nose with the emphasis that's placed on the heart being the center of transformation. The irony of Jennifer Connelly emphasizing Russell Crowe's heart in *A Beautiful Mind* harkens back to Jim Carrey's `two sizes too small` heart in *How the Grinch Stole Christmas*. The film that would be the highest grossing blockbuster of the year 2000, and Howard's highest grossing film in the United States[3], would be followed exactly one year later by the film that would earn him 2001's Best Director and Best Picture Oscars – making the variances between the two "heart" scenes all the more ironic in hindsight. There was some intention with Carrey's portrayal of The Grinch that the character would be mentally ill, by way of the different voices and radical mood swings. The heart transformation scenes when Jim Carrey and Russell Crowe make their switch are tremendously different. Carrey reacts bombastically to his inevitable change with crass remarks, whereas Crowe is somber and it's a harder moment to watch because the audience realizes, momentarily, how isolated he is. Even James Horner's scores are juxtaposed to some degree: while Carrey is vocally spazzing out on the mountainside, Horner uses loud brass, choir, chimes and strings, until reprising back to the instrumental theme of the film (the song, "Where Are You Christmas"). Whereas the intimate quiet setting of the bedroom for Crowe and Connelly relies on lighter strings and harp, and finally builds into a crescendo of the theme, (the song "All Love Can Be").

In both heart scenes, it's the persevering female leads who brings the scene to a close, and into the final act of the films. Little Taylor Momsen wanders back up the mountain Christmas morning, and her peril at almost falling off the ostentatious sleigh of Christmas decorations gives Jim Carrey the strength to lift the entire sleigh, keeping it from falling off the mountain side. (The near tipping the sleigh over the ledge is illustrated in the children's book, but the Grinch's lifting of the sleigh over his head after his heart grows in size was added in the animated short. The little girl, Cindy Lou Who is not present on the mountain top in either the short story or the cartoon.) This mirrors Jennifer Connelly's `"You wanna know what's real?"` scene from *A Beautiful Mind* in that she goes back upstairs, and it's from emphasizing the heart that Crowe begins his difficult recovery. The comparison is a bit of an authorship stretch, however as so many of Howard's narratives ultimately center on emotion and a strong heart, the two scenes certify the motif, regardless of genre or tone.

Strong moms:
The Missing

Prolific directors that turn in a bountiful résumé tend to suffer a "forgotten film." A title that may have received good, lukewarm or negative reviews, but began to quickly disappear from the circuit following home video release. The general consensus would agree that Steven Spielberg's *Always* (1989); Martin Scorsese's *Bringing Out the Dead* (1999); Ridley Scott's *A Good Year* (2006); or Robert Zemeckis' *Welcome to Marwen* (2018) fit the bill as their "forgotten film" within their bodies of work.

As it stands, *The Missing* is Ron Howard's.

To answer the question why a film performs well or poorly at the box office requires examination of over a dozen factors beginning with the year of release, time of year, the other films released during that timeframe, including previous years, trends in the genre, the popularity of the main stars attached to the project, critical reception of subsequent projects including that of all key players. With all these factors in mind, the "forgotten film" shouldn't automatically mean that the movie itself is bad – good products fly under the radar all the time. Given Howard's body of work, *The Missing* is an anomaly, which may have more to do with the Thanksgiving 2003 release date, the R-rating, and a crowded holiday release slate that year more than anything else. Either way, *The Missing* is one of the most unique entries in Howard's filmography.

To date, *The Missing* is the only western Howard has directed, but that maybe more on account of his desire for change. Keeping the "never make the same movie twice" concept in mind, what we see in *The Missing* is similar to what we saw in *Ransom*, but an entirely different set of circumstances. The two kidnapping films complement each other nicely because they are so different with the same crew at the helm: director Ron Howard, producer Brian Grazer, casting directors Janet Hirshenson & Jane Jenkins, second unit director Todd Hallowell, editors Dan Hanley & Mike Hill, and composer James Horner – and yet – the physical landscape of *The Missing* is ruggedness, which is dramatically different from the urban city life of *Ransom*. Mel Gibson is a multi-millionaire living in a New York high rise penthouse. Cate Blanchett is introduced to us defecating in an outhouse.

Based off the fictional novel by Thomas Eidson, the book was one of several by the author that focused on endearing women in the wild west.[4] Being that so much had been memorialized about "Cowboys & Indians," Eidson wanted to focus on the women who took the brunt of the labor and sorrow toiling away in rural America. Although the book spends an equal amount of time with the lead characters, by the finale, the character of "Jones," the character portrayed by Tommy Lee Jones, can't help but marvel that he's spent his life "surrounded by strong women."[5]

The Missing is the first time that Howard has a woman in the leading role and Cate Blanchett is subjected to the same abuse that Howard's other protagonists go through. Not once throughout does *The Missing* bend to the "girls can kick butt too" mantra, because it's set in such a coarse world. Blanchett and her two daughters are isolated in the barren desert of New Mexico in the mid-1880s, only with Aaron Eckhart, her lover, and another hired rancher as their only line of defense. In an added twist that says more about Howard's attraction to messy family dramas – in Eidson's novel, the Aaron Eckhart role is simply the husband and father to Blanchett and the two girls. In the film, that family dynamic is way more complicated: Blanchett admits she doesn't know what happened to the father of her older daughter played by Evan Rachel Wood, and Jenna Boyd's father is dead. In the film version, Aaron Eckhart is her lover and is slowly becoming stepdad to both girls. Tommy Lee Jones is the one who points out, `"There's places where a father would kill a man for doing what you're doing. You know that, don't you?"` Although the audience knows that Jones' familial past is dark, there's something to be said about the Anglo-Saxon ranchers of 1880s rural New Mexico having disjointed families. (Given the accounts of early homesteads throughout American westward expansion, it's probably more historically accurate that the frontier families would be disjointed like that).

Something *The Missing* does peculiarly well is the presentation of how remote and vast the United States' western desert feels when you're alone in it in every direction (something that is appreciated if one has physically experienced it). With Hollywood, the capital of movie making being relatively close to the desert states of Arizona, Nevada, New Mexico and Utah's – the desert backdrop has been embedded into cinema history because it's been so frequently revisited for over a hundred years. *The Missing* was Howard's first collaboration with cinematographer Salvatore Totino who embraced a more spontaneous approach to filming that would become in vogue by the end of the decade as the handheld aesthetic began to be used more often in action films. A decade prior, Howard's *Far and Away* was set in the 1890s, which is essentially the same era that *The Missing* takes place, showcasing the mountainous splendor of the west, with a grandiose John Williams score as the soundtrack. In *The Missing*, the colors are bleak due to the strong sunlight on snow-covered plains which accentuates the shots of emptiness and openness. James Horner's score uses a lot more instruments from the time period to buffer the ambiance and reflect the Native American culture, while still using similar sweeping musical swells akin to *Far and Away*. An added parallel to *Far and Away* is that both lead actresses, Nicole Kidman and Cate Blanchett, grew up in Australia, are close in age in real life, are both Hollywood royalty – but the casting of Kidman fits the polished spectacle that *Far and Away* embodied. The casting of Kidman's then husband, Tom Cruise also played into a romanticizing of the settlers' pioneering west. We do not know whether or not future audiences, specifically the 2050s, 2060s or 2070s are going to be conscious of the on-screen couple's real life relationship and history – however the youthfulness, freshness and chemistry of the Cruise and Kidman casting help glorify this period of American history.

But in 2003, Ron Howard throws that romanticism right out the window. Defaulting for a more spontaneous type of shoot, thereby doing away with precision planning, Totino's camera shows us a stark landscape with Blanchett, who is not portrayed as effeminate when compared to Kidman. A mother with two daughters; a teenager played by Evan Rachel Wood, who is disgruntled with life on the frontier, and therefore is beginning to challenge her mother's authority, as well as a ten-year old played by Jenna Boyd. Although a fictional story, *The Missing* pulled from various scattered records about the American west.

In the bank of Ron Howard's leading characters there's an argument to be made that Cate Blanchett in *The Missing* is the toughest of the group. One of the first actions we see her perform, without a moment of hesitation, is extracting a decaying tooth from a resisting old woman (in a graphic scene that was intentionally placed at the beginning of the film to set the tone for the brutality to come).[6] The audience sees that Blanchett is bilingual in both

English and Spanish, isn't making good money from being a "healer," therefore has resorted to the physically taxing work of farming on her homestead. Within the first quarter of the film, we see Blanchett chopping wood, tending to animals with her bare hands, as well as riding a horse while leading a second horse behind her, which is a maneuver that takes skill to learn. In the research for the film, journals of frontier women were consulted, and entries reflected two feelings: perseverance and gloom.(7)

The tenacity of Blanchett's character is reflected throughout her family. The two daughters share in this difficult lifestyle: we see the 15-year-old Evan Rachel Wood carving up a deer, and the 10-year-old Jenna Boyd milking a cow. The desolation of the territory leads to Evan Rachel Wood clashing with her mother about wanting to attend a fair and see a phonograph that plays a recording of voices back. The general concept implies that Evan Rachel Wood longs for a life far away from the barren snow covered New Mexico – probably out east towards urban life. Once captured, Wood brandishes her bravery and strength by trying to escape and save the other girls in captivity. As for the youngest, Jenna Boyd, she is the most innocent but she's just as determined of an individual akin to her mother, sister, and her grandfather, Tommy Lee Jones, whom she's particularly fascinated with.

A great deal of *The Missing* is embedded into the subtleness of the acting performances. When Cate Blanchett (Maggie), Tommy Lee Jones (Jones) and Jenna Boyd (Dot) decide to track the kidnapped girls and the Apache gang, a momentary rift arrives – one of several between the daughter and father throughout the film. One of the captivating traits of Jones is his unapologetic audacity in the way he speaks; the vast majority of his "dialogue" is expressed through physical statements:

```
INT. STABLE - DAY.
DOT, on horseback, and MAGGIE, walking - enter the
stable barn. As Dot rides in, a small bell makes an
audible ring coming from her horse.
```

Maggie is packing bullets into a side saddle on one of the other horses. As she does this, she turns to Dot and gives her a wink.

JONES walks into the barn with his horse. He looks to Dot, then back to Maggie.

                    JONES
    Taking this child out there is awful
    foolish.

                    MAGGIE
    (Adjusting the contents of her side saddle)
    I know my daughter. Leave her behind she'll
    just be followin'.

                    JONES
    No way to care for a young girl.

That strikes a nerve.

                    MAGGIE
    What would you know of any of it?

Maggie finishes packing the side saddle and walks away. Jones looks after her with a sad expression, and then turns his attention back to Dot.

                    DOT
    I'll be just fine - thank you.

Jones walks towards Dot and pulls out a knife.

Dot stares right back at him, unflinching.

Jones grabs the front reins of Dot's horse and the leather strap with the bell on it, cutting it loose off of the horse. The horse mildly jumps back.

Jones brandishes the bell, rings it, looks at it, and then looks to Dot while tossing it across the

```
barn, where it falls to the ground and ceases
ringing.
```

This ad hoc family reunion of estranged father, disgruntled daughter and curious granddaughter is Howard's comfort zone: a messy family unit. Additionally, Cate Blanchett and Tommy Lee Jones have the same antagonistic relationship that looks all too familiar by this point: a culture clash. However, this isn't Tom Hanks and Daryl Hannah (*Splash*), or Michael Keaton and Gedde Watanabe (*Gung Ho*), which are "safe" movies because even while watching them we inherently know that they're going to be lighthearted. Post-1989, or post-*Parenthood* and onward, the caliber of films that Howard directs over the next two decades almost always have an edge or a sense of foreboding. Jones is the one who sets the bar at approximately the halfway point of the film, telling Blanchett that, `"If they make it to Mexico, your child is lost."` This entire rescue mission plays out in the middle of a family drama that takes a unique approach to the collective history of the Native American and colonialist narrative. The voluminous records of hostilities between settlers and Natives that fills history books has few detailed accounts of family relations, and so for the fictional film (as well as the 1995 book), creates a tale about a father who "goes Native" causing hefty domestic complications that Howard layers into the subtext of *The Missing*. Consider how much of an *implied* backstory there is to Tom Hulce's past in *Parenthood*, that hangs in the air. The same sense of a dark backstory is in *The Missing* with Tommy Lee Jones. It's worth pointing out that Blanchett's youngest daughter is quietly fascinated by her grandfather's rituals, giving another maternal strife that she's burdening throughout the film.

In a later scene, Jones offers shoes to the 10-year-old when she complains about her feet hurting. In front of Blanchett, Jones says that the moccasins belonged to his Native American wife (the woman, and indirectly the lifestyle, that he abandoned Blanchett for when she was a child). There's an innocence in the way that Tommy Lee Jones speaks of his Apache ties and the culture he openly embraces almost unaware of the heartache it still causes for his now adult daughter. In turn, this provides *The Missing* with an undercurrent of racism, particularly from Blanchett's character since the Apache way "kidnapped" her father. The anti-indigenous fervor is embedded into Blanchett's character make-up. As the drama goes on, Blanchett requires her father's skill and knowledge to traverse the dark world of human trafficking in the 1880s American west. On the flipside (because Howard loves dualities), we see glimmers of admiration from Jones of his daughter being a healer. In a sense, Blanchett has to confront her own racism on this journey, adding a mental component to this physically strenuous rescue mission.

CHAPTER 8
PARTNERSHIP/DUALITY:
OPPOSITES ATTRACT

There is a symmetry between the lovers that Ron Howard puts on screen, specifically a healthy amount of antagonism that makes their relationship interesting to watch. Tom Hanks & Daryl Hannah in *Splash*; Tom Cruise & Nicole Kidman in *Far and Away*; Alden Ehrenreich & Emilia Clarke in *Solo*. There are similar antagonist relationships with the non-romantically entangled characters and this juxtaposition is seen routinely:

- *Backdraft* | William Baldwin & Kurt Russell – sibling rivalry, specifically that of the younger brother in the shadow of the older brother.

- *How the Grinch Stole Christmas* | Jim Carrey & Anthony Hopkins – the neurotic behavior of Carry's Grinch is countered balanced with Hopkin's serious narration.[1]

- *The Missing* | Cate Blanchett & Tommy Lee Jones – the daughter and father are both stubborn, but they need each other's skill set in order to survive.

- *Cinderella Man* | Russell Crowe & Paul Giamatti – the reserved sports star and the wily manager. The opportunities allotted to Crowe are possible because of Giamatti's witticism.

- *The Dilemma* | Vince Vaughn & Kevin James – similar to the boxer and manager in *Cinderella Man*, James is the brilliant engineering mechanic, and Vaughn is his marketing person.

- *In the Heart of the Sea* | Chris Hemsworth & Benjamin Walker – a qualified seaman is asked to be subservient to a lesser experienced captain.

- *Thirteen Lives* | Colin Farrell & Viggo Mortensen – the optimist and the pessimist. Farrell is the family man and Mortensen is the straight shooter.

- *Jim Henson: Idea Man* | Jim Henson & Lew Grade – two ambitious television producers with very different backgrounds, but develop a working relationship that made way for *The Muppet Show*.

In all forms of art, the spectator is naturally going to be intrigued by a contrast, even something as basic as a contrast of colors. This is why the dynamics of Abbott & Costello, Tom & Jerry, R2-D2 & C-3P0, and of course Bert & Ernie has stood the test of time. The contrast of the characters brings subtext to the stories themselves and inadvertently presents two different perspectives on any given topic. The way we see the influence of female leads progressively develop throughout Howard's career and films, is similar with this dichotomy between characters. *Night Shift* may remain the funniest contrast of polar opposites. In *Splash* a love story is made out of the contrast of a man and a mermaid. With *Gung Ho*, the contrast between Michael Keaton and Gedde Watanabe becomes extended to the American and Japanese cultures and work ethic, signaling Howard's beginning to dig deeper in the minutiae of his films. We start seeing anecdotes of two paradoxical mindsets needing to come together and learn from each other.

"I'm gonna make a man out of you":
Night Shift

At the time of its release in 1982, the marketing component of Henry Winkler in a movie directed by Ron Howard, playing the polar opposite of his famous "Fonzie" character from *Happy Days* was ideal fodder for a worthwhile gag; (Winkler agreeing to be in the film was what got *Night Shift* greenlit). In many ways, Winkler's role in *Night Shift* is the ultimate Ron Howard caricature of the common man. Intentionally playing the opposite of his cool-sway "Fonzie" from *Happy Days*, Henry Winkler turned the dial way down. His first couple seconds on screen in *Night Shift* is unassuming and subtly brilliant; he's treated like a side character in the conversation taking place at the morgue regarding the identification of a body. While the detective and the escort are talking about what happened to the dead pimp, their conversation commands our attention, which emphasizes Winkler's lowliness. Winkler is centered between the two speaking and it takes a while before he's able to get a word in edgewise in *his* introductory scene. Mere seconds later, in the following scene, Winkler receives a pseudo demotion being given the night shift, protesting: `"Night shift? I started on night shift. I'm here six years - I thought I was getting a raise."` in which he's swiftly cut down by his superior. Winkler being demoralized is a recurring moment throughout the film, but his plainness is the perfect arena for Michael Keaton to barnstorm in and dominate. The irrational excitement that Keaton brings to their job is counterintuitive to Winkler's ardent desire to remain a simpleton, yet Winkler *needs* the outlandish behavior.

Around the half-hour mark of *Night Shift*, the audience is shown a breakup *and* resolve between Henry Winker and Michael Keaton. For the first act of the film, Keaton is a nuisance to Winkler, upsetting the uptight mortician's routine while spouting off nonsense. Eventually Winkler goes off telling Keaton to `"Shut up!"`, and really puts his co-worker down. In the following scene, Winkler finds Keaton hiding in one of the morgue's cold locker drawers and apologizes. What's special about this moment is that Keaton slightly opens up about his past just enough that the scene doesn't get overly emotional, or make it difficult for the audience to accept Keaton as a wacko for the remainder of the film. (Audiences tend to push back if a wild comedic relief starts to be too humanized. It's much easier to laugh at an off the wall screwball.) Keaton's initial aversion to Winkler's apology is just brief enough for Winkler to reconcile properly with his co-worker, and thereby solidifying the relationship. This conflict and resolve between the two allow for all additional antics by Keaton to be met with laughter. The two have an equilibrium, allowing for Winker to be the perfect "straight man" to Keaton's uncontrollable behavior.

The development of their partnership comes by way of the Thanksgiving scene, when Winkler gets a phone call from Shelley Long, his neighbor down the hallway who works as an escort, who needs to be bailed out of jail. Winkler's embarrassing situation pushes him over the edge to go along with Keaton's crazy `"love brokers"` concept turning the city morgue into an escort service.

The wild concept, spurred from Michael Keaton using the morgue's hearse as a make-shift limo service, is the maverick that piques the audience's interest (an impossible concept). The crux of the story comes from the relationships Winkler has with Michael Keaton (partnership) and Shelley Long (romance). They both live on the wild side, and lure Winkler out of his monotonous existence where everyone took advantage of him. Later, when Winkler begins complaining about the laundry list of ailments that the illegal escorting service is causing him (the headaches, stomach aches, the chills, bleeding gums, hair falling out), Keaton pulls out the tape recorder he carries around with him and announces, `"This is Bill. Mission in life: make Chuck [Winkler] a man."` Granted, this exchange is completely overshadowed by Keaton shoving tissues down into his pants crotch as the humor is dominate (and frankly, should be) – yet this ying-yang between the two is the heart of *Night Shift*.

While the nonsensical silliness of *Night Shift* is for comedic value — the fiancé with obesophobia, the frat party in the morgue, and the organized crime subplot, an impracticality is created. How much opposition will the protagonists get thrown at them? Even when in prison, Winkler says, `"My life is over. Do you know, at this moment, I've sunk as low as I can go?"` only to be taunted by an inmate who makes a goofy homosexual pass at him. The joke is for comedic purposes, yet it continues the trend of Winkler getting browbeat.

In this hilarity, a romantic tryst between Winker and Shelley Long becomes keynote, and enters *Night Shift* before the final act. Unlike rom-coms that get heavy with the romance in the second half of the film, *Night Shift* gives plenty of screen time for the comedy to return. The love affair between Winkler and Long have two effects on the story: first, it brings about a positive change in Winkler's flat demeanor. More importantly, the romantic entanglement starts to dismantle the mortuary escort operation, setting up for a conflict between the odd couple business partners. One of the reasons why Keaton's performance is deserving of praise is that the character keeps the film alive from, what could have been a very sappy final act. His spontaneity keeps *Night Shift* interesting. When the cash is raking in, Keaton awards himself with a new car, a Stutz IV-Porte, a nod to the automotive theme Howard loves so much.

After being caught, the two get off scott free on account of it being an election year. The irrational Keaton decides to take advantage of their lucky break and push for more – granted, it's never clear what Keaton wants to blackmail the legal system with – then again, none of Michael Keaton's antics in *Night Shift* need an explanation, and if we were given one, it would probably sullen the film. This spurs the deterioration of the friendship. Winkler (Chuck) wants his old life back and he needs Keaton (Billy Blaze) to cease his brazenness for this to happen. `"I have thought about this through the entire time in jail. What I want is to go back to my old life. Please, Bill`

[Keaton]. Please let me have my old life back." Not to read into a screwball comedy too much, but isn't it unique that Winkler (Chuck) pleads to Billy Blaze? It's as if Keaton (Billy Blaze) has some sort of divine authority over him, and yet, Keaton (Billy Blaze) responds in kind: "No. Chuck, if I did that I'd never be able to sleep with myself again." This provokes the break of the friendship, but because *Night Shift* remains first and foremost a comedy, the fight in the fancy office has more laughs. The audience really isn't too concerned with Winkler and Keaton no longer being friends. The audience inherently knows everything is going to work out in the end.

Dispensing with Michael Keaton from his life, Winkler quickly reverts back to the mundane. Although it's conventional, all of Winkler's problems return in one scene: Shelley Long seems to be out of his reach again, there's another improperly made sandwich, and the rabid dog in his apartment building that's always trying to bite him comes back. Nearly as a reflex, Winkler has the backbone to react to all these problems and become the "man" he was always supposed to be. Someone with a banal outlook on life who successfully comes out of his shell. Winkler doesn't turn into a version of, or even mirrors the Michael Keaton character – rather Winkler's character arch has come full circle to who he was meant to become from the start of the film.

Cultural duality:
Gung Ho* and *Hillbilly Elegy

In the full scope of *Gung Ho*, Micheal Keaton and his pals are the central focus, yet the Japanese are also prominently featured throughout to showcase a compelling juxtaposition of both cultures and work ethics.

There is a touch of drama throughout *Gung Ho*, (albeit decorated in comedy), hinging on the question of work ethics. *Gung Ho* doesn't hesitate to explore the social differences between the Americans and Japanese. The blue collar automakers are shown with prejudices, an air of disrespectfulness and a sense of laziness when confronted by the Japanese. There is a learning curve between the cultures that Howard is contemplating throughout his comedy.

What's particularly interesting is that Keaton is (another) flawed man with smug over-the-top behavior. Although primarily done for comedic effect, *Gung Ho* uses the love story between Keaton and Mimi Rogers to accent his flaws. Keaton's dismissiveness towards Rogers brings out his shortcomings to the point that the audience might be hesitant to root for him. On the other hand, the American's critiques of the Japanese are somewhat legitimate, eventually bringing Gedde Watanabe, the person responsible for overseeing the factory, and Keaton's doppelganger in *Gung Ho* to tell his Japanese colleagues: `"There are things we can learn from Americans."` There is no doubt that Ron Howard intends to show the foreigners embracing the American worth ethic.

***

In *Hillbilly Elegy*, Howard shifted his lens to rural Ohio of the 1980s and 1990s at a time when he started getting more introspective. There's a bit of a mental challenge with Howard's cultural identity because he is so ingratiated into American pop-culture that we forget his roots. On the other hand, the lore of *The Andy Griffith Show* does a nice job of reminding us of Howard's small town origins (despite that the show was filmed in Los Angeles). Regardless of what we bring to the film, Howard's *Hillbilly Elegy* is a reaction to the "us" vs. "them" elements of the mid-to-late 2010s. It is the updated version of *Parenthood*; a true story, moved twenty-years into the future, and looking at a single nuclear family instead of a wide spread of characters. *Parenthood* shows us all fictional characters, so we can choose to laugh or be shocked by their behavior as we see fit – whereas *Hillbilly Elegy* are real people and real stories.

In the comedies of the 1980s, Howard is going into familiar communities under the guise of fiction: *Cocoon*'s Florida retirement homes; *Gung Ho*'s steel mills; *Parenthood*'s Midwestern suburbia. In the 1990s and 2000s, the locations themselves serve a practical purpose for the characters: the inner workings of the news industry in *The Paper* and *EDtv*; highfalutin academia in *A Beautiful Mind*; desolate New Mexico in *The Missing*; the Great Depression in *Cinderella Man*. Once we get to *The Da Vinci Code*, Ron Howard heightens interest in the locations themselves. There's a small shift that becomes more gradual in the 2010s, where Howard starts to use the environment, landscape and settings to service the story: the full urban sprawl of Philadelphia in *Made in America*. Consider how much hands-on the physical work of whaling and life at sea is shown to the audience in *In the Heart of the Sea* as compared to the other industries displayed in past films. Make no mistake, this isn't something Howard neglected in his previous work – rather an element he utilizes in his storytelling more in later years.

Although not usually considered a controversial director, *Hillbilly Elegy* was the third time that Howard's movies caused commotion,* this time on account of predisposed political beliefs that critics thought *Hillbilly Elegy* should commentate and contribute. Howard was dismissive of the attacks saying:

> Critics have a job which is to see something [and] run it through their lens and write and talk about it, so I can't argue with it. I do feel like that they're looking at political thematics that they may or may not disagree with that honestly aren't really reflected or not front and center in this story. What I saw was a family drama that could be very relatable. Yes, culturally specific and if you're fascinated by that, I hope you find it interesting. If you're from the region, I hope you find it authentic because that was our aim and effort. I felt it [*Hillbilly Elegy*] was a bridge to understanding that we're more alike than we are different.(2)

---

*In early 2002 there was controversy regarding past antisemitic remarks and a homosexual relationship John Nash allegedly had that was omitted from *A Beautiful Mind*. The hit pieces about the film were orchestrated by Harvey Weinstein during the Oscar campaign, in trying to discredit the film. Yet that story, and even the *Hillbilly Elegy* controversy, pale in comparison to *The Da Vinci Code*, which was a hotbed of trouble since the book's publication in 2003 with widespread denunciation by Christian organizations months before the film's release.

The reason for the backlash against the film has to do with the political environment of the late-2010s and early-2020s. Additionally, J.D. Vance's book reads akin to a collection essays rather than a linear narrative. Vance uses his life story to show how much of a quagmire the system is, therefore the book has more political commentary. Vance's observations on how behavior influences the local economy and self-worth is key to the book. The film doesn't openly communicate on such things – rather it's in the subtext if we want to look for it. As Howard responded to the critics at the time, we can translate the film adaptation as we see fit.

What *Hillbilly Elegy* showcases with regards to culture is the way an elite class sneers at those from the outside. At a formal dinner, which is understood to be a social test for perspective recruits of a summer internship through Yale University, the adult J.D. Vance, played by Gabriel Basso, is unsure what forks to use throughout the dinner. What does he do? Basso excuses himself to call his girlfriend, played by Freida Pinto, an Indian and another cultural minority, who instructs him how to correctly use the dinner forks. The couple are the two outsiders making their way through Yale's elite environment (in real life, Vance would marry Usha). What we see in Basso/adult Vance, is another common man who works incredibly hard to disassociate himself from the unimpressive chaotic life back home. That chaos, and the events in the Appalachian region captures our attention, but the heart of the story is the relationship between Basso & Pinto, which is intricately tied into the screenplay.

When Basso is asked to come home due to his Mom's relapse, Pinot expresses genuine concern for him. When Basso/adult Vance, is in Ohio and on the phone with Pinto relaying the news that he got a call for an interview for the internship, he won't open up about what's happening. Basso/adult Vance tells his sister, "I just don't want to drag her [Pinto/Usha] into it, you know?" The film is a hot mess of family dysfunctionality and racked with drug abuse.

With the exception of Russell Crowe's struggle with his pills in *A Beautiful Mind*, the subject of drug use is something

Howard hadn't dabbled in prior to *Hillbilly Elegy*. The implications that drug abuse is an epidemic in the Appalachian area is something the book delved into, but in Ron Howard's version, he accesses drug addiction by looking at the insidious effect it has on the family members. Through this struggle, we are presented with the story of a man trying to keep two cultures apart, where in fact he needs to embrace the good of his heritage to excel as a person. Finally, there is no way that he'll survive the trial without letting Freida Pinto in; an overnight car drive back home isn't the most edge of your seat nerve racking finale – but it's the most appropriate. Someone trying to escape dysfunctionality finds functionality in a caring and strong woman.

Two perfectly contrasting leads:
Frost/Nixon* and *Rush

The duality of *Skyward* or *Far and Away* consists of two strong-willed people, nearly at one another's necks in frustration with each other, but the audience roots for *both* leads simultaneously. A similar duality of equally opposed forces is presented in *Ransom* through Mel Gibson and Gary Sinise. Both are squared off against each other, and the audience is primed to root for Gibson on account of Sinise's vileness. These are traditional story structures: the teacher and the student (*Skyward*), lovers that bicker that we ultimately want to see be together (*Far and Away*), and the well-matched protagonist vs. the antagonist (*Ransom*).

When you get to *Frost/Nixon*, and especially *Rush*, Howard doesn't bend the audience towards either of the lead characters. *Rush* in particular is able to remain totally unbiased, as it doesn't have the Watergate scandal and Nixon's faux pas looming over it.

The duo films, both written by Peter Morgan, are Ron Howard's celebration of the mid-1970s. What makes this an interesting case study is that we get Howard's retrospective take of this era. Recalling *Eat My Dust!* (1976) and *Grand Theft Auto* (1977) they are a paradigm, specifically on account of the atmosphere of car racing. Howard doesn't offer much in the arena of political activism during the mid-1970s; even his memoir is skimpy on the subject. He lets three decades elapse before returning to the nostalgia of his early twenties, a time frame of young adulthood that many tend to reflect on. The Formula 1 season that the dramatic events of *Rush* unfold took place between January through October 1976; the interviews between David Frost and Richard Nixon began in March 1977 and were broadcast throughout the month of May.

***

In the interview-based publicity for *Frost/Nixon* during the movie's release, it was referred to with boxing metaphors, specifically two guys having it out with words. With that concept in mind, we see that the title characters are surrounded by a team of people prepping them for the interview taping. In a sense, "ringside coaches."(3) The supporting character's time on screen is spent readying their man (i.e. fighter) for the upcoming bouts – consulting, encouraging and critiquing how they should handle different subjects. The film omits familial details about David Frost and Richard Nixon, and so the two groups of advisors become a surrogate family around the two men. This same concept is seen in *Rush*: outside of the respective love interests, family information about James Hunt and Niki Lauda are downplayed; both get one scene briefly acknowledging dissatisfied parents. Their pit crew and confidants become their ad-hoc family.

With the boxing metaphor promulgated for *Frost/Nixon*, we can't help but think of *Cinderella Man*, however the films are set in two different eras with different motivations. Russell Crowe is "fighting" to make money, whereas Michael Sheen is trying to fund the fight himself. The only unique parallel between the two film's philosophy is that the "fight" has an aura of honor and respectability to it. It's the corner men, Paul Giamatti in *Cinderella Man*, or Kevin Bacon and Sam Rockwell in *Frost/Nixon*, that are fiery about the opponent. Michael Sheen (David Frost) wants to do something intellectually stimulating, distancing himself from his smug, off-the-cuff talk show host persona. Given that Frank Langella (Richard Nixon) is not taking well to retirement, he recognizes an opportunity: "It would be so good to go back to where the action is. The hunger in my belly is still there, Jack." he tells Kevin Bacon (Jack Brenan), who was Richard Nixon's valued "corner man." Michael Sheen (Frost) and Frank Langella (Nixon) are two ornery characters that are looking for a way to raise their profile. In *Rush*, the two racers are constantly pushing each other through their rivalry to the point of a unique fusion, but in *Frost/Nixon*, both in pursuit of scoring a good interview for different purposes. Michael Sheen is not obsessed with the ex-president the same way that Chris Hemsworth and Daniel Brühl are obsessed with each other; rather their fixation comes from doing something historically significant.

Frost/Nixon can be viewed as a lesson in façade, in that we see two people putting on an act in front of each other, and in front of the world. As for *Rush*, both racers openly wear their personalities on their sleeves. But *Frost/Nixon* is full of lies. Where is the money coming from? Why is the British guy actually pursuing this? Will Richard Nixon come clean about a role in a cover up?

There are moments peppered throughout the film where Michael Sheen is torn between the depth of research and living the celebrity circuit lifestyle he's "supposed to" play. (David Frost did in fact executive produce a musical, *The Slipper and the Rose*, that released during the prep for the interviews). There's a moment in the drama when Michael Sheen's people, i.e. the "ring men," constructed out of anti-Nixon political pundits, are profoundly concern that they are participating in something that will become a puff-piece for Nixon. In that exchange, Michael Sheen makes an honest, yet semi-strange invitation for his birthday party. The intention of this moment was to display that David Frost still had to put on a happy face in the midst of all the drama.[4]

As for Frank Langella, the film in of itself is a perfect example of President Richard Nixon's inability to escape the

Watergate scandal. Langella is shown being very successful during the interview, making his "corner men" proud, while upsetting Sheen's "corner men." It's at the subject of Watergate that Langella is forced to be confronted with evidence that he escaped public cross-examination for, and the façade slowly brakes away. Specifically, Michael Sheen is able to illicit the mental reasoning and justification for the ex-president's actions – an intangible object Langella and his "corner men" want hidden.

In *Rush*, Daniel Brühl and Chris Hemsworth introduce the film with their own narration. Unlike *Frost/Nixon* where the "corner men" do the commentary, the audience is much more locked in with the two Formula 1 racers. Therefore, because the viewer is in tune with the rival racers, the women play a more significant role in *Rush*. Yes, Rebecca Hall in *Frost/Nixon* has an influence in the story (both in the film, and in the real story), but she has a minor role in directly influencing the interviews. The two wives in *Rush*, Alexandra Maria Lara and Olivia Wilde, have dramatically more influence over their husbands which becomes major plot points in the film.

Historically speaking, Sir David Frost had a media reputation prior to his interview with Richard Nixon. What Frost's interview did accomplish was altered the mindset on political commentary. Niki Lauda (Daniel Brühl) comes out of nowhere, walks into the racing industry and is intent on upending and improving the system for himself. Brühl (Lauda) "common man" traits are present in the sense that he's the unassuming person who shows up and proves himself a maverick. Brühl is arguably the first character since Mel Gibson in *Ransom* with poignant masochistic tendencies. Aside from all the machoism we hear the racers talk about, (i.e. willing to take life or death risks on the track), after the near death accident, Brühl embraces the pain required to get back into the competition.

Rush is the perfect showcase of rivalry: Brühl discloses that he was frustrated with Hemsworth gaining points in the Formula 1 championship, personalizing the antagonistic rivalry between the two. This pushes Hemsworth to admit his inability to express his emotions about the crash; the very masculine celebrity has difficulty accessing his authentic emotions. The very "Howard-esque" way these two find a perfect reconciliation comes through a press conference (again, the recurring theme of the media). When a reporter snidely remarks about the burns on Brühl's face being grounds for his wife to divorce him, the insult evokes the end of the press conference, but more so a visceral reaction from Hemsworth, who takes the reporter aside and roughs him up.

Although some light understanding of either the Watergate scandal, or the Ferrari family's influence on car racing would help one appreciate the films – the story's emotion is truly cultivated through the leading characters. To grasp the politics of either film requires two screenings because the acting performances are so dynamic, especially the aesthetic of *Rush*. Similar to *Cinderella Man*, the racing scenes of *Rush* have an announcer providing play-by-play commentary, which gives the audience some guidance through the mayhem of the scenes. (Additionally, there is momentary confusion at the end of the final race, when Chris Hemsworth doesn't know if he came in third or fifth, which is akin to *Cinderella Man* when the final round has ended, yet the viewer is placed in a moment of confusion and suspense about the outcome).

Frost/Nixon doesn't offer the audience an honest exchange between the leading characters due to undertone of deception. There is an exchange, in a fictionalized scene, but it's one sided coming from an inebriated ex-president ranting about being undermined by the elite class – therefore it tells the audience more about Langella (Nixon) than it is about his juxtaposition with Sheen (Frost). At their final meeting after the interviews air, Langella rightly predicts that the news commentators were rough on him in their reporting of the interviews, and Sheen sheepishly admits this. We realize that Michael Sheen is uncomfortable in admitting this. Even when Langella tells him `"You were a worthy opponent."` Sheen doesn't quite know how to accept the compliment, minus an eye roll, brushing the remark off. Here we arrive at an impasse in that Sheen doesn't know how to close out this relationship. There's an effort on the part of Langella to reach Sheen on his level, expressing how unique it is to have a life in the celebrity circuit, while Langella admits that he doesn't like the limelight. There's almost a hint of regret in Langella in that he is, or was, trapped in a job that forced him to be a people pleaser. This is how the film closes on the subject of President Nixon: Langella isolated from the world in his home, La Casa Pacifica.

Rush on the other hand offers a deep post-mortem on the events of the film. The final exchange between Daniel Brühl (Niki Lauda) and Chris Hemsworth (James Hunt) is one of the most preeminent moments in all of Ron Howard's cinema. At the end of all the drama, their respective success is contributed to each other. The closing scene of the film takes place in a hanger off a tarmac of a private airport, when Hemsworth (James) arrives with a small group of friends and sees his rival working along on a small airplane:

EXT. RUNWAY - DAY
A group of "beautiful people," all FRIENDS, cross the tarmac towards their waiting jet, when JAMES stops. He's seen something. Someone familiar has caught his eye.

James sends his friends on ahead to their waiting jet, and walks over to another small, private jet. NIKI is there working on it.

                            JAMES
        Niki! Good to see you.

The two shake hands. Niki's wounds have healed a little more.

                        JAMES (cont'd)
        I heard you were spending more and

more time in one of these...

NIKI
Do you fly?

JAMES
Ha-ha, no, I don't think they'd insure me.

NIKI
You should try. It's good for discipline, you have to stay within the rules, stick to regulations, suppress the ego, it helps with the racing.

JAMES
(lighting a cigarette)
There I was thinking you're about to wax lyrical about the romance of flight.

NIKI
No, it's all bullshit.

Niki indicates James' friends...

NIKI (cont'd)
What brings you here?

JAMES
A friend's wedding - or at least I think it was a wedding. Might have been a birthday or something - it's all a bit of a blur.
(beat)
How about you, have you been at Maranello?

NIKI
Pre-season testing.

Niki begins to walk around and check the airplane, with James following.

                    JAMES
          You're relentless.

                    NIKI
          Thank you.

                    JAMES
          Not sure I meant it as a
          compliment.

                    NIKI
          When do you start testing? Next week?

                    JAMES
          No, what are you? Nuts? I didn't just
          win the biggest thing of my life so I
          could get right back to work.

                    NIKI
          Why? You have to - to prove to all the
          people who will always say you just won
          it because...

                    JAMES
              (cutting him off)
          Because of what?
              (beat)
          Because of your accident?

Niki turns.

                    JAMES (cont'd)
          You sneaky - is that other people or
          is that you? I won, okay. On the all
          important day when it came down to
          it, we raced on equal terms. Equally
          good cars. And I put my life on the
          line and saw it through.

                    NIKI
And you call that winning?

                    JAMES
Yes!

                    NIKI
The risks were totally unacceptable.
You were prepared to die. To me
that's losing.

                    JAMES
Yes, I was! I admit it, I was
prepared to die to beat you that day,
and that's the effect you have on me.
You pushed me that far and it felt
great! I mean hell, isn't that what
we're in this for? To stare death in
the face and to cheat it?

Niki begins to walk to the other side of the hanger.

                    JAMES (cont'd)
Oh come on there's nobility in that,
it's, it's like being knights!

                    NIKI
You English. You're such assholes.
          (beat)
You know my position. 20% risk...

                    JAMES
No no no, Niki, don't bring the
percentages into this. Don't be a
pro. The minute you do that, you kill
what's good about this. You kill the
sport.

Niki stares, momentarily thrown. The plane load of James' friends call out...

      FRIENDS
 James! C'mon, James...!

      JAMES
 I've got to go.

James begins to walk off.

      JAMES (cont'd)
 Careful in this thing.

Niki considers something for a moment.

      NIKI
 James...

James turns around.

      NIKI (cont'd)
 You know in hospital, the toughest
 part of my treatment was the vacuum.
 Pumping the shit out of my lungs. It
 was hell. While I was doing it, I was
 watching television - you winning all
 my points.

      JAMES
 Your points?

      NIKI
 "That bastard, Hunt." I would say. I
 hated that. And then one day the
 doctor came in and said, "Mr. Lauda,
 may I offer a piece of advice? Stop
 thinking of it as a curse to be given
 an enemy in life. It can be a
 blessing too. A wise man gets more
 from his enemies than a fool from his

friends." And you know what? He was right.
(beat)
Now look at us. We were both a pair of kids when we met. Hot-headed jerks in Formula 3.

This makes James laugh.

                    NIKI (cont'd)
Disowned by our families, headed for nowhere. And no we're both champions of the world. It's not bad, huh?

                    JAMES
No. It's not bad.

                    NIKI
So don't let me down. I need you busting my balls. Get back to work.

                    JAMES
I will Niki, I will. But I intend to enjoy myself first. Some of life needs to be for pleasure. And what's the point of having a million cups and medals and planes if you don't have any fun. How is that winning?

                    FRIENDS
We're gonna leave without you! James!

                    JAMES (cont'd)
I'll see you on race day. Champ.

                    NIKI
You will. Champ.

                    JAMES
          You look good, Niki. You're the only
          guy to have his face burned off and it
          be an improvement.

Niki gives James the middle finger. James smiles
walking off to his beautiful friends in the plane.

CHAPTER 9
FAMILY

Let's return to the exchange between Jeffrey Tambor (Mayor Maywho), and Taylor Momsen (Cindy Lou Who) in *How the Grinch Stole Christmas* the morning after all the decorations and gifts are stolen. The original short story (published 1957), and the animated short film (1966), make no mention of a family for little Cindy Lou Who, but she is given one in the 2000 version. The scene is worth revisiting because two prominent Ron Howard motifs jump out at us courtesy of the father, Lou Lou Who played by Bill Irwin.

Jim Carrey (the Grinch), and Jeffrey Tambour (Mayor Maywho) have a very antagonist relationship throughout the film. During the big heist, Carrey (the Grinch) places a big hook on the lower bedframe of Tambor's (Mayor Maywho's) bed. Here we note Howard's love for deception: it's never clear what or why Carey (the Grinch) does this – it's merely just one thing he does in the Christmas stealing montage. On Christmas morning however, we see the village police officer run out of his house and into a car – which turns out to have a heavy industrial chain attached on the back of it, linked to Tambor's (the Mayor's) bed. The bed is launched through a large picture window and dragged through the streets, with Tambor (the Mayor) still in bed, eventually stopping in the town square of Whoville next to the giant Christmas tree.

EXT. TOWN SQUARE - MORNING
A collection of WHOS begin to gather in the town square around the bed with the MAYOR still in it. The Mayor begins to get out of the bed.

> **MAYOR MAYWHO**
> Well, I wonder who could have done this.

The number of Whos gathering gets larger. The Mayor's assistant, WHOBRIS starts to help him put on his robe.

> **MAYOR MAYWHO (cont'd)**
> Tell you people one thing: Invite the Grinch, destroy Christmas.

Then in a flash of anger, Mayor Maywho begins to pound his fists on the bed mattress.

> **MAYOR MAYWHO (cont'd)**
> INVITE THE GRINCH, DESTORY CHRISTMAS!!

The crowd murmuring goes silent. CINDY LOU WHO is up near the front witnessing this.

> **MAYOR MAYWHO (cont'd)**
> But did anyone listen to me?

> **WHOBRIS**
> I did.

> **MAYOR MAYWHO (cont'd)**
> (talking over him)
> Nooo. You choose to listen to a little not-to-be-taken-seriously girl,
> (beat)
> who hasn't even grown into her nose yet.

The Mayor points his finger at Cindy.

> **MAYOR MAYWHO**
> Cindy, I hope you're very proud of what you've done.

The Mayor waves his finger "no" at her and turns away. Cindy hangs her head.

LOU steps in front of her.

> **LOU**
> If she isn't, I am.

The crowd gasps.

> **LOU (cont'd)**
> I'm glad he took our presents.

> **MAYOR MAYWHO**
> What?

The crowds continue to murmur amongst themselves.

> **LOU**
> I... Well, I'm,

Lou glances down at his daughter, Cindy, who is now smiling.

> **LOU (cont'd)**
> I'm glad.

> **MAYOR MAYWHO**
> He's glad. You're glad. You're glad everything is... is gone.

The Mayor beings to walk back and progressively gets into Lou's face.

> **MAYOR MAYWHO (cont'd)**
> You're glad that the Grinch virtually wrecked... no, no, no, not wrecked, pulverized Christmas. Is that what I'm hearing from you, Lou?

>   **LOU**
> You can't hurt Christmas Mr. Mayor,
> because it isn't about the gifts ore
> the contests or the fancy lights.
> That's, that's what Cindy's been trying
> to tell everyone!
> (beat)
> And me. She's been trying to tell me.
>
>   **MAYOR MAYWHO**
> What's wrong with you? This is a child.

Lou takes a step forward towards the Mayor and gets into his face.

>   **LOU**
> She's my child. And she happens to be
> right by the way.

Lou touches the upper chest of the Mayor with his finger. The murmuring of the crowd gets louder and more positive.

Lou turns back and puts his arms around his family.

>   **LOU (cont'd)**
> I don't need anything more for
> Christmas than this right here, my
> family.

The crowd gives an audible "aww."

>   **LOU (cont'd)**
> Merry Christmas everybody!

The group of Who's begin to repeat "Merry Christmas" to each other.

 Once again, neither Dr. Seuss' children's book or the cartoon short explain why the Who's wake up Christmas morning and are celebratory. The Ron Howard film provides an explanation using family. The scene is edited in such a way that once Irwin (Lou) says the line and puts his arms around his family, the reverberations of holiday greetings starts to pass through the crowd. What's even more telling is that when Tambor affixes blame on Momsen (Cindy Lou) for provoking the robbery, her father steps in to defend her. For all of the buffoonery and mischief that Jim Carrey does to the little girl, the viewer isn't concern that Carrey would actually harm her – but Tambor's belittling her in front of a crowd results in the parent snapping at him.

Threatening families is the lynchpin that increases the tension throughout Howard's movies. Harm to the family brings about a visceral reaction: see Mel Gibson in *Ransom* or Cate Blanchett in *The Missing*. The constant presence of families is a concept rooted at the core of the stories. *A Beautiful Mind* isn't a difficult film to watch, however the most shocking scene is the baby's near drowning in the bathtub. In *Grand Theft Auto*, Nancy Morgan's domineering family is the problem for the two lovers. The mystery of *The Da Vinci Code* comes from Audrey Tautou's family and their blood line lineage.

In films where a traditional family is not present, the structure of an ad-hoc family is there be it the old folks in *Cocoon*, or the crime gangs in *Solo*. This is clearly seen through The Beatles in *Eight Days A Week* through the emphasis of the four votes that they all made together in dealing with obstacles such as playing to non-segregated crowds. The documentary makes a point to acknowledge that Paul McCartney and John Lennon lost their parents at a young age, thereby underlining the closeness they developed through that loss.

Dual families:
Ransom

There's no doubt that by the time of *Ransom* in the mid-1990s, Howard had successfully reinvented himself as a director of dramas and thrillers. *Ransom* was the furthest Howard had descended into grimness and macabre. In 2023 it would become public knowledge that attempts to kidnap Howard's daughter, Bryce, influenced his decision to direct the film. It's important to point out that Howard said *Ransom* was the hardest film for him to make from an emotional standpoint and that he was working in a genre he was not used to.[1] Although *Backdraft* had dark elements, the film had a lighter aesthetic thanks to the humorous comradery of the firemen and the music video montages. Hardly any moment of lighter flair is present in *Ransom*, and the idea of willingly harming a child has a significantly dark tinge. The film addresses elements that coincide with Howard's fascinations, specifically families and the media. When Gibson decides to turn the tables on Sinise, offering the $2-million dollar ransom money as bounty for the kidnappers, he uses the media. Dare we go back to Howard's first film, *Grand Theft Auto*, (which shares aesthetically nothing with *Ransom*), the radio DJ in the helicopter exploits the young couple's peril, creating a frenzy out of the situation. So too as the conflict progresses in *Ransom*, the media latches on and turns it into "a story" for the networks. One could certainly do a kidnapping drama without the news media being so present, yet in Howard's film, it's a tool Gibson uses to fight his opponents which is a concept we see him dabble with in later films. Specifically in the context of *Ransom*, the news is the link between the two "families" – one functional and the other dysfunctional.[2]

Howard intentionally structured the film to be an examination of two families: the *functional* "victims" (Mel Gibson & Rene Russo), and the *dysfunctional* "kidnappers" (Gary Sinise & Lili Taylor). Two different "households" are presented in contrast, Mel Gibson and Rene Russo in one household, is cross-cut with Gary Sinise and Lili Taylor in the other. Gibson and Russo fulfill the quintessential Howard couple as they are strongly united, are joined in the hardship, they reach a breaking point, and ultimately reconcile. When Gibson (falsely) believes he causes his son's death, it's in his devastation that Russo goes to counsel him. Meanwhile, the alternate "family" of kidnappers are never coherent and are perpetually in conflict. The angrier they get, the more mistakes they make. A subplot between Liev Schreiber and Donnie

Wahlberg as two brothers brings a layer of complexity to the villains that tells the audience about their agenda they have in assisting with this crime. This only adds to our understanding of the internal messiness of the dysfunctional family. When someone is in it for themselves and/or becomes selfish, everyone suffers.

***

It must be highlighted that Mel Gibson is a "star-teur": taken from the terms "auteur" and "[movie] star." Gibson belongs in the same category alongside Woody Allen, Tom Cruise and Clint Eastwood: major Hollywood celebrities that have a direct influence in their body of work.[3] Obviously, movie stars picks and chooses what films he or she wants to be in, yet the "starteurs" have more personalized investment as they are often producers and/or writers on the various films. Gibson's own Icon Productions was not directly involved with making *Ransom*, yet given Gibson's celebrity and influence in the mid-1990s, his tropes are clearly at work. Therefore, if we look at *Ransom* through the perspective of "the authorship of Mel Gibson," it actually resonates more than looking at it from the perspective of "the authorship of Ron Howard." Make no mistake, *Ransom* is a brilliant co-op between the two directors, but it feels like Howard is working in Gibson's territory. The same can be said for *How the Grinch Stole Christmas*, in that Howard is working in Jim Carrey's territory[4] and *Jim Henson: Idea Man* as he pulls from Henson's style to decorate the aesthetic of the documentary.

Gibson is readily willing to address the concept of "sins of the past" and retribution in his films. Audiences will often find a protagonist, especially if Gibson himself is playing the part, hiding a dark secret. In *Ransom* the subplot of a dishonest business partner sitting in prison on account of Gibson's airline business was something he himself encouraged be added to film. Of course, this deal is what provoked the kidnappers to blackmail him for money, forcing Gibson to confront his past. It leads to marital strife between him and Russo, forcing him to take matters into his own hands. There is a form of confession on Gibson's part, admitting his own pride was at fault; once Gibson makes that omission, he begins to take control over the situation.

Masochism is a regular theme of Gibson's mantra, therefore in his taking control of the situation, Gibson takes responsibility unto himself. He goes through the wringer of trying to get his son back only to fail. An interesting behind-the-scenes to make note of is that Gibson thought up diving into a pool, fully clothed, to grab a key, just to make the situation more difficult for his character.[5] Therefore, when he's unable to get the kidnapper to release his son, and believes he himself responsible for his son's death, that pain is shown to be taken personally. The emotional stress that Gibson brings to *Ransom* is significantly more poignant than what any of Howard's other leads had suffered in his films prior to *Ransom*. The beating Tom Cruise takes in *Far and Away* or the astronauts nearly getting blown up in *Apollo 13* might be more physically painful, but there is a hint of sadistic torture the viewer is put though watching Gibson's stress in *Ransom*.

Howard points out that *Ransom* is not a traditional happy ending[6] being that no one really exits this conflict better off than they were before it started. Although the villain is defeated, Gibson doesn't end in his posh apartment, but rather bruised and bloody on the street (again, another Gibson encouragement on set was the amount of visible blood in the final confrontation,[7] which adheres to Gibson's authorship as gore is gratuitous in his films). *Ransom* ends with a camera pulling up and away from the scene of this clash, which gives the audience a "God's eye" point-of-view on the scene — given Gibson's affection for theology in his films, the final shot is fitting.

This concept is reflected in James Horner's score, which is yet another parallel as Horner and Gibson were collaborators*. For the music Ron Howard said:

> There's nothing celebratory about it [James Horner's score]. Even the end music has a bittersweet quality. It

---

*Horner did the score for Gibson's *The Man Without A Face* (1993); *Braveheart* (1995) and *Apocalypto* (2006). He was slated to do *Hacksaw Ridge* (2016) but died before getting to work on it.

acknowledges that the hero has survived, but at a cost. So on the one hand, the suspense and action of the story needed to be dealt with. And on the other, *Ransom* is very much a film about personal anguish. I wanted that to be scored in a simple, dramatic way.(8)

Pointing the lens at families:
Rebuilding Paradise* and *We Feed People

The two documentaries are a unique Howard-esque pair because of their juxtaposition: they're both about natural disasters in the late-2010s, but handle the subject matter very differently. In the case of *Rebuilding Paradise* we look at one specific natural disaster and the recovery process for several different people in the context of one town. *We Feed People* covers several natural disasters across the globe, viewed through the eyes of one group, the World Central Kitchen. A crucial similarity between the two films is how the topic of family is utilized.

Rebuilding Paradise spends a relatively small percentage of its screen time devoted on what caused the fires. The simplicity of the causation of the 2018 Camp Fire is disturbing, yet we, the audience, learns it matter-of-factly through the residents of Paradise. Although it does come up, one would be hard pressed to call *Rebuilding Paradise* a political drama because the cameras spend a lot more time capturing a variety of families affected by one horrible event and their coping with the after effects. This includes town hall style explanations from Pacific Gas and Electric Company (PG&E) which provides the viewer with an answer as to how and why the fire started, but that's not Howard's focal point. A lot of *Rebuilding Paradise* is compiled from footage of various families and watching them deal with not having a neighborhood anymore, let alone a house. There's a lot of time devoted to families looking at and/or explaining what the charred out remains used to be. Although it's a profoundly traumatic event, the documentary embraces cinéma vérité, simply capturing people in a state of shock as they go about the arduous process of reconstruction. The age variety between young families and older ones present a balanced spread of what a major event can do to people of varying ages. This allows the viewer to hone in on different people and lets the audience pick and choose who they'll follow in the course of 90 minutes. One family's circumstance is entirely different than someone else's, despite that they all live in the same region.

With the exception of one character, the pyrogeographer, all of the characters are presented to the audience in the context of their families. Their stories are comprised of testimonies about their domestic status. The condition of the schools is a key element as the future generation cannot develop properly, which is accented with b-roll footage of kids loitering at temporary housing or in the ruins.

***

With the myriad of disasters shown in *We Feed People*, the documentary doesn't spend a lot of time with the victims on the ground. Focused more on the logistics of World Central Kitchen and its founder, José Andrés, the film gives us a brief expose of his past and what brought him into undertaking the challenge of bringing food to areas of crisis. (There's a "blink and you'll miss it" shot of Andrés serving food after the fire in *Rebuilding Paradise*). The celebrity chef material has to be outlined in the film for an explanation for how Andrés has been able to do what he does, but it's not a fixation for *We Feed People*. In both Howard's live action films and the documentaries, the celebrity trappings of his biographical subjects aren't something he spends a lot of time weighing in on. If it comes up, (such as John Nash's Nobel Prize or Jim Henson's success on *Sesame Street*), it remains part of the story, but its laurels of are not extensively scrutinized – unless it directly affects the character. The pop-culture trendiness of David Frost wanting to move into politics in *Frost/Nixon*, or the dissonance of how the Formula 1 racers' view victory in *Rush*, and the endangerment of The Beatles in *Eight Days A Week* are examples of when Howard locks on the subject of fame, but it's usually shown with an omen. *We Feed People* spends time acknowledging Chef José Andrés status in the culinary arts world, but it pales in comparison to how much screen time is given to Andrés' family and their home when the documentary turns its attention to his literal home.

There's something about the 30-minute mark in Ron Howard's films because that's when the daughters come into the narrative. *We Feed People* establishes who Andrés is, how World Central Kitchen got started and what they do – but we almost sense that Howard *needs* to tell the viewer about Andrés as a person from the domestic perspective. Andrés' family is the prism used to access who he really is, by way of his wife and three daughters. All three share their perspectives on who their father is, while splicing it together with home video footage from a smart phone. It's as if Howard needs to bring the audience into Andrés' own kitchen and show you the interactions between family members. Why? Family is generally Howard's access point in his narratives. How a man or woman treats their family is crucial to unlocking the character and flushing out who he/she is. For a boxing movie, *Cinderella Man* only has one short training montage; a majority of the time spent is with the Braddock family. So too with *We Feed People*; the family interviews are regulated to one entire section of the documentary, but the adventures Andrés goes on now have that familial anchor established while he's on these dangerous charitable efforts.

CHAPTER 10
THE ENSEMBLE CAST

Of all Ron Howard's collaborators, Todd Hallowell has one of the longest and steadiest track records working with him as production designer or second unit director dating back to the late 1970s. With regards to *Frost/Nixon*, Hallowell said:

> Ron loves an ensemble. You watch him on set handling six people, six characters simultaneously in a scene, which could completely traumatize an awful lot of directors, [but] he's in his element. One of my favorite things about this movie [*Frost/Nixon*] is the way he works with an ensemble in a scene with half a dozen different characters or more. It's like a phenomenally complicated three level poker game and he tracks it as a director in a way that every time I see it, I go 'Wow, this is so cool.'"[1]

With the motif of families being so present in Howard's body of work, it's no surprise that a multi-person cast comes as a regularity. It is unlikely that Howard will direct a film akin to *My Dinner with Andre* (1981) or *Gravity* (2013) — movies with one or two characters throughout the entire picture. Howard is roused by a large cast, often with a hefty amount of contention thriving between all the characters.

Cotton Candy, co-written by Ron and his brother Clint Howard, demonstrates the power of an ensemble with the teenage garage band. Although the film bends to the romantic storyline between Charles Martin Smith and Leslie King, it's the band working as a team that comes through in the end. The blueprint of *Backdraft*'s screenplay is a spider-webbed story between various characters, including two romances, intermixed with city politics and the firemen's own concerns. Consider how the little girl interviews the citizens of Whoville in *How the Grinch Stole Christmas* in attempt to give a backstory to the film's title character. The supporting cast in *Frost/Nixon* give subtext to what the title characters' agendas are, which is particularly crucial for a good political drama. *Rebuilding Paradise* isn't just about the governmental coordination after the destruction, rather individuals are zeroed in on despite not being directly related with each other.

Philosophical questions on set:
Cocoon

Before addressing the way *Cocoon* utilized it's cast of esteemed Hollywood professionals, we need to revisit the ending of *Splash*, and more importantly, the two science-fiction blockbusters by Steven Spielberg that unofficially inspired them. Following the unfathomable success of *Jaws* (1975), Spielberg was given the green light to make whatever he wanted next, which became his self-penned *Close Encounters of the Third Kind* (1977). The film was financially successful which paved the way for Spielberg to, essentially, have carte blanch access to whatever he wanted to do. Following a hiatus from space-aliens, Spielberg returned to science fiction with *E.T.: The Extra Terrestrial* (1982).

Splash was released in early 1984 and it's worth noting the vast popularity of *E.T.* which had become the highest grossing film of all time in the U.S. box office.* With this in mind, we need to be mindful of "copy-cat" movies which inevitably arrive in the wake of a mega-blockbuster, and Howard's *Splash* and *Cocoon* draw some distinct parallels. How much of this was unintentional or in the screenplays prior to *E.T.*'s release is hard to say, nevertheless, with *Splash*'s debut two years after *E.T.*, the mermaid flick

---

*E.T.'s standing in the U.S. box office would be surpassed in 1997. However, should one adjust the numbers for inflation, *E.T.* still ranks in the top-five most lucrative films in box-office history.

becomes an easy target for accusation. Howard said his daughter, Bryce's, reaction to *E.T.* influenced his desire to direct *Splash*.[2]

An "alien" developing a relationship with a human, the government clandestinely hunting the "alien," the capture and experimental tests that harm said "alien" are strikingly similar. There is a flower pot in *E.T.*, a physical object/token, that connects the "alien" with the humans. In *Splash*, Daryl Hannah trades her neckless for a 14-foot tall fountain that she gifts to Hanks. Although the large water fountain with a mermaid perched on top is a sight gag, there is an emotional bond to the oversized fountain that Hanks clings to when Hannah is taken away — not unlike the flower pot in *E.T.* Of course, one of *E.T.*'s most famous scenes is the bicycle chase when the alien is smuggled out from the government's supervision. So too with *Splash* – the mermaid is whisked away from the government's science lab and a car chase through New York City ensures (granted, a car chase with more gags than actual suspense).

In the end of *E.T.*, the alien leaves Earth, whereas with *Close Encounters*, the human leaves with the aliens. In the finale of *Splash,* Hanks is given an ultimatum: if he goes under the sea with Hannah, he cannot return back home and will be destined to live underwater with her forever. He initially decides to stay on land, but then worried that she'll be re-kidnapped, Hanks joins her and they swim off together. (In an earlier version of the script, Hanks originally let the mermaid leave, but the wives of Ron Howard, Brian Grazer, Lowell Ganz and Babaloo Mandel all disagreed and said they were nuts if Hanks didn't leave with the mermaid).[3] If one watches the first 90-seconds of *Splash*'s end credits, the final shot of the film reveals, then fades out on, an underwater kingdom in the distance. *Splash* sides with the ending of *Close Encounters of the Third Kind*; the human leaves his life to go be with an alien.

This very concept returned in *Cocoon* only to be much more heavily debated. With this in mind, Howard reportedly had mixed feelings with the first drafts of *Cocoon* in its similarities to Spielberg's *Close Encounters of the Third Kind*.[4]

The accusations of the two films, *Splash* and *Cocoon*, being copycats of Spielberg's two sci-fi mammoth success is a fair observation. Aliens coming to Earth, then returning home, heartfelt goodbyes, the emphasis on family, an ending chase – one could argue that Howard was cheapening himself with two films that seem to ride the coattails of the blockbusters, yet we should be mindful that Ron Howard and Steven Spielberg have been in the same circle of friends since the 1970s. *Cocoon* was a Zanuck & Brown production, the same team that worked with Spielberg on *The Sugarland Express* (1973) and *Jaws* (1975). The special effects in *Cocoon* were done by George Lucas' Industrial Light and Magic studio. Not only are Lucas & Spielberg are friends, but Lucas had directed the commercially and critically successful *American Graffiti* (1973), which Ron Howard had a leading role in. Additionally, the co-lead of *American Graffiti* was Richard Dreyfuss who was also a close friend of Spielberg's, and say nothing of another *American Graffiti* actor, Harrison Ford whom became globally recognizable through his subsequent work with George Lucas (*Star Wars*) and Steven Spielberg (*Indiana Jones*). Finally, although it's a joke, the use of "May the Force Be With You" in *Cocoon*'s final scene was something Howard had to get permission from Lucas for – a request Lucas didn't typically grant but made an exception for. Howard quotes Lucas saying, "Well, you did a good job in *American Graffiti*."[5]

With Tom Hanks abandoning his life to be with Daryl Hannah forever under the ocean in *Splash*, and with the senior citizens abandoning Earth to live with the aliens in *Cocoon*, we see this striking parallel to the end of Spielberg's *Close Encounters of the Third Kind*, where the main character abandons his life on Earth to be with space aliens in the finale of the film. Instead of it just being one person, in *Cocoon* it's six people that are taken.

Herein spurred a question that became a recurring dialogue between the cast ensemble of *Cocoon* during the filming, which was in credit to the cast members themselves. Many of them debated the idea of cheating death with the power that radiated from the alien's cocoons – a philosophical debate that the younger

Howard was not intellectually investigating himself in at the time of production, yet cites as giving the performances some weight in retrospect.[6] A brief passage from Howard's memoir offers more substance to the concept of multiple perspectives on *Cocoon*:

> When I directed *Cocoon*, Mom made her first tentative noises about returning to acting, having forsaken it three decades earlier to focus on her family. I put her in the movie as key extra, a background actor who has no dialogue but appears in a lot of the scenes. True to form, she charmed everyone in the cast. She had some heart-to-heart conversations with Maureen Stapleton, Jessica Tandy, and Gwen Verdon in which they, for all their success, voiced regrets about their life choices. They all expressed to Mom that they envied her for having spent that amount of time she had with her children. There is no one correct way to achieve work-life balance, of course, and the conditions for doing so as a working actress in the twentieth century were brutal. But Mom was buoyed by her talks with Maureen, Jessica, and Gwen. "They made me realize that, for me, I did it right," she told me.[7]

Despite the charm of the film, there is a gravitas seen through the three main leads: Wilford Brimley, Don Ameche and Hume Cronyn. After getting kicked out of using the pool house, it's Brimley who quips to the other two: `"You know, I can't remember the last time I really took a risk."` prompting them to stubbornly sneak back in. Although *Cocoon* is a fantasy movie, lines like this carry more flavor when delivered by actors who have lived life. The authenticity of *Cocoon* is in credit to the collection of aged wisdom courtesy of the leading cast members. Although Wilford Brimley is positioned as the de facto main character, *Cocoon* gives a considerable amount of screen time to the other cast members thereby offering various perspectives on the concept of cheating death. Each of the three leads, their wives, the other characters living tangentially to the pool house, including the cranky Jack Gilford, all view the appropriateness of the predicament differently. Knowing that this question was debated by the cast themselves while making the film, explains why it boils over so well into how the performances came across on screen.

Approximately twenty years after the release of *Close Encounters of the Third Kind*, Spielberg disparaged his own film saying that the ending reflected a youthful naiveté about himself. Spielberg pointed out that becoming a father with responsibilities would never allow him to get into a spaceship and fly away.(8)

Therefore, it's worth asking the same question of Ron Howard with the adventurous spirit seen at the end of *Splash* and *Cocoon*. Keeping in tandem with Spielberg, Howard has similar observations regarding *Cocoon* about twenty-years after its release:

> Despite the philosophical controversy that we discussed during rehearsal, that the actors talked about amongst themselves of whether it was the correct thing to try to roll back the biological clock, whether if it was even right to consider going on a spaceship and going off on that kind of adventure where you'd live forever. I felt that one of the important ideas that the movie offered, one of the themes, was that you must never at any point in your life ignore the possibility of something extraordinary coming along; some force of change, some unexpected turn at any point in your life that could present itself, and you needed to be prepared to make a choice about that — but be aware enough to recognize it when it came your way.
>
> At that time, when I was 30 years old, [there was] no question in my mind I would get on the spaceship and go, if I could, live forever. As I've lived a little longer, and understand the way of world a little more, I understand why the actors were raising the philosophical question — although I think in my heart I'd probably still be getting on the mothership.(9)

Howard's acknowledgement of an "unexpected" and "extraordinary" opportunity coming along is something that we see throughout the résumé. A chance to migrate to the United States (*Far and Away*); a chance to land on the moon (*Apollo 13*); a chance to box again (*Cinderella Man*). The darker side of this question is what one does when bad things happen, be it children being kidnapped (*Ransom* & *The Missing*); or your home being wiped off the map in the timespan of a day (*Rebuilding Paradise*). In all these situations, Howard showcases different people reacting to the unexpected creating a pseudo kaleidoscope presentation of thoughts and opinions. Howard behind the camera is not a filmmaker easy to pigeonhole. Yes, moral stances are taken: it's wrong to steal, kidnapping is evil, don't be condescending, feed the hungry, don't cheat on your significant other, etc. He's vocal about his opinions when asked, but we almost sense that Howard regularly says, "Well, what do you think about 'this?'" in the way that he functions. This is mirrored by the amount of commentary in the live-action movies provided by other characters.

An examination of the media:
The Paper* and *EDtv

Even before his stint as a 6-year-old in *The Andy Griffith Show*, Ron Howard is one of the few child stars who would be a lifelong player in the industry.* Additionally, his fame has never been adjudicated to personal scandal (a la Bill Cosby, Robert Downey Jr., or Lindsay Lohan). Therefore his commentary on the subject of the paparazzi is uniquely poignant. The most significant way Howard addressed this came by way of his autobiography, *The Boys*. One of the reasons the brothers wrote the book was to pay tribute to their parents, Jean & Rance, sheltering them from the intensity of "celebrity" as well as instilling character building values in them. Decades later, we see how that parallels the way

---

*Aside from his brother Clint, Shirley Temple Black, Jackie Cooper and Baby Rose Marie are the rare others who've achieved lifelong "Hollywood" celebrity status in the U.S.(10)

Howard uses wholesome family values as an avenue to address the pitfalls of the gossip-driven media industry.

Howard revisits the subject of bad media quite a bit in his body of work: *Grand Theft Auto* has a radio jockey who exploits the young lover's escapades for his own show's programming. In *Splash*, the media make the reveal of Daryl Hannah's mermaid that much more of a disappointment and embarrassment for Tom Hanks. It's in the 1990s that Howard really starts to debate the issue and cross examines the media's influence throughout his films (*Backdraft*; *The Paper*; *Ransom* & *EDtv*) by way of making their power a focal point of the narratives. The *Life* magazine cover photo in *Backdraft* which looms over William Baldwin's character, and *Apollo 13*'s use of the news reporting from the time of the event. Should one watch the bonus features of *Apollo 13*; *Ransom* and *EDtv* in order, Howard progressively philosophizes about the media more and more.

We see the "ensemble" concept at work with Howard's two dissertations on the media: *The Paper* and *EDtv*. The pair are separated by five years and neither got a huge reception upon release (*The Paper* fared much better in comparison, coming in as the 36th highest grossing film of 1994, with one Oscar nomination for Best Song. *EDtv* on the other hand ranked as the 81st highest grossing film of 1999). They each have their own aesthetic despite being produced in the same decade and highlighting the same industry, but they inadvertently reflect the transformation of the media seen throughout the 1990s.

There is one event from 1991 and 1992 that requires revisiting, particularly to appreciate *The Paper*: in the early morning of March 3rd, 1991, twenty-five-year-old Rodney King, along with two passengers, was pursued by law enforcement for speeding, resulting in a car chase with police helicopter that stretched for approximately 8 miles through the San Fernando Valley of Los Angeles. King was slightly drunk and high, and didn't want to risk getting a DUI. After being cornered by several police cars, all three individuals exited the vehicle, yet King resisted arrest. King was tased, and then struck repeatedly by four police officers with batons which resulted in a broken leg, missing teeth and skull fractures. The beating was captured on video by a resident across the street filming the commotion from his apartment balcony. The video was brought to local media two days later and sparked public outrage. The footage of Rodney King's beating has become referred to as "the first viral video," even though it predated widespread access to the internet. On March 15th, just shy of two weeks since the initial arrest, the four police officers were charged for assault.

Over a year after the incident took place, on April 29th, 1992, the four officers were found not guilty which sparked the LA riots of 1992, which resulted in $1-billion dollars in property damage, over 2,300 injuries and 63 deaths.

With the exception of *The Da Vinci Code*, (only on account of the book's vast popularity at the time), Ron Howard was never one to make beelines into contemporary hot-button topics the way Paul Greengrass or Spike Lee have. In the late-2010s and early 2020s that changed with the likeness of *Rebuilding Paradise* and *Thirteen Lives*, including some of the Imagine Entertainment documentary content, although Howard himself has personally avoided "hot button" controversy. Anytime that Howard traversed modern events, it was done so from a distant vantage point and repackaging of the material. Beverly Gray's biography references an interview with Ron Howard in the mid-1990s that's worth noting:

> Though the plot of *The Paper* touches on questions of racial profiling and the power of the media to expose injustice, Howard admitted at the time that he had yet to delve deeply into social issues: "I don't think I've pushed any boundaries yet as a director. I may be a little braver in the future."(11)

The Paper and *EDtv* offer a lot of commentary about culture's relationship to the mainstream media, and the Rodney King "viral video" can be seen as a starting point for what Howard was contemplating with these films. For audiences in 1994, merely two years after the traumatic events in Los Angeles (not to mention additional federal prosecutions that took place in 1993), the tensions certainly maintain a presence in *The Paper*'s subtext, however the concept of voyeurism was undoubtedly an element inspired by the Rodney King story. A lot of the Rodney King and L.A. riot history has to do with what the world saw, or rather, what was broadcast to them. *The Paper* is an anecdotal film about the early 1990s – uniquely staged on the opposite end of the United States, New York City.

Opening with two young black teenagers coming across a crime scene (that the audience eventually learns was staged by hired hitmen to look like a black-on-white hate crime), *The Paper* starts off with racial tension. It's not until later in the film that *The Paper* blatantly winks to modern events when Michael Keaton warns colleagues of the consequences of getting the story wrong and `"igniting another race war"` should they accidentally exploit the arrest of two young black men (who the viewer already knows are innocent). For a film that's just under 2-hours in length, there are a lot of different characters, subplots and running jokes, with a significant increase in the amount of handheld camera work Howard had used up until that time. While *Parenthood*'s story was about accepting the `"roller coaster,"` the cast of *The Paper* are already strapped in. It's not an easy film to write a synopsis for on account of all the different drama and humor at play. *The Paper* is similarly messy, but the difference is that all the little side plots slowly begin to merge onto one subject: the awareness that the business of the media, their profession, has the ability to change lives for the better, or the worse.

Without looking it up… what was Steve Martin's job in *Parenthood*? Don't remember? Exactly. (The audience is never told). Where *Parenthood* explored marriage and families with kids, *The Paper* can be viewed as the alternate presentation of marriage with an emphasis on the career. *Parenthood* and *The Paper* are a unique doppelgänger as both films have a striking different tempo, (the "loudest" *Parenthood* ever gets is the drag race scene, whereas *The Paper* is non-stop noise). Yet the "roller-coaster" concept that Steve Martin is reluctant towards in *Parenthood*, is applicable for *The Paper* because that metaphorical "roller-coaster" is one that husband and wife Michael Keaton and Marisa Tomei, love to ride. Steve Martin's boss in *Parenthood* is not a likeable character and one he harbors animosity towards, yet Robert Duvall in *The Paper* is a pseudo-father figure to his motley crew of journalists. Furthermore, both films end in a hospital immediately following the birth of a new family member, and both films are scored with Randy Newman's recognizable music.

The problem Michael Keaton has in *The Paper* is that he's in a Ron Howard film. While in the middle of a time sensitive issue, and trying to keep his newspaper from printing a false story, Keaton also has the stress of a job interview from the larger rival newspaper, a pregnant wife whose family is in town, and his co-worker, Glenn Close, becoming more contentious about production costs. When Keaton has enough confirmation to be convinced that they are running with a false narrative and needs to stop the presses, he get into a physical tête-à-tête with Glenn Close. Despite Keaton successfully hitting the red button to cease the paper roll, it's not enough to override Close's influence on the production floor – the incorrect headline continues to be printed.

The ultimate goal for Michael Keaton in *The Paper* ends up being that he rallies everyone, the ensemble, to the cause. As the night wears on, the realization of *their* collective actions begins to settle on all the contributing parties, making it a collective effort for all of them to change the headline cover story. Keaton's determination in pressuring fellow reporters to seek out the right police officers and get the appropriate quote to put a pause to the sham story eventually guilt trips Glenn Close. Keaton himself doesn't even realize the triumph of his achievements until the next morning. He does the right thing, inspires others to take action, but once the health of Tomei and their newborn are in danger, the priorities change and everything else becomes secondary.

***

Every once in a while, directors will undertake an official "do over." These movies should not be thought as remakes or improvements. Spielberg's *Close Encounters of the Third Kind* was followed five years later by *E.T.: The Extra Terrestrial* and are two different versions of aliens coming to Earth and how people react to them. Martin Scorsese has made an array of crime movies, but he's revisited the Italian mob several times throughout the span of his career in *Mean Streets* (1973); *Goodfellas* (1990) and *The Irishman* (2019). For all the heavy dramas that Edward Zwick directed, he gave an early comedy of his, *About Last Night...*(1986) a "cousin" over twenty years later with *Love & Other Drugs* (2010).[12]

The Paper and *EDtv* look very different: one takes place within a 24-hour window timeframe, while the other takes place over the course of a few months. One strictly looks at the newspaper business, and the other television broadcasting. A further juxtapose is that news anchors and reporters are seen in *The Paper*, but they don't have much of an influence in the story (minus the paparazzi mayhem outside of the courthouse when the novice photographer is trying to get a picture). As for *EDtv*, we see physical magazines and newspapers and hear people read from them, but the audience only sees inside the television executive offices. *EDtv* doesn't show us other news outlets or network studios reacting to the phenomenon that the reality tv-show has caused.

As time has gone on, both films seem slightly prophetic. In *The Paper* when Michael Keaton and Randy Quaid have the police sergeant locked in the bathroom, and the officer discloses how weak the evidence was for the arrest of the two innocent youths, we see an example of what depravity the news media is potentially capable of causing. Not only are the higher ups who made the decision to target two kids *knew* they had weak evidence, but that the whole news media can run with a false story without being able to verify information. As time would go on, the damnation of the mainstream media would progressively increase as the reporting of false information would spike in the 1990s, 2000s and especially the 2010s. This was of course in part due to the 24-hour news cycle, which we can see foreshadowed in *EDtv* via the concept of following one person around non-stop for 24 hours a day, 7 days a week, 365 days a year.

Released in early 1999, *EDtv* really embodies the late 1990s era on account of the soundtrack and the ambiance. The trendiness of San Francisco reflects the pop-culture of the late-1990s in a way that few films from the era were able to. What's most unique about *EDtv* is how it truly anticipated social media's livestreaming capabilities of the late-2010s, arguably making the movie a full 15 years ahead of its time. The concept of self-exposure would become something that people had the ability to do with a smart phone and the proper app (be it Facebook, Instagram, OnlyFans, Twitch or YouTube), and would go mainstream for both entertainment and journalism. *EDtv* wasn't the only film from this era to predict a future that wasn't too far off, particularly with regards to social media. The obsession of controlling reality in *The Truman Show* (1998), and the ability of companies to do targeted advertising in *Minority Report* (2002), would become common by the late-2010s.

In the case of Matthew McConnaughey, he signs a contract allowing for something akin to a voyeuristic reality tv show. Even before the "EDtv" show begins broadcasting, everyone in his circle is suggesting how McConaughey should behave. The perceived fame has them worked up, and once the show does begin to broadcast to the country, everyone wants in on it… except Jenna Elfman, the love interest. The one person McConaughey would rather spend time with wants nothing to do with the show, and eventually becomes appalled by the 24/7 coverage. Elfman becomes "hated" for simply not being in lock-step with what the audience (i.e. strangers) want. Even Rob Reiner says he "hates" her just because he wants something new tossed into *his* reality tv show. This becomes an emotional tug on McConaughey, which in-turn effects his brother, mother, step-father and long lost biological father.

Unlike Jim Carrey's character in *The Truman Show* who was born into the fantasy and grew up with a skewed perception of reality, Mathew McConaughey had freedom and liberty until he signed it over to the TrueTV network. Ellen DeGeneres and Rob Reiner try to control McConaughey, but ultimately they can't. All they can do is influence him via the world around him to the best of their ability, such as putting someone like Elizabeth Hurley in his way to spike ratings. Unlike *The Truman Show*, they don't have a nonautonomous set they can control. The problem the "EDtv" showrunners have is that something can backfire. Therefore the source of *EDtv*'s conflict comes not just from McConaughey, but from those around him. The concept of a girlfriend falling for a brother is rather in-tune with something Ron Howard and company would do in a comedy (or, potentially Matthew McConaughey and Woody Harrelson for that matter as they were friends prior to doing *EDtv*). Yet, the problem boils down to McConaughey's fame becoming its own hurricane and causing havoc to everyone within his orbit; rather appropriately McConaughey begins to feel isolated, alone in the eye of the storm. Howard said that he intended for the film to be observational rather than judgmental.[13] In *EDtv*, all of the characters are watching McConaughey, but we the audience are watching the supporting cast. Howard spends a significant portion of *EDtv*'s runtime on the other characters and showing us a kaleidoscope of different people throughout the weeks long broadcast, giving us their reaction to the pivotal events happening to McConaughey.

The telling moment of *EDtv* is when the network decides to turn cameras on all members of McConaughey's family. There is a brief scene of McConaughey watching his family resist assaults by camera crews on a bank of monitors in Clint Howard's truck. It's a vulgar prefiguration of what social media would actually do to some people after it became common place by the mid-2010s. Would an audience in 1999 appreciate the shock and gravity of having something broadcast to the world that they didn't want? Undesired content going out into the public forum is a concept that most of the modern culture has likely experienced in some form, thanks to the speed at which content travels and cameras being everywhere. The effect and the danger of what Rob Reiner decides to do is arguably appreciated more and better understood by a viewer in the 2020s, as the potential of something like that happening had become more common throughout the 2000s, and excelled further in the 2010s. Audiences of the 2010s and 2020s know what that's like and it's a shame that we don't have a way of measuring how audiences in Spring 1999 reacted to that scene in the monitor truck. No one watching *EDtv* on opening weekend had a camera on their cell phone, let alone experienced what having the world wide web in their pocket was like yet.

CHAPTER 11
AUTOMOTIVE, DECEPTION, MUSIC & RELIGION

If you take a college level class on the authorship of Clint Eastwood, you can't *not* acknowledge his love for jazz music. You're not getting through a Martin Scorsese class without at least one discussion about the real-life gangsters that some of his fictional crime dramas were inspired by. If you dive into Steven Spielberg's cinema, you'll quickly see that the subject matter of fatherhood is the dominate motif, but it would be odd to have that discussion without addressing the recurring aliens. These subjects aren't necessarily the central themes that these filmmakers are debating within their body of work, but those topics are present and it would seem rather odd to omit them. Additionally, Eastwood's jazz, Scorsese's gangsters, and Spielberg's aliens – are the subjects their fan bases recognizes them for.

With this in mind, there are several themes that can be cherry picked from Howard's cinema that don't have the same consistent presence throughout his body of work. Nevertheless, they are definitive traits that make up Howard's versatile authorship, and not something that he fell into a routine of doing for monetary purposes, or made an effort to shift away from doing.

Automotive

Chris Hemsworth's formal introduction at the beginning of *Rush* involves him hooking up with the nurse (Natalie Dormer), whom be brings to one of his Formula 3 races in the following scene. While Hemsworth preps for the race and first notices his soon-to-be rival, Daniel Brühl, his manager, Lord Hesketh, (played by Christian McKay) is talking to Dormer. As the cars are revving up, Lord Hesketh (McKay) can't help himself and begins to wax lyrical about cars:

LORD HESKETH
Ahhh - what music! They could never have imagined it - those pioneers who invented the automobile that it would possess us like this in our imaginations, in our dreams. Now see, men love women, but even more than that - men. Love. Cars!"

On the word "Cars!," the film cuts to one of the first races of the movie. *Rush* has a lot of energy from the get go, so the enthusiasm by McKay's character perfectly complements the sentiment that all the characters share about their industry. Although Howard had been a successful working director for over thirty years by the time he got to *Rush* the film really plays more like a passion project for himself, particularly with sentiments like the one McKay pontificates about moments before the first race.

Director Sam Rami is famous for his Easter Egg of putting a yellow 1973 Oldsmobile Delta 88 somewhere in all his films. Pixar Animation Studios has yet to fail to clandestinely slip in the Pizza Planet truck into one of their films. Yet these examples are mere trivial fodder (yet the Easter Eggs represent that the filmmakers pay fan service to their base). For Ron Howard, the automobile is embedded into the DNA of his cinema. Even when cars are not particularly relevant for the story, the usage of vehicles are omnipresent, even something as rudimentary as a scene taking place while someone is driving. Additionally, cars are used for sight gags as Howard's humor is more confined to physical than verbal. For example, Michael Keaton throws his mail out the window of a moving vehicle when reuniting with Mimi Rogers once getting back to the U.S. in *Gung Ho*; the attempt on Mary Steenburgen's part to relieve Steve Martin's "stress", resulting in an accident in *Parenthood*; and the very last scene of *We Feed People* when José Andrés realizes that he was so busy that he forgot to put gasoline in his truck.

The strange irony is that for a filmmaker who's been affiliated with automobiles since his teenage years, a la *Happy Days*, that the car chase isn't something Ron Howard is known for, although it's repeated ad nauseam in his films. Going back to *Grand Theft Auto*, it's somewhat poetic that a Rolls Royce takes center stage in the action and everyone's attention is directed onto it, despite the irrationality of taking such a car off the freeway and onto the backroads desert of California & Nevada. (Should the reader have ever driven that terrain, a greater appreciation is had for the impracticality of driving a Rolls Royce across those grounds). Throughout *Grand Theft Auto*, the chronic switching of automobiles is as nonsensical as the characters, such as hijacking police cars, a bizarre makeshift wedding love truck and an ice cream clown truck. We don't see Howard attempt the car chase again until the finale of *Splash*, which takes place throughout Manhattan and is also layered with comedic value. There are short car chases in both *A Beautiful Mind* and *The Da Vinci Code*, but those are in the center of the narrative and inevitably overshadowed by other more dramatic events.

On the other hand, the most gripping chases from Howard's movies are not a "car chase" in the traditional sense. The Oklahoma land rush in *Far and Away* is the major finale of the film, with one of John Williams' most grandiose, (and underappreciated) pieces. Howard's own family history is linked to the film's finale,[1] a depiction of the September 1893 Oklahoma Land Run as the crown jewel of the story. The 1893 Land Run (also referred to as the Cherokee Outlet Opening) was the fourth in the time span of a decade and the most chaotic. The Panic of 1893 had already plagued the U.S. economy throughout the previous summer which affected farming, and direct governmental supervision was late to arrive at the site of the land run. The shot of the long lines in *Far and Away* when Tom Cruise goes to register for the land race are accurate in reflecting the numbers that descended on the territory the week before the land race; a conservative estimate suggests that over 100,000 people showed up. With a lack of registration offices and staff to handle the surge of interested participants, drunkenness and fighting was breaking out,(2) which we see Cruise become subject to the night before the land race. In many ways, *Far and Away* is the romanticizing of a historical event, where a fictional love story is put into the center of a larger event, such as the Civil War in 1939's *Gone with the Wind*, or the sinking of the Titanic in 1997's *Titanic*. It's really not a surprise that Howard, who was a writer on the film, would structure a story that positions a race as the grand finale. With horses, carriages and a significant amount of crashes, the chase sequence strikes similarities to the Americana epics of the 1990s era such as *Glory* (1989); *Dances with Wolves* (1990) and *Gettysburg* (1993).

There is a tense cat-and-mouse pursuit in *Ransom* between Mel Gibson and Gary Sinise, which is appropriate as the film is a mind game, so the car chase functions as intrigue without dramatic crashes and spin outs. The opening landspeeder chase of *Solo* is the most "by-the-books" thematic car chase Howard has included in his films. Of course the irony being that *Star Wars* landspeeders are not technically cars, but the sequence plays out exactly as we expect it would in an action film. Finally, some of the most frightening footage in *Rebuilding Paradise* comes from video captured inside of a car during the opening. Through the vantage point of driving in a car, and seeing night time darkness during the day, does one get an authentic sense of how encompassing and powerful the 2018 Camp Fire was.

Vehicles as characters:
Apollo 13*, *In the Heart of the Sea* and *Solo: A Star Wars Story

Occasionally filmmakers might refer to an inanimate object as a "character" in the story; no doubt that the "object" may feel like a character on set to the cast and crew, but conveying that concept on screen is very hard lest the object physically moves on its own. Some of the most hallowed "cars" in Howard's films are not in fact cars, but still vessels of transportation: the Aquarius and Odyssey in *Apollo 13*; the Essex from *In the Heart of the Sea*; and the Millennium Falcon in *Solo: A Star Wars Story*.

***

Without a doubt, the safety of the astronauts in *Apollo 13* is the most important, but after the accident, every decision made is centered on the well-being of the spaceship. The central fixation of every character gets focused on the carriage holding the three men. This directly pours the audience's concern into the inanimate object. Mission Control decides that shutting down half of the spaceship, the Odyssey Service Module, is the best solution. It's treated like the death of a character, albeit temporarily. In the final act of the film, the astronauts (and audience) finally see the physical damage inflicted on the Odyssey. It's one of the most unique reveals in the movie because the audience understands that the astronauts and Mission Control are fighting toxic air and physics — elements the audience and characters can't physically see but are physically present. With the exception of a few very quick seconds of screen time showing the start of an explosion inside the ship, no one actually sees the damage. *Apollo 13* hinges on the fear of an unseen antagonist. The reveal of the blast debris puts the harrowing situation into context and visually reinforces the tension regarding the sustainability of the heat shield protecting the astronauts upon re-entry to Earth.

***

The pressing question author Herman Melville, played by Ben Whishaw, has for the last survivor of the disastrous shipwreck, Brendan Gleeson is: `Tell me what happened to the Essex?` The viewer knows the *actual* reason the author has shown up to query the final living member of the Essex is to garnish information about the whale, yet the narrative is shaped around the fate of the ship. Gleeson is the one who recounts his story from the perspective of the Essex's two leaders – the duality of the captain, Benjamin

Walker, and first mate, Chris Hemsworth. We also can't help but notice that Brendan Gleeson's resistance to speaking with the author is overruled by his wife, played by Michelle Fairley, showcasing once again the acute persistence from the feminine figure. Gleeson's wife knows that the conversation will function as a form of self-exoneration for her husband who has spent nearly three decades suffering from post-traumatic stress about the event.

With the exceptions of the flashbacks to Brendan Gleeson retelling the story, once the Essex sets sail, the audience is stuck with them. There are no flashbacks to the financiers on Nantucket, Chris Hemsworth's family or Benjamin Walker's prestigious family of mariners. *In the Heart of the Sea's* "family" is the crew.

When the Essex is damaged by the gigantic whale and the abandoning of the ship takes place, we see items from the captain's quarters get damaged beyond repair; the ink from the pages of the ship's logs dissipate into the water and the large fancy compass shatters. When the Essex's oil supply catches fire and the ship begins to explode, the death of the Essex becomes accentuated. Roque Baños scores the ship's slow explosion and sinking into the depths of the ocean with a cello, contrabassoon and a metal scraping on metal sound effect playing over the Essex's death. Does the film need this sequence? Not really. There's several ways the sinking of the Essex could have been edited, but in Howard's cinema, the destruction of a vessel of transportation will be given a little more screen time. The death of this grand ship is worthy of a dramatic moment.

***

Of all the films on Howard's directorial résumé, *Solo: A Star Wars Story* is arguably the best litmus test for honing in on his definitive motifs. While the *Star Wars* franchise has hosted a variety of different directors – especially since the advent of the various television shows – the studio has avoided hiring filmmakers with a defined aesthetic. No doubt fans would love to see, (or watch in horror), the likes of Woody Allen, Wes Anderson, Terrence Malick or Quentin Tarantino get the opportunity to direct a chapter in the ever-expanding fictional universe due to their very distinct visual and narrative styles. Nevertheless, *Solo* fits perfectly within the pantheon of Howard's cinema. Howard is not a director whose work has a visually distinct aesthetic that the viewer instinctually senses after watching a couple minutes of. After all the ink that has been spilled on what the Walt Disney Company, or George Lucas himself, has done to the beloved franchise, to date no one dared tried something as experimental as letting an auteur with definitive traits into the Galaxy Far, Far, Away. Hence, Howard's chameleon efforts play to his advantage in *Solo* since aesthetically there is nothing that openly reflects the film being "a Ron Howard film" – yet it's blatantly present.

The whole premise is centered around a love story of two young people trying to make it on their own. Alden Ehrenreich is an outcast without anything special about him, minus his ability at flying and being a smooth conman. Ehrenreich insists on getting himself involved in a gang and wants to be part of the galaxy's underworld crime syndicate. The problem is that he's actually a good guy at heart, but idles in a world of crime, reflecting a duality of his nature. He's betrayed several times throughout the film by Paul Bettany, Woody Harrelson and Emilia Clarke – yet still has a surrogate "family" in whatever group he teams up with.

What of the strong female character? Audiences don't need to look further than the ship that the Han Solo character made famous: the Millennium Falcon. The droid, L3-37, played by Phoebe Waller-Bridge, is an opinionated bleeding heart liberal. Despite that droids technically don't have a gender, it's telling that *Solo* makes it abundantly clear that L3 is supposed to be a woman robot. She's introduced in the film as being an advocate for "droids rights" – meaning that robots shouldn't be subservient to other species. One of the unique elements of the *Star Wars* franchise is that the robot droids have varying personalities, which means that there is leeway in the different attitudes and emotions the robots express. The relationship she has with her captain, Donald Glover as Lando Calrissian, is one of quick-witted banter. When they quip about having Phoebe Waller-Bridge (L3) re-set on account of her boisterous rebellious attitude, Glover (Lando) says, "I actually would have her memory wiped, but she's got the best damn navigational database in the galaxy."

In the heist to steal "coaxium," a fictional substance that is a combustible fuel from a mining facility, Waller-Bridge (L3) takes it upon herself to remove the restraining bolts off of one of the droids. This begins a domino effect of the other droids removing their restraining bolts off of each other and spurring chaos. Although Waller-Bridge (L3) works for Donald Glover (Lando), her agenda to do the admirable thing is a telling trait. When she's shot, Ehrenreich suggests that they download her navigation system into the ship, the Millennium Falcon, to help them escape. The download concept works and Waller-Bridge (L3) becomes part of the ship itself, thereby sowing an inanimate vehicle with an opinionated programing system. It's rather fitting that in Howard's chapter of *Star Wars* he places a strong feminine mind into the brain of the famous Millennium Falcon. With that said, the *Star Wars* franchise has narrative rules that it needs to adhere in order to compliment the other films. In *Star Wars Episode V: The Empire Strikes Back* (1980), another droid makes a comment to Han Solo while working on the Millennium Falcon: "Sir, I don't know where your ship learned to communicate, but it has the most peculiar dialect." Whether or not the installation of Waller-Bridge (L3) into the Millennium Falcon was penned into *Solo* prior to Ron Howard getting involved, it gives a personality to the ship that wasn't there before. Placing Ron Howard's spirit of the "strong feminine character" into the "automotive" spaceship that's present in so many of the stories is a retroactive continuity, (also known as "retcon"), to the *Star Wars* universe, yet it's a rather fitting development.

Deception

We don't consider Ron Howard a cinematic manipulator of elaborate story subterfuge on par with the likes of Alfred Hitchcock, Christopher Nolan or M. Night Shyamalan.

Nevertheless, there are a surprisingly high number of turncoat characters: Scott Glenn in *Backdraft*; Ian McKellen in *The Da Vinci Code*; Ewan McGregor in *Angels and Demons*; Felicity Jones in *Inferno*. Although the reveal of these villains is intended for shock value, there are other instances where the audience is let in on a plot reversal such as Gary Sinise in *Ransom*, or Woody Harrelson and Emilia Clarke in *Solo*. (The brief reveal of a famous Sith Lord at the end of *Solo* was in service for what the *Star Wars* franchise had planned going forward, rather than a typical Ron Howard-ism, even though it's one of the most memorable moments from *Solo*). Nevertheless, in every case the plot twist doesn't upend the entire movie as a Hitchcock, Nolan or Shyamalan film might do. Without a doubt, *A Beautiful Mind* is the closest Howard came to a narrative caper, being that the film plays half way before letting the audience in on its secret: three of the characters we've gotten to know are not real and nearly everything having to do with Crowe decoding Russian intelligence is fictional.

While these examples are plot devices, there are similar moments of visual deception that are used to great effect. With so many sight-gags in the comedies, it's no surprise that Howard finds ways to visually deceive the audience in small ways. These jokes point the attention of the audience in one direction, and then quickly flips the scenario around. For example, *Night Shift* embodies a certain amount of "sit-com"-isms through the use of props for humorous object work; the ending of *Gung Ho* when Michael Keaton begins to drive away in his new car, only to have it fall to pieces while he's inside of it; and of course Randy Quaid in *The Paper* shooting a gun into the stack of old newspapers. Ron Howard also uses visual deception for dramatic purposes such as Amy Adams getting caught trying to shoot heroin into her arm in *Hillbilly Elegy*. Adams' past addiction to the pills is shown to the viewer, as well as her disrespectful behavior, but we aren't expecting a relapse so suddenly after the gratitude and tenderness she shows to her son. Brief and intense, it has just enough shock value to really moor the audience into comprehending what J.D.

Vance (played by both Owen Asztalos & Gabriel Basso) went through in both his youth and young adulthood.

Backdraft was Howard's first use of a sinister twist, with the reveal of Scott Glenn's involvement with creating the backdraft fire bombs. The reveal remains well-hidden from the viewer, buffered by Donald Sutherland's brief, but very memorable role as a pyromaniac. Scott Glen is also presented as a stand-in paternal guardian of the two brothers played by William Baldwin and Kurt Russell. The film even lets the audience falsely believe Kurt Russell is the villain for about 4-minutes of screen time. With the emphasis on "fire" itself as the monster of the story,(3) the suspense of saving lives becomes the central concern for the viewer. It's also worth contemplating how Scott Glenn, Donald Sutherland and T.J. Walsh become a "stand-ins" for *Backdraft*'s villain. What, or who, are William Baldwin and Kurt Russell fighting? The fires? Their own family legacy? Or, these corrupt characters? The political scandal gives us something tangible; a physical character(s) to root against. Baldwin is not only trying to discover something in himself, but he also needs to outsmart people conspiring against him.

The Scores

The concept of performance art entertainment (concerts, dance, plays) are unique in that the consumers are essentially purchasing an experience that will make the audience either cry, laugh or educate them, but ultimately change their emotions. When we go watch a film in the cinema, we don't get to take a piece of the actual movie home with us (albeit a ticket stub, collectable popcorn tin or large plastic cup are a version of this), but we only exit with a memory. Purchasing a BluRay, DVD or VHS is the closest we can come to physically having the film, however the rights do not belong to us. We can collect posters or merchandise, but those only emphasize the memory of the feelings that the film gave us. And of course, one needs to be a seasoned collector to know how to obtain props used in the production, which is an underground market unto itself being that physical items belong to the production companies.

The soundtrack however is arguably the most practical item from a movie as it can give us a mental stimulation of, at least in part, re-experiencing the movie in our head vicariously through the score. Even this falls into the realm of the intangible since we cannot physically touch music itself. Music stimulates a section of the brain called the nucleus accumbens – technically the part of the brain that receives dopamine. This means that if we want to relive a favorite moment from a film, the soundtrack allows us one way to access this favorite moment without having to actually rewatch the scene(s).

***

Film score composers are not too unlike the film directors in the sense that we can audibly hear similarities in their collected body of work. Thomas Newman's credits span from action, to comedy, to drama, to family-friendly. There's no question that with over eighty titles under his name there are departures in style, but Newman is able to be distinguished. His two scores for Ron Howard are twenty years apart: *Gung Ho* in 1986 and *Cinderella Man* in 2005. If you played the two soundtracks back to back they don't sound the same… until you come across certain melodies. The song "Bucket Of Ice" from *Gung Ho* doesn't really fit the ambiance of the comedy at-a-glance (or "at-a-listen" in this case), but one can instantly tell that the soft piano, violin and wind instruments are akin to the recurring theme in *Cinderella Man*.

Howard follows the trends of the time which is heard through the music in his films. The usage of the song, "Grand Theft Auto" that we hear at the very beginning and periodically in instrumental rendition throughout *Grand Theft Auto* stands out due to its unapologetically 1970s sound. There are a few 1980s music video sequences in *Cocoon*, and more in *Gung Ho* with antics around the auto factory. Even in *Backdraft* Howard still included a few "music video" numbers, but the phase had plateaued by then. The music montage did not fade entirely, however one would be hard-pressed to find something so MTV inspired in the 2000s and 2010s. These are worth highlighting because they reflect Howard embracing the contemporary cinematic trends, which is something that he continues to do in the subsequent decades. Howard isn't a director who stayed mainstream for two or three decades and then receded (consider Brian De Palma or William Friedkin whose films from the 2010s, unfortunately came and went unnoticed by the mainstream). Howard doesn't stubbornly stick with a style considering that the "music video cinema" isn't something we see Howard doing in later years. *Gung Ho* is unapologetically a product of its time, fitting to the 1980s spirit. Just the same, consider how the visual aesthetics changed to more handheld as the 2000s progressed, that by the end of the decade, and into the start of the 2010s, that handheld style became mainstream. As the 2010s continued, a slick stylized usage of cinematography would become more in vogue.

Given that Howard has directed over thirty films, the music has grown wide in variety and since he has had the luxury to explore multiple genres, consistency between scores is hardly present. With the exception of James Horner, there isn't a definitive "sound" throughout the films. Composers too transform their style: by 2024, Howard has collaborated with Hans Zimmer the most, yet even those soundtracks share little consistency. The tense ticking and violin we hear in *Frost/Nixon* sounds nothing like the Gregorian chants from *Angels & Demon*. However – one of Zimmer's trademarks is the Shepard tone (also referred to as the Shepard-risset glissando); the increasing or decreasing of a melody that sounds like rising or descending, but it's not. The pieces "Watergate" from *Frost/Nixon* and "160 BPM" from *Angels & Demons* are similar in their use of the Shepard tone. Yes, one is more bombastic than the other and they clearly don't appear to be by the same director/composer duo, yet it reflects Howard's desire to adapt for whatever serves the film best.

Sometimes the music gives a form of authorship to what we anticipate from a director. Sergio Leone and Ennio Morricone; Tim Burton and Danny Elfman; Sam Mendes and Thomas Newman – regardless of the variety of genres, there is an equipollence that the filmmaker and composer give to each other. On the other hand, Terrence Malick has worked with a variety of famous movie score composers, but the collected soundtracks from his films all evoke Malick's aesthetic more than they do the individual composers.

The musical diaspora of Howard's filmography is hard to pinpoint simply because it's as wide ranging as the genres themselves. Two less ostentatious soundtracks would be Lee Holdridge's *Splash* from the mid-1980s, all the way to Hans Zimmer and Lorne Balfe's *Rebuilding Paradise* from the early-2020s. Two completely different films, with two completely different scores. James Horner always maintains a grand orchestral presence in the seven films he scored for Howard, whereas Randy Newman's work in *Parenthood* and *The Paper* are nowhere as ambitions, nor do they need to be. That should not be interpreted as a slight against Mr. Newman's talent; rather his ambiance is perfectly suited for those films.

This brings us back to the idea that choices are made on account of whatever services the film best. Howard has expressed as much saying:

> The composer and I have to find a melody that will be worth putting center stage. Ultimately, I think everything has to do with music. Even the decision not to score a scene is a musical decision. Occasionally, a scene might be working on several levels, and there's one of them that you'd like to underline with music, whether it's tension, emotion or to remind the audience of a character's history. That means bringing in a thematic idea that's been established earlier in the film.
>
> One of the wonderful qualities about film music is that it's one more way to focus an audience, almost in a subliminal manner.[4]

With this in mind, should one put the themes of Zimmer's *Backdraft*; *The Da Vinci Code* and *Hillbilly Elegy* together in one tribute piece, you're not going to instantly think "Ron Howard." The scores reflect the versatility of the director. The scores don't default to ambient or tonal music as the work of Trent Reznor and Atticus Ross can, which can be difficult for easy listening.

James Horner

Of the various composers that Howard collaborated with, James Horner was the most frequented, (until surpassed by Hans Zimmer). The composer/director duo are unquestionably linked in a variety of ways: they were nearly the same age, both grew up in the Los Angeles area, and the first couple of movies scored by Horner were produced through Roger Corman's New World Pictures. James Horner often utilized a large orchestral presence in his soundtracks and that element of his artistry is present in all seven of the scores he did for Ron Howard. Additionally, Horner's eerie, spooky and lyrical squibbles that can be heard in his music from other movies are periodically present in the seven he did for Howard. For *Cocoon*, brass, strings and woodwinds are used in combination to create an "outer space" undertone, building into the film's aria. This is not much different than the usage of woodwinds, strings and percussion in *The Missing* to create the sense of the Native American frontier, and culminating into in a single grand orchestral theme.

There's no way of knowing for sure whether or not Howard and Horner would have partnered again. Between Spring 2012 to approximately late 2014, Horner took a hiatus from composing feature-length film scores, yet had begun working on movies again. On June 22nd, 2015, at 9:30am, Horner, an aviation enthusiast, crashed his small airplane in the Los Padres National Forest in the town of Ventucopa, California.(5) A little over a year following his tragic death, Howard said:

> There's certain people that I enjoy collaborating with. James was one of those. I've worked with Tom Newman twice, Randy Newman twice, Hans six or seven times – but I really miss James. It was always in the back of my mind that we'd work together again. In fact, I had a great lunch with him a couple of months before he died. It wasn't about a particular project or anything – he was very busy working on a lot of different movies, but he had really fallen in love with flying. People don't realize what an avid hobbyist James was. He could make radio controlled

helicopters from scratch and fly them. He collected gemstones and would go all over the world and into caves. Here's this very sophisticated guy, and you wouldn't think he'd be in a cave with a pick and a helmet with a light on it finding these gems and mineral deposits – he had a vast collection.

But he'd really fallen in love with flying, so that crash was devastating for me, but I knew from my last conversation that he was doing something that he truly loved. We were exactly the same age so we kind of grew up together advancing our careers at a similar pace. James was really the composer who helped me understand how the performances and the camera movements could influence a composer. It's not just a great piece of music that happens to work over a scene – it's about reinforcing nuances and ideas that literal language can't quite convey.(6)

Keeping Howard's motifs in mind, let us consider three quotes of Horner's, two from projects that were unaffiliated with Imagine Entertainment. Looking at the perspectives of a director's chief collaborators often works as a great access point for assessing authorship, and of Howard's regular collaborators, there is no doubt that Horner is one of the keenest. While being interviewed regarding the score for *Enemy at the Gates* (2001), Horner says:

> I need something I can spiritually feel like I can create something for. I don't do it for income. It's like an art piece. I don't mean to sound pretentious. I have to feel like I'm part of this fusion of a film. It's like a classic composition to me, and if it's just a crass commercial film, I always regret doing it. I really don't do those. I try not to. Obviously, everyone wants their movie to be a big hit and that [*Titanic*] success was an after-the-fact. Jim [Cameron] made the movie knowing he wasn't going to take a salary. You see, there's something very exciting about working with a major director who is going way off on a limb to make a

> movie he believes in – and that's the magic of film music for me. Those are the kind of people I search out, who are taking a big risk with something. They're not just doing the same movie they've already done four times and just collecting a paycheck. Those kind of experiences are very very hard to find."(7)

Of course, by that point in his career, Horner had the luxury to pick and choose what he wanted to score. Yet we notice his attraction to filmmakers who take chances and want to branch themselves out. Looking at one of those big "commercial films," here is what Horner had to say regarding his work on *The Amazing Spider-Man* (2012):

> It's a big action hero movie, but I wanted to add colors and pull out emotions that aren't associated with a movie like this. The action stuff will take care of itself. It's gonna look great and it's gonna sound great. The part that is really important are the in between bits: what's Peter [Parker] thinking? When he gets pensive. When he loses a family member. When he's developing this relationship with Gwen [Stacy]. It's really important to bring out the under story, the human story – for me. That's just the way I like to write scores.(8)

What makes this quote all the more interesting is that Horner turned down the job to do the music for the sequel, *The Amazing Spider-Man 2* (2014) because he didn't care for the direction that the franchise was going in.(9) Yet what's unique about the *Spider-Man* quote is that if we backtrack to James Horner's first collaboration with Ron Howard on *Cocoon*, he approached the job nearly the same way:

> When I write a score, I don't look for the obvious things. I find something or somebody that means more to me than what's on the screen. *Cocoon* touched me because it was about getting old and the frailties of life. I wasn't worried about what I would write for the

science fiction stuff. It's already all over the screen, looks massive and that takes care of itself. I was much more concerned about the inside story of the characters, their relationships and what happens when some of them pass away.(10)

Religion

Before the mid-2000s, Ron Howard really didn't have much use for Christianity in his films, let alone religion in general. Howard has said repeatedly that when he and his wife, Cheryl, first started dating he would attend church with her, but he always admits it was an excuse to spend time with her that his protective parents would approve of.(11) The zany preacher in *Grand Theft Auto* is one of the few times that the subject was actually relevant to the film's story, however being that everything is a farce or a joke in *Grand Theft Auto*, it's really not all that telling. One could say that mocking a Christian preacher in his first movie was a foreshadowing of what Howard would be accused of three decades later, yet then why do flawed Christians never come up again? A couple years later, the children's pilot turned movie, *Through the Magic Pyramid*, concludes with the new pharaoh giving an endorsement for religious tolerance, after learning from the time-traveling kid that in the United States, no one is forced to worship any specific god. *Cocoon*'s subject matter offers a narrative opening to discuss the afterlife and mortality, but doesn't. On the other hand, Rance Howard's cameo as the priest in *Apollo 13* is appropriately placed and works perfectly as a subtle accent to the tension. In other words, there are narrative opportunities to address the subject of Christianity in his films, but Howard doesn't do much with it.

Adaptations and devotions:
The Missing, The Da Vinci Code, Angels & Demons** and **Inferno

Once we get to *The Missing* and *Cinderella Man*, the subject of religion and spirituality starts to make a presence, yet even then it's an auxiliary plot. In the book, *The Last Ride* by Thomas Eidson, (which was later republished as *The Missing* when the film adaptation released), the contrast between Christianity and Native American spiritualism is heavily present in the novel. Throughout the book, Maggie (the Cate Blanchett character in the movie) is appalled by her estranged father's devotion to his pagan rituals and repetitive soft chanting. A significant quandary throughout the book is the youngest daughter, Dot's (the Jenna Boyd character in the movie), attraction to her Grandfather by way of his spiritualism. In the film adaptation this is present, but it's in a practical familial attraction that Jenna Boyd (Dot) has to Tommy Lee Jones (Jones) – it's not explicitly his religious beliefs, although she's seen witnessing them. In the book, the debate between Jones' "creator" and Maggie & Dot's Christian God is a regular subject of conversation. Furthermore, in Eidson's book, the Christian God is ultimately dismissed on account of Apache spiritual warfare being the vessel in which Maggie is saved from a curse. In the film as well, the actual voodoo of the main kidnapper does successfully put a curse on Cate Blanchett, thereby giving the Native American spiritualism credence.

On the other hand, the outwardly anti-Christian rhetoric is absent in the film adaptation. Aaron Eckhart announces to Jones that Blanchett maintains a Christian household and that they are averse to the Apache customs, but unlike the book, the estranged father never outwardly proclaims that the Christian God is of no help. Jones in the movie is so devoted to Apache spirituality that he's captivating, as pious individual expressions can be particularly alluring to watch; not in the sense of a crazy lunatic, but rather moved by reverence. The magnitude of his absorption into Native American customs is so poignant that we don't question his devotion to the Apache way of life he chose.

Recalling that Howard allowed for more religious themes in his work in the 2000s, we'll pause for a moment on *Cinderella Man*. The usage of the neighborhood parish in 1930s America was reflective of the culture at the time. What's interesting is that the film paints Russell Crowe as having a slight aversion to religion: he tells the priest he skipped Sunday Mass to get extra work on the docks. Later, when Crowe and Zellweger are about to say grace before dinner, they hear one of the kids coughing across the room. When they take hands and try again, Crowe's hands fall, saying `"I'm all prayed out."` Cliff Hollingsworth, who has "story by" credit on the film, said that likely never happened as James J. Braddock was always a religious person, but the moment was kept in the film.(12) Considering that the controversy of *The Da Vinci Code*, which would release the following summer, (*Cinderella Man* was a June 2005 release; *The Da Vinci Code* a May 2006 release), small indications like these, specifically moments where Christianity is dismissed, we would expect to see littered throughout Howard's résumé, but in fact they're not. This begs the question: how anti-Christian or anti-religious is *The Da Vinci Code*? There is a fair argument to be made that the film downplays the crimes of the medieval church, but ultimately the widespread outcry over the novel prior to the film going into production, Imagine Entertainment knew what they were getting into.

There are two conversations that need to take place in tandem with regards to the Robert Langdon films: one is the topic of spirituality, and the other is the topic of contemporary bestsellers-turned-movies. If we look at other astronomically popular novels from the year 2000 and onward (*The Lovely Bones*; *The Girl with the Dragon Tattoo*; *Twilight*; *The Hunger Games*; *Gone Girl*; *Where the Crawdads Sing*) – we get a mix of films that received very different receptions, both from audiences and critics. Therefore, when discussing cinematic adaptions they need to be thought of as "remakes," and especially a remake of an uber popular title, they always come with the guarantee of being compared to the original. It doesn't matter if one is a novel and the other a film. Movies to stage adaptations, or vice versa, and even video game adaptations to either a film or a television show are all part of the repackaging of content. The art form is what changes.

Books have a lot more leeway to go off on tangents, and in particular all of the Dan Brown novels in the Robert Langdon series, despite each of them taking place within 24 hours, do a lot of departures from the plot to explain something. The time rush in the books aren't as much of a precedent because our brains process the information at a speed at which we consume it by reading. In a movie or television show, we are going to receive the information at the speed it's delivered to us, which is why even when cutting away from a suspenseful moment to another scene, our mental clock is still ticking at a "real time" of events happening in another location. In a book, that time sensitive pressure is dramatically decreased. This is why the five Robert Landgon novels all "feel" like they are moving at a comfortable speed for us, whereas the three Ron Howard adaptations have a set pace. We decide how many hours it will take us to read Dan Brown's 400-plus page novel. The running time for the movies is set at two and a half hours, and within those windows of time, the pace is controlled by the filmmakers. *Angels & Demons* and *Inferno* move much faster because they're edited at a quicker tempo, whereas *The Da Vinci Code* takes it time with the tangents, with full sequences of historical flashbacks happening during the time of the crusades. The Knights Templar, Priory of Sion, the Sangreal, the Council of Nicaea all get an explanation in *The Da Vinci Code*, whereas the traditional beliefs/folklore material in the other two adaptations gets quickly incorporated into the dialogue as the drama continues.

***

There is a theory that *The Da Vinci Code* got significantly more popular than Dan Brown or the publishers anticipated, thereby inviting a level of scrutiny from historians that it was never intended for.(13) There were two lines of defense from Dan Brown at the time: the first being that the novel is a work of fiction and therefore detractors look silly getting bothered by something that was openly made up. On the other hand, the book was touted as being impeccably researched and opens with a disclaimer saying "All depictions of artwork, architecture, documents, and secret rituals in this novel are accurate." That said, it bears emphasizing that "accurate" and "precise" mean two different things.

If you go through the press interviews and behind-the-scenes bonus features of *The Da Vinci Code*, you're not going to find much commentary about the controversy from the filmmakers themselves. There's almost a conscious effort on the part of the production to *not* acknowledge it. When Howard does address it, he only brings it up in the context of Paul Bettany's character, Silas, using the word "devotion" and refers to said "devotion" becoming possessive of some people.(14) Paul Bettany makes for an interesting contrast to Tommy Lee Jones in *The Missing* as they are both zealots with a dark backstory. The pain is etched on both of their faces and the films withhold the finite details of what drew them into their newfound devotion. (Granted the novel that *The Missing* was adapted from explains Jones' backstory, but it's omitted from the 2003 release – as well as the extended cut of *The Da Vinci Code* has a scene detailing some of Paul Bettany's backstory, but it was omitted in the original 2006 release). When adapting the novel for the movie, one of the goals was to bring out the complexities of the albino monk and personal hitman for the Opus Dei bishop. At one point, they discussed shaping the whole film around Bettany's character.(15) Instead, *The Da Vinci Code* film sets out to examine a range of emotions that religious devotions stir in people. The ensemble of characters, particular Ian McKellen, Alfred Molina, Jean-Pierre Marille and Jean Reno are all motivated by their religious convictions, with Paul Bettany being the most extreme of the group. Or is he? Ian McKellen is just as much of a radical slandering Catholic dogma as Bettany is aggressive to preserving it. In the end, they are both murderers.

Tom Hanks is in the center of all this, essentially hijacked by Audrey Tautou, and acts as a translator to what the other characters are opining about with regards to the illusive messages left by the museum's slain curator. *The Da Vinci Code* movie doesn't let the audience in on Hanks' own belief. He begins by dismissing Ian McKellen's interpretation of Leonardo Da Vinci's The Last Supper painting implying that John the Apostle is actually Mary Magdalene. We're never told if Hanks reverses his opinion on the painting, but when it comes to the Priory of Sion, the cult murdering people with evidence proving that a lineage of Jesus of Nazareth exists, Hanks begins to understand the implications why they want to keep the ancestry a secret, specifically the female lineage. *The Da Vinci Code* movie spends more time contemplating the "sacred feminine" than it does crafting a spy-thriller. There are so many revelations in the source material that a filmmaker could have honed in on any of them; should *The Da Vinci Code* have been directed by Mel Gibson, Terrence Malick or Martin Scorsese, (all three who've been cinematic theologians periodically throughout their body of work), it's safe to assume we would have seen a movie adaptation crafted off a different axis point from the novel. Ron Howard, who typically does not gravitate in the direction of spiritual awakenings, puts more emphasis on the feminine influence throughout the "hidden" history, albeit soft-pedaled. The ending of the film is faithful to the short epilogue of the book, but Howard assembles the revelation of Mary Magdalene's tomb as the gargantuan reveal. The unassuming woman from the early foundations of Christianity is the one who has posthumously influenced world events.

***

It's when we get to *Angels and Demons*, as well as *Inferno*, that Howard modifies the source material closer to what we would expect him to do by placing a significant amount of pressure on Tom Hanks, rather than Hanks merely being a participant. The sequel feels like a cousin of *Ransom*, with the same sense of intrigue that *The Da Vinci Code* embodied, yet more immediate and imminent. The horror of *The Da Vinci Code* was affixed to Paul Bettany and the disturbing medieval history, whereas *Angels & Demons* brings the cult-like secret society lore, in front of news cameras for all the world to see. *The Da Vinci Code* is about keeping a secret; *Angels & Demons* is about exposing a scandal.

The sequel is more of a test for Tom Hanks as he's surrounded by people predisposed to dislike him. The only narrative link the two films have is a vague implication that Hanks published something that upset the Roman Catholic Church. (We can assume that Hanks made the "sangreal" discovery from *The Da Vinci Code* public, but this is never confirmed in any of the films). Since Hanks has traversed through conspiracies that slander, or at least call into question the Church's teachings about the divinity of Jesus of Nazareth – he's not going to get through the sequel without facing a cross-examination. *Angels & Demons* doesn't spend time rearguing the lineage of Jesus or correcting the history from the previous film (neither do the novels), but rather calls into question the integrity of the leading character. Again, Tom Hanks is more of a spectator in *The Da Vinci Code* helping push the action along, whereas *Angels & Demons* he has much more authority and influence, therefore the emphasis is placed on him.

After agreeing to help decipher the threats from the Illuminati assassin, Hanks (Robert Langdon) requests access to the Vatican achieves. Before being allowed in, Ewan McGregor (the Camerlengo) takes him aside to another room. The audience is taken just up to the starting point of this adventure, yet before being allowed to continue, the events of *The Da Vinci Code* require a coda, particularly its leading character and what his role is in all this. In the novel, Robert Langdon is given little pushback on his request to get into the archives. In Ron Howard's film, his request to examine the Vatican achieves becomes an avenue for the movie to reaffix emphasis on Tom Hanks, personalizing the sequel in a way that *The Da Vinci Code* didn't do. In a scene added to the film that's not in the book:

```
INT. LARGE OFFICE - DAY
The    CAMERLENGO   enters   the   room   with   LANGDON
following.  The  CAMERLENGO  closes  the  door  behind
them.

The Camerlengo walks into the large room and Langdon
follows.
```

       CAMERLENGO
  Mr. Langdon, you are correct that I may
  grant you access to the archives.

       LANGDON
  Thank you, Padre.

CAMERLENGO
I... I... I said that you were correct that I may, not that I will.
(beat)
Christianity's most sacred codices are in that archive. Given your recent entanglement with the Church, there is a question I would like to ask you first...

Camerlengo gestures to the room they are standing in.

CAMERLENGO (cont'd)
...here, in the office of his Holiness.

Camerlengo takes a few steps closer to Langdon.

CAMERLENGO (cont'd)
Do you believe in God sir?

Langdon stares him down.

LANGDON
Father, I simply believe that religion...

CAMERLENGO
(Interrupting)
I did not ask if you believe what man says about God. I asked if you believe in God.

Langdon realizes he's being challenged.

LANGDON
I'm an academic. My mind tells me I will never understand God.

CAMERLENGO
And your heart?

Langdon is caught.

> **LANGDON**
> Tells me I'm not meant to. Faith is a gift that I've yet to receive.
>
> **CAMERLENGO**
> (beat)
> Be delicate with our treasures.

The rest of the film follows the Ron Howard textbook of thrillers: Hanks is paired with Ayelet Zurer, both determined to find the canister with the antimatter that could cause a nuclear detonation. Zurer is a stronger force than Audrey Tautou as she's invested in the consequences of the bomb going off. Additionally, there is a hint of flirtation between Hanks and Zurer throughout the rush of *Angels & Demons*. Tautou and Hanks have a 20-year age difference, so there was intentionally no romantic insinuations between the two in the previous installment. Hanks and Zurer have a 13-year age difference so the hint of flirtations is acceptable, not to mention that Zurer did not just lose a close family relative the way Tautou does at the beginning of *The Da Vinci Code*. The sequel is relentless in the number of hurdles that Hanks and the police need to surpass in order to find the bomb and save the remaining Cardinals held hostage. *Angels & Demons* as well as *Inferno*, uses a "ticking time bomb" plot device, (which in both cases are literal bombs). Other filmic examples of this narrative structure would include *High Noon* (1952) and *Armageddon* (1998), where the story is centered around something that *will* happen. In *The Da Vinci Code*, the threat to Tom Hanks is Paul Bettany pursing them and trying to steal the cryptex, which is essentially because Hanks got involved with the wrong people. The threat is not personalized until the end, which is a common trait of "airport novels" or literary series with multiple volumes centered around a single character. Hanks is a voyeur in *The Da Vinci Code* book and movie – but the action is refocused on him in Howard's cinematic sequels.

***

What happens when we get to the third installment, *Inferno*? Will the theology of Hell be debated, or will Tom Hanks continue to be put through the meat grinder?

Between May 2006 and May 2009, there was a three-year gap between the two films, while the Robert Langdon character was still in the mainstream conscious of pop-culture. Even though two other novels in the Langdon series were published – the *Inferno* movie did not release until seven years after *Angels & Demons*, and over ten years since *The Da Vinci Code*. With some of the same key filmmakers brought back (director, producer, cinematographer, editor and composer), there was an intention to make a different kind of film with the third installment, specifically a horror film. There are disturbing images in the two prequels, however the nightmare Hanks is thrusted into for the third installment is a different element entirely. They also went out of their way to install a past romantic intrigue with Sidse Babett Knudsen and Hanks to give more depth to his character.(16) In the novel, the director of the World Health Organization (WHO) has no history with Robert Langdon, let alone one with romantic feelings.

What the film does retain from the novel is the secret romance of the Ben Foster and Felicity Jones characters. They are the third bad screen couple we see in Ron Howard's filmography (*Ransom* and *The Dilemma* being the previous two). In the vein of trying for new material – Howard uses *Inferno* to give us two lovers that are essentially mass murderers. Furthermore, while *Ransom* showcases an unhealthy relationship between Gary Sinise and Lili Taylor, with *Inferno*, Ben Foster and Felicity Jones are academic fanatics, which uncomfortably synchronizes better to a modern audience. Dan Brown's 2013 novel maintains an uncomfortable prognostication to anyone reading the novel *after* the Wuhan Coronavirus pandemic in the early 2020s, particularly by the end of the book. The accusations of population control that were leveled at the Big Pharma funded doctors, scientists, and viral labs in the wake of the pandemic in 2021 and 2022, (some with credible evidence, some uncorroborated conspiracy theories), the majority of the unethical doctors cooking up deadly viruses did so under the banner of "academia" research. The concept of two ideological academics via Felicity Jones and Ben Foster is a more credible villain in the 2020s, than in the 2010s. As a final nod to deception, we cannot forget that Felicity Jones entraps Hanks into helping her unleash the virus, which given what happens in the prequels, we should expect a turncoat character in the series by this point.

For all of the energy that went into denouncing *The Da Vinci Code* for its incorrect history and its illusion to a secret dogma within church teaching, by the third movie installment, Howard really doesn't do much with any of the religious undertones that *Inferno* offers. It's almost as if Howard came back full circle to not bothering with religion in his films unless he has to. In the post *Da Vinci Code* era, it starts to have a recurring presence in his film, albeit relatively minor. The shipwrecked leaders from *In the Heart of the Sea* are allowed a conversation about their isolation and God's intentional punishment for them killing whales. The Beatles get push back from Christians for John Lennon's comparing his popularity to Jesus Christ in *Eight Days A Week*. However the continued omission of religion is almost obvious: *Solo* is one of the only *Star Wars* movies that doesn't make use of the Force, *Rebuilding Paradise* doesn't highlight any faith communities from the destruction or Christian charitable organizations, and *Hillbilly Elegy* as a biopic of J.D. Vance who is open about his Christian faith, doesn't address the subject.

Spirituality:
Thirteen Lives

Of the produced material about the Thai cave rescue, it's Ron Howard's movie that really makes the religious aspects of the story a recurring theme. Although some of the books and documentaries available address the subject, it gets regulated to a minor theme. The content about the "sleeping princess," or "crying princess," in conjunction to the Tham Luang mountain comes from residents in the local region and the Buddhist traditions. Although the sleeping princess is not in the focal center of Howard's version, the way in which this religious belief subtly repeats itself throughout *Thirteen Lives* nears to the point of wanting to categorize the movie in the "faith-based film" genre. That phrase has different meaning to western audiences: faith-based movies are explicit in declaring that *only* through the divine power of God, most often the Christian Trinitarian God, are obstacles conquered. While *Thirteen Lives* omits any overt miraculous moments with humans encountering something unexplainable, *Thirteen Lives* is edited to imply that something spiritual was unfolding with the events at Tham Luang. This concept is presented through the eyes of the Thai locals; they're not trying to convert others to their belief systems, nor is the film attempting to convey that the sleeping princess was irrefutably influential. All the same, should the viewer want to believe that she's playing a role, *Thirteen Lives* doesn't explicitly say that she isn't. The concept is left open-ended.

    Just before the soccer team enters the cave, the boys and the coach pause, with hands folded, bowing to show reverence to the statue of the sleeping princess outside of the entrance to the large first chamber of Tham Luang. In the mix of all the various subplots that are taking place throughout the movie, there are cutbacks to the faithful praying in front of the statue with incense, and leaving offerings of sweet snacks. More often than not, the audience is given close-ups of the statue's face, which innately implies something. Rain fall is just rain fall, but cut to a dull placid face of a pseudo-goddess whose tears supposedly have something to do with the region, and the contextual reading of the scene changes. Should *Apollo 13* have spliced in imagery of the Judeo-Christian God while the three astronauts were in space, the implications of the rescue mission, let alone the mindset of what the movie was saying about space travel would have drastically altered. Apart from the actual number "13" in the title, Howard's two rescue dramas offer a nice compare and contrast of each other. The viewer is meant to be enthralled with the technical marvels displayed in both films, yet *Apollo 13* doesn't tell us that Kevin Bacon, Tom Hanks and Bill Paxton are blasting off into "God's outer-space." As for the UK divers, when the rescue operation begins, we are shown the faithful praying to `"the Garden Spirit of the Forest"` asking for forgiveness for any wrong doing. The usage of the Reverend seen at the house of Hanks' family towards the end of *Apollo 13* watching the news with them accents a pastoral presence that's appropriate for the tense drama, without making a religious overture. (Apparently there was a longer scene with Rance that was ultimately cut from the movie).(17) In *Thirteen Lives*, the presence of the Buddhist monks becomes its own minor subplot in the film, segueing into the blessed prayer beads for the boys. There is a fundamental belief held by a large number of the supporting characters, (i.e. the Thai locals), therefore the religion and their collective devotion is baked into the narrative of *Thirteen Lives*.

CHAPTER 12
AUTHENTICITY

Since the release of *Splash* in 1984, with commercial and critical success, Howard solidified that his endeavors as a filmmaker were not just a temporary experimentation in the showbiz industry. He continued his vocation moving through a variety of genres, cultivating achievements and moving past any financial or critical disappointments. In nearly forty years of directing we don't see him paint himself into an artistic corner with a selected fanbase the way Wes Anderson, David Cronenberg, Terrence Malick or John Waters – all whom earned respected reputations – but cater to a specific audience. Howard has successfully gone from the mainstream into the more nuanced, and then been able to return back to the mainstream. Furthermore, there is no doubt that the variety of (in release order), *Frost/Nixon*; *Angels & Demons* and *The Dilemma*, at a later stage of his career strikes an odd mix of movies. Consider what the critics might say: there are those that may take umbrage to the depiction of President Nixon in *Frost/Nixon*, both from the political right and left. Others may criticize *Angels & Demons* for being too ostentatious. Finally, there are those who may simply watch *The Dilemma* and think of it as a disposable romcom. Nevertheless, the one element that all the films share is a level of authenticity. Regardless of how exaggerated the reenactment of the interviews were in *Frost/Nixon*, the logistics of a nuclear explosion happening over Vatican City in *Angels & Demons*, or someone perched on a small apartment balcony snapping photos in *The Dilemma* – the stories are buttressed with an honesty embedded into the acting, ambiance and dialogue.

On the subject of films based off true events, some mainstream Hollywood directors adapt the material to fit their narrative style, and Howard is no exception. Taking the mammoth subject of World War II, we can see this through the work of three separate directors who had very different approaches to the material. Terrence Malick's *The Thin Red Line* (1997) and *A Hidden Life* (2019), focus on self-reflection and spirituality. Christopher Nolan's *Dunkirk* (2017) and *Oppenheimer* (2023) make use of a non-linear plot in their story structure. Quentin Tarantino's *Inglorious Basterds* (2009) is complete historical fiction, yet is intended to be a glorification of the World War II genre.

Howard's historical adaptations are approached from the perspective of accuracy, strictly to put weight on the emotions of the characters while conflicts unfold. In his fictional films, this same concept is at work.

***

Robert Duvall is a bit of a curmudgeon in *The Paper*, and therefore a kindred spirit to Jason Robards in *Parenthood*, and Glenn Close and *Hillbilly Elegy* in the pantheon of Ron Howard's filmography. The presentation of the older generation in these three films are the sages of wisdom, but not in a traditional or stereotypical sense, such as the old martial arts master in a Kung Fu flick, or Gandalf from *The Hobbit* and *The Lord of the Rings*, or Yoda in *Star Wars*. The older generation in a Ron Howard film speak with an unfiltered frankness. That doesn't necessarily mean they are all downcast grumps – see Wilford Brimley in *Cocoon*, or Martin Landau in *EDtv*. The vast majority of people gravitate to those who speak with honesty, which is probably why it makes these characters very believable.

This is nicely succinct in an exchange between Robert Duvall (Bernie) and Michael Keaton (Henry) early in *The Paper*, when the office learns about their co-worker potentially taking another job elsewhere. Stressed with the responsibilities of marriage and impending parenthood, Keaton (Henry) picks Duvall's (Bernie's) mind:

EXT. ON TOP OF A BUILDING - DAY

Both HENRY and BERNIE have their arms resting on the railing overlooking the city.

                HENRY
      Hey Bernie, you've got kids - how'd you keep doing the job?

Bernie waves his hand.

                BERNIE
      Don't ask marital advice from a guy with two ex-wives and a daughter who won't speak to him.
      (beat)
      The problem with being my age is everybody thinks you're a father figure, but you're really just the same asshole you always were.

Minus a gender swap, we can easily imagine Glenn Close in *Hillbilly Elegy* saying something like that. The dialogue has a blunt honesty – not for the sake of shock value, but to convey to the audience an authenticity about the characters within the ensemble cast. Is *The Paper*'s story premise about a group of reporters reversing false accusations in less than 24-hours in a high-profile story likely? Not really. On the other hand, *The Paper* gives the viewer an honest representation of the sorts of people that make up the journalism business.

An authentic sense of mental illness:
A Beautiful Mind

Make no mistake, Russell Crowe has high ambitions in the field of mathematics, but we would be hard pressed to call him a fame seeker. In actuality, the character is more of a social outcast (see Tom Cruise in *Far and Away*, or Jim Carrey in *How the Grinch*

Stole Christmas). In the true story of John Forbes Nash, he would receive the Nobel Prize in 1994 at the age of sixty-six. The best-selling biography by Sylvia Nasar that released in 1998 granted Nash fame that he didn't particularly seem to be striving for.

Yet decades before any of that, loneliness was the avenue in which John Nash became susceptible to schizophrenic episodes. In actuality we don't know what those episodes were like: Nasar's book doesn't detail the hallucinations, and Nash himself says that leaving them was like waking up from a dream. The film adaptation uses actual people giving the viewer a tangible antagonist to what Russell Crowe is facing. This is not unlike Jeffrey Tambor as the mayor in *How the Grinch Stole Christmas* — a character created for the film to give a face to the Christmas materialism that enrages Jim Carrey. *A Beautiful Mind* does essentially the same thing: Paul Bettany, Ed Harris and the young Vivien Cardone were created for the film and appear when Russell Crowe is either the most isolated, or when he's reached a depression of sorts. The delusions are a comfort to Crowe, always *heard* on screen before actually being shown to the audience from Crowe's perspective.(12)

A unique element that correlates to the impossible conquest motif, is withheld until the final third of the film, when Crowe and the audience realizes that a major portion of his life is a delusion. *A Beautiful Mind* is a version of the man vs. himself conflict in the most brutal form. The viewer also shares a unique sense of disappointment when realizing that all the effort put into cracking Russian codes was a farce. It's as if we, the audience, get cheated out of the spy-thriller that we thought we were going on, thereby getting a little sense of how debilitating living a fantasy might be. Any typical Film School 101 class will dictate that leading character(s) have an arc of some kind, specifically a change from who they were at the start of the movie, to who they become by the end credits. Russell Crowe's grand quest is to separate fantasy from reality, and this journey of curing himself makes for a very difficult task on account of his audience *also* being jibbed out of what we thought was a spy thriller.

The maturation of self is something Howard plays with in his body of work. For example, Tom Hanks has to learn to love in *Splash*; Michael Keaton needs to commit to making tough decisions in *Gung Ho*; and Steve Martin needs to accept the roller-coaster in *Parenthood*. Each of these protagonists need to confront their own shortcomings before they can achieve success. But how to do this for someone who is emotionally disturbed? *A Beautiful Mind* makes the decision to play the game again, and lets us watch Crowe begin to rebuild his conspiracy. The film does not explicitly tell us this is a conspiracy or a hallucination – the viewer is simply ushered back on the ride with Russell Crowe again, this time in his backyard. Those who noticed him not taking his pills in a previous scene may have had a hint that what was happening in his shed was fake. Jennifer Connelly discovering the thousands of news clippings in the shed is one beat, but it's her running back into the house and her seeing that Crowe is speaking to an empty space (Ed Harris) is the moment that we realize the hallucinations are true. It's definitive proof for herself and the audience. Again, the three imaginary characters that Russell Crowe communicates with throughout the film were not concrete visions of John Nash – they were created for the film to give context to understand someone in Nash's state. Crowe (Nash) never realized that the little girl, "never gets old" – it's a narrative device to reflect John Nash's brain power in overcoming his schizophrenia.

There is no documentation of actual people that John Nash was speaking with, yet the three fictional characters accurately relates to the audience what a giant crisis it would be to have a whole quota of your life removed. Cinematic depictions of schizophrenia are either an outsider looking in (2009's *The Soloist*), or inside the mind of the victim (2010's *Shutter Island*). To strive for cogency in depicting the illness, Howard chose the path more often used in edgy films, yet schizophrenia is handled in a way that viewers can have empathy towards someone suffering from a complex mental disorder. It's a compassionate approach by definitively taking the fantasy away from us in the final acts of the film.

American Filmmaker

There can be a bit of a misperception with the term "American filmmaker" in the sense that it could imply several different things. One might presume a director like Ken Burns or Oliver Stone, both who have made the subject of United States history a recurring topical theme in their body of work. Consequently, someone else might automatically think of George Lucas or Steven Spielberg – filmmakers who have authored modern classics that have become hardwired into American pop-culture. Then of course the immigrant, Frank Capra, who has directed several films that compel audiences to the prefect the American spirit.

As for Ron Howard, one might pin the title "American filmmaker" to him on account of being born and raised in the industry that has become the predominate American art form. Throughout his memoir, Howard indicates he was offered many off-ramps to leave show business at his choosing, yet he continued to make a career in it.(1) After the commercial and critical success of *Splash*, we see Howard embrace his native country in a way few other American filmmakers have. He began by pointing his camera lens pointed at Manhattan, New York (*Night Shift* and *Splash*), he then shifted to a Tampa Bay, Florida retirement community (*Cocoon*), then to the blue collar Midwest of Pennsylvania (*Gung Ho*), and then suburban St. Louis, Missouri (*Parenthood*). In the 1990s Howard began exploring the quiddity of the country's spirit (*Backdraft*; *Far and Away*; *Apollo 13*), and the sociological relationship the United States has with the media (*The Paper*; *Ransom*; *EDtv*). Further exploration of these themes are seen in the 2000s, even as Howard turned his eye to international material, particularly with *The Da Vinci Code*. However, Howard doesn't remain overseas once he goes there – he does comes back to America in due time and continues to make films rooted in the United States.

Howard's first documentary, *Made in America*, is littered with little moments showcasing the "American dream" becoming a reality. Although it very much is a concert film, *Made in America* can't help but demonstrate how the American dream is not applicable just for the music performing artists, but also for the common folk. Howard privileges these people throughout the film, such as a mother with her taco truck or the music managers. Routinely throughout the documentary, the audience is given a story recounted by a popular musician or group, but it's quickly cross-cut with the plight of a different musician of lesser stature. *Made in America* implies that hard work will be rewarded in due time.

There is one short exchange in *Made in America* that's of worth highlighting. In the middle of the film there's an interview with a security officer that's being conducted by Howard himself. It's spliced into a sequence, but the conversation goes as such:

ABDUL GOODMAN
You gotta have more than one hustle now-a-days. Everything is hard – get yourself up, go to work, do the right thing. But you know what though? [This] is a time when we look back and say, "There's a guy out here no worse than me. I'm living the dream."

RON HOWARD
What is the dream?

ABDUL GOODMAN
The dream to me is just to have the opportunity. You know, realistically, having ambition beyond just regularly getting up and going to sleep. If you have no dream, you're not dreaming – you're sleeping. You're dead. Success is a journey, not a destination. When you stop seekin' it, you've already lost.

The moment concludes with a fellow security officer ribbing Abdul, accusing him of stealing what he said off of a generic inspirational Facebook post. Even if that was the case, the exchange is one of the many endorsements of determination, and hard work championed throughout the documentary.

With respect to the musical performances in *Made in America*, Howard doesn't present them the way most concert films would; the documentary remains focused on telling a multipart narrative. The film is intended to be a glamorous cosmopolitan presentation of different individuals. The various stories reflected throughout are probably what Jay Z intended for the music fest. Philadelphia, the city where the continental congress voted for, and signed the Declaration of Independence in the summer of 1776 is an ideal setting for Ron Howard to flex his patriotism. The finale of *Made in America* embraces the concert film aesthetic by letting Jay Z and Kanye West perform on stage without interruption, (i.e. cuts to interviews) that encapsulate all that's required to facilitate these events.

Director on director:
Jim Henson: Idea Man

Between 1977 to 2024, there are three radical shifts in Ron Howard's aesthetical directing choices. The first arrives in the late-1980s and early-1990s with the successive releases of *Willow*; *Parenthood* and *Backdraft* where the subject material incorporated into the stories indicate a progressive shift towards more serious matters. Throughout the 1980s, there are heartfelt moments of conflict scattered throughout the comedies, but it's with *Willow* that some fairly frightening imagery is merged into what could have remained a light hearted story. *Parenthood* openly addresses the adult topics of abortion, divorce, out-of-wedlock births, pornography, and runaways. *Backdraft* is Howard's first bona fide suspense drama with action sequences and a real danger threatening the characters throughout the film. Although Howard does not abstain completely from directing comedies, by the late-1990s, he successfully rebrands himself into a filmmaker that the general public takes seriously.

The second radical shift arrives in 2013 with both *Made in America* and *Rush* – two films that visually break from Howard's modus operandi. Howard kicks off the 2010s with a sojourn to romantic comedies via *The Dilemma*, but then tackles the Jay-Z lead concert film with a handheld, boots-on-the-ground approach of showcasing the inaugural "Made in America" music festival over Labor Day weekend 2012. The other cinematic extreme arrives courtesy of *Rush*'s cinematographer, Anthony Dod Mantle who used the cameras like Go-Pros by placing them in tight corners, thus giving radical depth of field to the shots. In literally the same month, September 2013, with the release of both films, Howard singled his shift to documentaries while also embracing a pseudo-immersion style of filmmaking. We've seen Howard attempt unique captivating techniques before such as having the audience live through Russell Crowe's fantasies in *A Beautiful Mind*; the camera being physically placed in-between the boxers throwing punches in *Cinderella Man*; or CGI allowing the audience to pass through the walls of the small cryptex in *The Da Vinci Code*. Yet with *Rush*, the camera technology and Mantle's use of extreme close-ups allow the audiences to be inside of, hear and ultimately "feel" the car engines in a way that Howard hadn't done to such extremes before. Following 2013, the environments of where the characters are present becomes accentuated in the use of extreme close-ups; the physicality of the areas they inhabit becomes part of the cinematic experience. *In the Heart of the Sea* and *Thirteen Lives* rest heavily on the close proximity that the audience is made to feel on account of where the camera is placed. It's really no surprise that *Inferno* spends so much time inside Tom Hanks' head and centers around the visions of torture he thinks he experiences.

The third shift arrives at the beginning of the 2020s when Howard becomes more retrospective about himself. Granted there are a couple of times in his career where Howard offered a personal perspective of his films in the various press junkets and interviews, but it's fleeting. Whereas the majority of Steven Spielberg's directorial features have their origin from topics that Spielberg himself was fixated on, Howard only does this periodically. With *Parenthood* being a combination of his, Lowell Ganz, Brian Grazer and Babaloo Mandel's experiences of raising kids, as well as *Far and Away* with Howard setting the story in Ireland on account of his family's Irish heritage and then in Oklahoma. The vast majority of the times when Howard's interviews get nostalgic, they gear towards his acting career on *The Andy Griffith Show* and/or *Happy Days* as well as any fun stories about any number of famous stars he acted alongside.* It wasn't until 2023 that Howard disclosed that one of his desires to do *Ransom* was on account of kidnapping threats made towards his 11-year-old daughter, Bryce in 1992.(4) It is oddly appropriate as this disclosure was made in the 2020s when Howard was routinely opening up more about personal connections. Beginning with *Hillbilly Elegy* on account of Howard's own rural roots, he spoke about connecting to J.D. Vance's autobiography on account of what he knew about the area and the struggles those communities were going through. Of course, although it's not a movie, the release of his and Clint's memoir, *The Boys*, indicates a willingness to talk about himself and display gratitude for his life.

As Howard gives indications that he's progressively becoming more retrospective, he does something particularly unique with the art form that he's devoted his life to.

***

It's no surprise that an industry that shapes culture tends to be self-indulgent, which is probably why we see directors make their own "love letter" to cinema. What's unique about this is that we see different directors hone in different elements of the business; they don't seem to collectively gravitate to one given topic. Paul Thomas Anderson ops for the pornography industry in *Boogie Nights* (1997); Ben Affleck looks at geopolitical Hollywood history

---

*The other films that Howard ties personal experiences to are *A Beautiful Mind* having witnessed a friend of Andy Griffith's have a mental breakdown on set when he was a boy(2); *Cinderella Man* having made a Great Depression documentary in high school; and *Eight Days A Week* having experienced unruly fans during *Happy Days* press tours.(3) It should be noted that Howard didn't pursue those films specifically on account of those reasons.

in *Argo* (2012); Tim Burton, the B-movie with *Ed Wood* (1994); Damien Chazelle, the advent of sound in film via *Babylon* (2022); David Fincher, the screenwriter in *Mank* (2020); John Lee Hancock, the literary adaptation in *Saving Mr. Banks* (2013); Sam Mendes, the movie theatre palaces in *Empire of Light* (2022); Martin Scorsese, the silent era in *Hugo* (2011); Steven Spielberg, the director's journey in *The Fabelmans* (2022); Quinten Tarantino's historical fiction in *Once Upon A Time... in Hollywood* (2019); and Billy Wilder on the after-effects of stardom in *Sunset Boulevard* (1950).

For one of the only people in history who can justifiably say that they spent the majority of their life in the filmmaking industry, it's profoundly unique and very fitting that Ron Howard didn't dive into the subgenre of "movies about movies" until later in his career. Furthermore, Howard does it in an altogether different approach: a documentary that mirrors the style of his subject. The closest Howard ever got to a "movie about movies" film was *EDtv*, but the comedy is fixated on making a social commentary about society's celebrity obsession. *EDtv* never dives into the practicality of how the show is broadcast, how the camera crew operates, or the business legalities of a reality tv-show. With *Jim Henson: Idea Man*, Howard uses a lot of stock footage exhibiting the nuts & bolts of what it took to put together the various puppet productions.

Jim Henson got his footing in television at the same time Ron Howard was growing up in it, (Henson was twenty years Howard's senior). Although they didn't work together, the choice of Henson isn't instantly obvious, but we see the parallels to Howard right away: Henson is from rural Mississippi, he has an older brother who dies prematurely which really affected him, which is a noteworthy motif as the theme of brothers is something Ron Howard repeatedly circles back to. Brian Henson, Jim's and Jane's son, points out the differences in the Muppets his parents created, and we see the concept of repackaging at work – Kermit the Frog and Cookie Monster were originally for adults, but were adapted for kids when *Sesame Street* came along. What is the sense that the viewer can take away from this? That everyone in Jim and

Jane Henson's circle did what they did because they were having fun, which in turn causes their own children to gravitate to the same industry. This familial legacy of the Henson's we see reflected in the Howard household from Rance & Jean, to Ron & Clint, to Bryce. The lure to filmmaking is on account of the enjoyment witnessed by the children when seeing parents having pleasure in doing it. We can almost tell that throughout the majority of his directing career that when Ron Howard takes on a film, regardless of the subject material, there is a sense of fun embodied (*Ransom* and *The Missing* being the possible exceptions). The thrill of making a suspense drama about an atomic bomb in Rome, risk taking Formula 1 drivers, or an eccentric Spanish chef gives the collection of films a sense of excitement. The devastation shown in *Rebuilding Paradise* is heartbreaking, but the audience is inspired by the towns peoples' determination in pulling themselves up from the ruins back to functionality. There is clearly excitement within *Jim Henson: Idea Man*, in that Henson was a director who used his work, particularly *Sesame Street*, to make the experimental films he loved doing. Watching someone or a group of people achieve critical and commercial success by doing what he, she or they loved, in the context of creating profitable art is innately pleasurable to watch.

For his sixth documentary, Howard embraces a new approach and crafts *Jim Henson: Idea Man* to mimic the style of Henson's own aesthetic through the usage of animated effect shots between scenes, allowing Howard to create an homage to Henson. Furthermore, we notice that Howard uses two other directors to provide commentary: Frank Oz and Orson Wells. Although the use of Wells is from stock footage from his unreleased talk show,[5] the bits Howard chooses indirectly adds credence to Henson's contributions to movie history. The usage of Frank Oz, Henson's longtime collaborator and a celebrity in his own right, gives the viewer direct insight to their working relationship and some of Henson's philosophical views on the business. Oz explains how these shows were made; not the tactical mechanics of puppeteering, but rather the intent of getting the characters right. The goal is to humanize inanimate objects, be it Bert & Ernie, or Miss Piggy. The documentary is aiming for the heart of the filmmaker, not to be a traditional retrospective akin to an encyclopedic retelling. Through *Jim Henson: Idea Man*, Howard very much wants to emphasize to us that the reason we enjoy the puppets is because Jim Henson and Frank Oz fused authenticity into these inanimate objects.

Comprehending Rocket Science:
Apollo 13

Regretful that one might be prematurely eulogizing Ron Howard by saying this: *Apollo 13* will likely be his best remembered film. Despite the comical antics that constitute the majority of Howard's total runtime from both the large and small screen, the 1995 space drama has maintained the longest legs of the filmography having been viewed by the widest audience and age range. To date, several of Ron Howard's other films are contenders for the claim of his "most popular film" on account of box office receipts, ratings or reviews,[6] yet *Apollo 13* has an accessibility and a rewatch value that will likely, and has already begun to, pass down through generations.

There are two key elements at work in *Apollo 13*: the technicalities that composite actual rocket science and the emotional tone needed to understand the film.

For a complex narrative, and yet a fairly straightforward plot, the challenge of the astronauts and Mission Control is simply overcoming one problem at a time. The editing, (for which *Apollo 13* won an Oscar), balances the whole narrative around one hurdle after the next from start to finish. When the crisis of losing CO_2 arrives, a new puzzle must be solved. When Bill Paxton gets sick, a new concern is added. The pent-up anger between Kevin Bacon and Paxton presents a development in the character dynamic. Given Howard's affinity for difficult situations presented to his lead characters, the set-up of `"the successful failure"` is rather appropriate.

In the opening act of *Apollo 13*, the historical significance of the moon landing, Tom Hanks' relationship with Kathleen

Quinlan (note a hint of sexual flirtation between them), the son in the bedroom asking questions about landing on the moon works, and finally the Apollo 1 fire.(7) These are all elements to root Tom Hanks family as the emotional center of the film. The aim is to condition audience to be on the edge of their seat once the explosion happens, and because the narrative is structured with the prime focus of family in the opening scenes, the viewer warms up to them. The same concept is at work in *Cinderella Man*; the importance of Russell Crowe's family is established at the beginning, making them the focal point for Crowe during the most pivotal moments of the boxing matches. The families of the trapped soccer team in *Thirteen Lives* are presented to the audience first before the other characters.

There is a balanced mix between excitement and intensity which reflects the seriousness of what NASA and the astronauts are trying to do despite already having landed on the moon less than a year prior. It's worth pointing out that the space program of the late-1960s and early-1970s was exhaustively mathematical and orderly. No doubt that *Apollo 13* gives the audience a sense of this, but in actuality, every single aspect of the Apollo missions were accounted for, tested and carefully monitored more than the film conveys. The movie establishes a camaraderie between the astronauts, even when Gary Sinise is forced off the team, which is crucial in getting the accurate tone for how these professionals handled the series of events that plagued their mission. Although *Apollo 13* is immensely accurate and often attributed as being one of the most historically accurate films ever made*, many movies based off real events will alter and/or compromise events in order to get the emotion across to the viewer.(9) Therefore, as a "movie," *Apollo 13* remains excellently composed and makes choices that

---

*Make no mistake, *Apollo 13* is historically accurate and has been given deserved praise for being so, especially from a technological standpoint. The construction of the sets and some of the very sentences came directly from transcripts. Little things were tossed in to give credence to the history. For example, Tom Hanks' line about `"bouncing off the walls"` was never actually spoken on the spacecraft, but it was something Jim Lovell did say after the fact; that phrase is easier for the common viewer to comprehend. *Apollo 13* did take artistic license in areas and made alterations to the history to benefit the narrative of the film. A list of changes has been included in the endnotes.(8)

convey how one should feel when watching or learning about these events. Throughout the film there are about a dozen times that something "breaks," such as a bowl of salad dropping on the floor, Kathleen Quinlan's wedding ring slipping down the shower drain, or the overhead projector burning out when Ed Harris goes to use it. Each of these were meant to underscore the concept of things breaking, a subtle prognostication about what had happened on the spaceship.

According to Jim Lovell's book from which the film was based, *Lost Moon*, there was a rotation of crews at Mission Control that came in throughout a cycle. However the primary characters remain in place throughout the film so that the audiences maintains some familiarity with the army of white shirts in Mission Control. Furthermore, one of the tricks of *Apollo 13* is that complicated ideas are repeated three times throughout the dialogue: first in technical terms, then in layman's terms, and finally repeated a third time again in technical jargon. This was so that the audience is able to understand the complicated maneuvers. Once knowing this cinematic "Algebraic equation," it's charmingly obvious how much *Apollo 13* repeats itself, yet it's brilliantly masked on account of how sentences are rephrased line by line. Even simple disposable phrases or expressions by other actors convey the appropriate emotion(s) the audience; it may be intended to feel casual, but the practicality of "common spoke" language is much easier for the viewer to understand. We may not be able to perfectly grasp the rocket science, but we have some comprehension of what's going on while not feeling confused for any longer than a minute before moving onto the next moment of drama.

An example of this narrative comprehension is utilized through Ed Harris who is a focal point for the astronauts, Mission Control, and of course the audience in consuming information regarding the spacecraft, its malfunctions and then the return home. Howard points out that Ed Harris and Tom Hanks have a significant amount of "scenes" together, yet they are in two different rooms for the entire movie; they are never on screen together.[10] Again, an example of the superb editing on the part of Mike Hill and Dan

Hanley, Howard's go-to duo, in cutting between Tom Hanks and another person in Mission Control as if they are having a conversation face-to-face.

***

At the half-way point of the film, the stakes begin to rise. Being that the vast majority of the audience (both those in 1995, and future audiences) knows how the film will end, all the complications add to the enigma of the drama, making the story uniquely compelling. The mindset of: "We know how it ended, but how did it happen?" gives the viewer a mental advantage over the film. In a fictional movie the audience is processing unknown information, whereas with *Apollo 13* (and/or any movie based off popular events), the audience is in a sense studying and/or observing the film more. We are watching a puzzle be solved even though we already know the outcome. This is why a simple moment as Gary Sinise shutting off the television seconds before he hears or sees the "Apollo 13 Special Report" breaking news alert adds a little tease, creating a jolt of concern to the viewer. Therefore, because the filmmakers assume that the audience already knows how the yarn will unfold, this becomes the perfect stage for Howard and company to showcase just how difficult a task returning the three astronauts was. When we talk about Howard being the filmmaker of the impossible conquests, entering into the realm of non-fiction, the energy has the potential to reach a grander level.

Ed Harris' Gene Kranz, has two of the keynote lines in the film that could serve as the tagline for all of Ron Howard's films, especially the movies released after *Apollo 13*. Despite that both Ron Howard and Jim Lovell have stated that the Grumman Team got an unfair wrap in the film, one of the exchanges with Ed Harris (Kranz) begins with:

INT. BLACKBOARD ROOM

GRUMMAN REP
We can't make any guarantees. We designed the LEM to land on the moon,

> not fire the engine out there for
> course correction.
>
> **KRANZ**
> Well, unfortunately, we're not
> landing on the moon, are we? I don't
> care what anything was designed to
> do. I care about what it can do.

Later, in the same meeting room after the spacecraft passes around the dark side of the moon, the issue of conserving power becomes the dominate problem. Again, Ed Harris (Kranz) delivers a brief monologue that rests at the heart of nearly all of Howard's films, particularly those in the post-*Apollo 13* era:

> **INT. BLACKBOARD ROOM**
>
> **KRANZ**
> So you're telling me you can only
> give our guys forty-five hours?
>
> Kranz writes "45 hrs" on the chalkboard and then draws a line, makes an indication on the map of where the space craft would be.
>
> **KRANZ (cont'd)**
> That brings them to about there.
>
> Kranz taps the chalk on locations indicating where they'll stop and where they need to land.
>
> **KRANZ (cont'd)**
> Gentlemen that's not acceptable.
>
> The room begins to get very testy with Grumann team members speaking over one another. Finally, JOHN gets his voice above the others.

                    JOHN
     Whoa, whoa, guys - power's
     everything. Power is everything.

                    KRANZ
     What'd you mean?

                    JOHN
     Without it, they don't talk to us,
     they don't correct they're
     trajectory, they don't turn the heat
     shield around - we gotta turn
     everything off. Now. They're not
     gonna make it to re-entry.

                    KRANZ
     What do you mean everything?

                    JOHN
     With everything on, the LEM draws 60
     amps. At that rate in sixteen hours
     the batteries are dead,

Looking back to the other Grumman Team members.

                JOHN (cont'd)
     not forty five.

Turning back to Kranz.

                JOHN (cont'd)
     And so's the crew. We gotta get them
     down to twelve amps.

The room explodes again with voices all in an outcry over this.

                 GRUMMAN REP
     You can't run a vacuum cleaner on
     twelve amps, John!

                         JOHN
We have to turn off the radars, cabin
heater, instrument displays, the
guidance computer - the whole smack.

                         JERRY
Whoa! Guidance computer?! What if
they need to do another burn?
(To Kranz)
Gene they won't even know which way
they're pointing.

                         JOHN
The more time we talk down here the
more juice they waste up there. I've
been looking at the data for the last
hour.

                         KRANZ
That's the deal?

                         JOHN
That's the deal.

                         KRANZ
Okay John. The minute we finish the
burn, we'll power down the LEM.

                         JOHN
Alright.

John quickly vacates the room.

                         KRANZ
Now in the meantime, we're gonna have
a frozen command module up there. In
a couple days we'll have to power it
up using nothing but the re-entry
batteries.

> **GRAUMMAN REP**
> Never been tried before.
>
> **ANOTHER GRUMMAN REP**
> Hell we've never even simulated it before, Gene.
>
> **KRANZ**
> Well were gonna have to figure it out. I want people in our simulators working re-entry scenarios. I want you guys to find every engineer who designed every switch, every circuit, every transistor and every lightbulb that's up there. Then I want you to talk to the guy on the assembly line who actually built the thing. Find out how to squeeze every amp out of both of these goddamn machines.
>
> Walking back to the chalk board, Kranz makes quick dashes indicating on the drawing board.
>
> **KRANZ (cont'd)**
> I want this mark all the way back to Earth with time to spare. We never lost an American in space and we're sure as hell not going to lose one on my watch. Failure is not an option.

These are arguably the "by-lines" of all Ron Howard's films, particularly the dramas. The quotes could be attributed to who the timid Henry Winkler becomes at the end of *Night Shift*, or how José Andrés marches his World Central Kitchen team into disaster areas in *We Feed People*. The refusal to succumb to defeat and the determination to never give up will reward when living in the cinema of Ron Howard. The adulation the viewer gets from watching *Apollo 13*, gives us some version of the celebratory feeling that those experienced in the Spring of 1970.

Success does not mean that sacrifices were not required. The death of Tommy Lee Jones in *The Missing*, or Joel Edgerton learning of his father's passing at the end of *Thirteen Lives* is part of the price paid. Even Tom Hanks missing his opportunity to land on the moon contribute to the authentic meaning of what it costs to pull off impossible conquests. To quote James Horner regarding the music he composed for the scene in which the astronauts pass over the surface of the moon, his description of his piece ("The Darkside of the Moon") perfectly captures what the scene is about:

> It's a terrifically lonely sequence when you hear it with no music or dialogue. You can image the feeling of training for so many years and realizing that the closest you'll ever get to the moon is touching the window on your spaceship. So, in a certain sense, that was perfect for my way of scoring. If I'd just played the scene as a lonely night cue, then it would mean nothing. That's exactly what's on the screen. But if you try and get deeper with the tremendous loss that everyone is feeling, then the music works much more powerfully.(11)

Apollo 13 ranks as one of the most patriotic films in the pantheon of pro-U.S.A. cinema. James Horner repeatedly uses a single horn to build into the moment. The "less is more" approach is the way Horner and Howard treat the determination of the astronauts and Mission Control. The lift off, the explosion, course correction the return trajectory and end credits all make use of Horner's grand prodigious orchestra, but it's in the quieter moments of the film that the music helps craft one of the most inspirational stories of the modern era.

One biography to snapshot a history:
Cinderella Man

> There is something inherently tough about Americans. They will not admit defeat. Failure is not an option. The astronauts of Apollo 13 would not give up. John

and Alicia Nash would not give up. And Jim Braddock would not surrender to poverty. As moving and inspiring as Jim Braddock's story is on the outside, it's only when you get on the inside – inside his love for his wife and the simple desire to take care of his family – that you see the real basis for his courage which makes his story so powerful and enduringly relevant.

– Ron Howard[13]

There are some historical events that are not practical to be put onto film because they are too large in scale on account of a lengthy timespan or the amount of characters. Sometimes a movie will focus in on one historical figure whose biography gives a nearly complete representation of something that cannot be neatly packaged into a single movie. There is no doubt that the film will fail to cover all the crucial elements, but it will bring an audience closer to understanding the essence of said event. More often than not, these bioflicks are about minor figures in context when compared to the popular figures we associate various historical events with.

The tensions of the American Civil War can be accessed through Colonel Robert Gould Shaw in *Glory* (1989) played by Matthew Broderick and his company of African-American soldiers. The holocaust is presented from the perspective of a Nazi, Oskar Schindler in *Schindler's List* (1993), played by Liam Neeson about his efforts to save Polish Jews from the gas chambers. An assortment of bankers, investors and hedge fund managers make up the players that gambled against the economy in *The Big Short* (2015), with the threat of the subprime mortgage crash looming. There are many recognizable names from the Civil Rights movement, yet *Rustin* (2023) focuses on one of the background players, Bayard Rustin, played by Coleman Domingo, and his behind-the-scenes in organizing the famous 1963 March on Washington.

This is what *Cinderella Man* does with the Great Depression and the story of James J. Braddock. There is no question that the drama is a boxing film, however through the themes of family, the romance between Jim & Mae Braddock, the film is equally as centered on how the 1930s Depression lifestyle effected those in the United States. *Cinderella Man* has very few explicit references to key events of Great Depression; it completely embraces that era and the poverty created by the stock market crash to such an extent that the historical context is not required because the audience connects with the plight of the characters trying to survive the current circumstances.

During his teenage years, Howard was looking for any excuse to make movies. For a school assignment, he petitioned to make a documentary on the Great Depression. Interviewing elder adults and using photos from the Burbank public library, Howard crafted a short film that impressed his teacher so much that she had him show it to all five of her classes.[14] Howard recounts that when doing that high school documentary, the theme of "despair" was what got repeated the most. Although the project originated from Russell Crowe, *Cinderella Man* touches on all the themes in Howard's authorship.

James J. Braddock (Russell Crowe) is not pretentious or a complicated person; he's wholeheartedly a family man. At the very start of the film Crowe and Paul Giamatti are two "business partners" on the up and up, which quickly disappears shortly after the opening scenes. The devastation of the Great Depression took several months before it began to really hit for many people; it proceeded to get worse as time went on for the first year or two. In a simple but effective time-lapse, the viewer is quickly taken to poverty. The historical play-by-play is not required, and thus the pattern of *Cinderella Man* is staged in the opening few minutes: one set back after another keeps Crowe and his family under the poverty line. Screenwriter Akiva Goldman pointed out that that the plot of the film is relatively simple, being that it simply recounts the stats of James J. Braddock winning one fight after the next. Therefore the story was written around his family and the continual diminishment the depression caused them.[15] Crowe facilitates getting a work shift down at the docks in one scene, and in the following scene their electricity gets turned off. Crowe scores a crucial victory in the ring, and then Paddy Considine goes missing in Central Park.

Rooted throughout the whole film is a romance between husband and wife, and the family unit. Russell Crowe and Renée Zellweger are truly inseparable as a twosome, and although we see them have differences, they never attack each other in arguments. Why? Because the children are the center of attention for the leading protagonists. We could argue they are one of the most wholesome parents in Howard's entire filmography. Yes, they make mistakes, but those errors are overruled by Crowe and Zellweger placing their union first.

For the audience, the boxing holds our attention: the matches were shot and edited to give the viewer a sense they were in the ring with the pugilists. Cinematographer Salvatore Totino himself wore a special suit with a Steadicam suspension that allowed him and the camera to be front and center of the punches. With this in mind, during one of the most crucial bouts, there are desaturated flashes of the kids to remind the viewer that poverty is at the heart of the story. Not unlike the cut aways to the "sleeping princess" statue at the cave entrance in *Thirteen Lives*, reminding the audience that spiritual beliefs are at the forefront of the Thai people's minds – so too are the flashes of despair used to highlight the threat of what poverty can do to Crowe's family. The Great Depression is the enemy. It's never explicitly said in the movie, but we're given the impression that if Crowe were offered a big pile of money to do something else to get his family out of poverty, he would have jumped at the opportunity. His boxing career was a means of support because he was talented at it. The debilitating circumstances forces Crowe to humble himself to those around him. One of Braddock's biographers notes that when the former boxer was working the docks, he was averse to talking about his glory days in the ring.[16] This is not explicitly declared in *Cinderella Man*, yet the ambiance of the film and Crowe's performance leads the audience to assume this on account of how Crowe carries himself with others. An observation by Ron Howard is worth noting:

It is most telling to me that James Braddock did not enter the boxing ring with a champion title on his mind. He stepped between the ropes with a much simpler goal, a selfless one in fact. As the hardships the nation faced grew more dire, the crucible of the times reduced dreams to the most basic. Here was a man trying to keep his family together, fed and sheltered during that dark period called the Great Depression. Boxing was the best way he knew how to do that. Just as much as moving loads on a dock, boxing was his job.(17)

The duality of the film comes by way of three characters in contrast to Crowe: Paul Giamatti his manager, Craig Bierko, his opponent for the heavy weight title, and Paddy Considine – a character completely made up for the movie.

Paul Giamatti and Russell Crowe are a perfect on-the-nose "opposites attract" partnership that Howard loves to construct his films around. The contrast between the calm, cool and collected Irishman and the high energy manager was part of their business in Braddock's actual career. Jeremy Schaap's biography of James Braddock paints this picture of the boxer and his manager:

> Usually in manager-fighter relationships, the fighter is the hothead and the manager spends large chunks of every day undoing the damaged caused by his rash gladiator. But when the fighter burns slowly, like Braddock, or not at all, the manager is the one who has to be aggressive, protecting their interests and making sure they get respected. [Joe] Gould was congenitally aggressive, a fighting bantam with his chin out and his tongue wagging. Most often Braddock had to calm *him* down.
>
> Braddock, of course, was accustomed to Gould's nervous habits. Somehow it had an equalizing effect, Gould's anxiety calming him.(18)

Again, the authenticity of the true story fuels the make-up of Russell Crowe and Paul Giamatti. They are two people who function smoothly with their personality contrasts. There is a hint of antagonism between them (see Henry Winkler & Michael Keaton in *Night Shift*, or Warwick Davis & Val Kilmer in *Willow*, or Viggo Mortensen & Colin Farrell in *Thirteen Lives*), yet the ease at which the two operate inside and outside the ring conveys a confidence about Crowe that doesn't need to be expressed by dialogue.

Once Craig Bierko's Max Baer comes into the story, the audience's fixation will be on him because he's appropriately teased earlier in *Cinderella Man* as being a powerhouse fighter. The contrast between Bierko living a lavish playboy lifestyle versus Crowe trying to keep his head above the poverty line plays into a contrast between the two pugilists. The undercurrent of death, being that two of Bierko's (Max Baer) opponents died in the ring, also loiters heavily in the final act of the film.*

The theme of death in the latter half of *Cinderella Man* is in credit to the composite character, Paddy Considine. Again, Paddy Considine's Mike Wilson was not an actual person, but rather a fictitious "evil twin" of Crowe/Braddock; a dark alternate version of what he could become should the hardships of the Great Depression overcome him. Of all the characters in the movie, he is the least voluminous character which is no error on Paddy Considine's performance – to the contrary, Considine is appropriately subdued and a tad inappropriately eruptive. Being placed between other big personalities on screen (Paul Giamatti, Craig Bierko, Bruce McGill), Considine is situated as a crucial undercurrent for *Cinderella Man* because of what happens to him. Intended to be a doppelganger for Crowe, the sad plight of

---

*It should be noted that in actuality Max Baer was heavily distraught about the death of Frankie Campbell, the boxer he gave a concussion to in the ring, who then died the following day. Baer provided financial aid to Campbell's widow and paid college funds for Campbell's children. The other boxer Baer is credited with killing in *Cinderella Man* is slightly deceptive; Ernie Schaaf died in the ring in during a different bout, however experts believe he was probably severely injured from a previous bout with Max Baer five months prior. With regards to the Braddock fight, Baer was concerned he would hurt him. More details about this are included in the endnotes.(19)

Considine's character affixes the emotions of *Cinderella Man* going into the finale, and recenters the story onto Renée Zellweger. A nice touch is that Considine's wife is played by Rosemarie DeWitt, who is the real life granddaughter of James and Mae Braddock. The fictional wife/widow becomes a cinematic refrain for Zellweger throughout the final act of *Cinderella Man*. Rosemarie DeWitt is in all black at her husband's mass graveside burial, and that becomes the image Renée Zellweger mentally imposes on herself. As much as the film is about Russell Crowe, *Cinderella Man* allows for Zellweger to have an influential role in the finale of the film. By the final prizefight, we already know the rhythmic banter between Crowe and Giamatti. Akin to Jennifer Connelly in *A Beautiful Mind*, Renée Zellweger takes ownership of the narrative. Her increasing distress about Crowe getting hurt, going to church and her insistence that the children aren't exposed to boxing, shifts our perspective of the finale and wants us to view the championship bout from Zellweger's perspective. *Cinderella Man* won't allow the final match to proceed until Zellweger visits her husband at the venue.

***

During production of *Cinderella Man*, the concept was brought up that a "fairy tale" is only a "fairy tale" for everyone hearing the story – but never those who are living through it. The body of inspirational work by Ron Howard truly lives up to this: we are given lessons in courage and inspiration from various "fairy tales" we're enthralled by watching, but would never want to experience ourselves.

For all the analytical auteur theory we've gone through, not counting all that we've omitted, the inspiration bestowed to us through Ron Howard movies is the crowning achievement of his films.

ACKNOWLEDGEMENTS

Let me start at the very beginning: thank you Ron Howard. I was eleven years old when I saw both *Apollo 13* and *How the Grinch Stole Christmas* during the Fall of 2000. Although I wasn't aware that both of those films were made by you, they had a significant influence on an impressionable youth and undoubtedly influenced my lifelong love affair with filmmaking. During the elongated time it took me to complete this book, I took inspiration from the Dutch angles in *How the Grinch Stole Christmas*, and the rule of repeating information three times from *Apollo 13*, applying those concepts to two separate projects. Ergo, those films are still inspiring me decades later.

Also, I need to thank my Aunt Rita who took me to see *How the Grinch Stole Christmas* that Thanksgiving weekend. I loved it, she didn't.

Skipping ahead to May 2009, I took an Intro to Speech class at a community college (the key words are "community college"), and for my final presentation of the semester I chose the authorship of Ron Howard as my topic. The outline of my talk became my first foray in composing the motifs about Howard's cinema. At the end of my presentation, the professor asked for my sources, but I didn't have any as the concepts were my own. (Oops. Be careful about who's classroom you're allowed to "think freely" in). She couldn't fathom that I came up with these themes without stealing it from someone else, which resulted in an awkward exchange in front of the class. To be clear, she wasn't a tough professor who students respect on account of setting the bar high. She was the typical annoying boomer who… okay, bottom line, I'm acknowledging her for being condescending because that was a helpful catalyst in wanting to write this book.

In May of 2018, I was looking for some extra cash to put a down payment on a car. In the timespan of one week, I was hired by a website to write an article on Ron Howard, and began a simple part-time job in the evenings. I am forever grateful to Lillian Yeh for hiring me at her store at Northbrook Court in Northbrook, Illinois. Not only was it a fun experience for seven months, but it was in that storefront I was able to first undertake a Ron Howard retrospective by popping in DVDs to write that article, and filling up the notebook that would become the first rough draft of this book. (The website I wrote the Ron Howard article for became delinquent on payment for other articles, so they're not getting a shout-out.) And one overdue acknowledgement is warranted to Lillian: that was same job was where I was able to binge read several political books which would influence the writing of my previous book, *Make Hollywood Great Again*.

Now, there's one name on the cover, but it's a tad deceiving because there's always a few key players that were fundamental in getting the book get made, say nothing of the people who get consulted along the way. *The Films of Ron Howard* owes two big acknowledgements to its existence...

I know that aside from this paragraph, Siobhán Regan will probably never read this book, let alone give a rat's ass about film studies – nevertheless, Siobhán was a recurring presence in the assembly of a few books and film endeavors. Towards the end of 2020, when I began writing this book — the same infamous year that, depending on what state you lived in, some libraries couldn't make up their mind about being open or closed — I was in desperate need of an area to work. Luckily, Siobhán managed a "speak easy" that remained open, which was a life saver when in need of a quiet place to pen this book. *The Films of Ron Howard* is the one book that I can honestly say Siobhán helped me out with the most... even though she's rolling her eyes reading this.

Secondly, drummer Bryan Hughey and I first met in summer 2021. A year later we hired Bryan to do some music recording on a production and he instantly became one of our favorites to work with. I had always intended on narrating the audiobook of *The Films of Ron Howard* myself, but Bryan jumped into the audiobook narration business in early 2024, was rather successful right away, and was looking for work. For my writing process, recording the recording of the audiobook is akin to pouring cement and finalizing the manuscript. On account of this, Bryan became the de facto editor through *my* tedious editing process. I cannot emphasize enough how importance Bryan's influence was in helping fine-tune the book.

On the topic of influence, being that books are judged by their covers: a major thanks to Derek Davidson at Photofest Digital who found the cover image after I spent an unusually long time trying to get something suitable. On that note, I need to give a shout out to Photofest's Todd Ifft, who first helped me in the summer of 2013 when looking at cover options for *David Fincher: Interviews*. Over a decade later, Photofest has never failed being a reliable source for a handful of my book's cover pictures.

There are those who helped me periodically along the way, some probably not realizing they were contributing to this book: Dr. Annette Bochenek of *Hometowns to Hollywood*, Laruen Candela, Clint Cottrell, Eric S. Cunningham, Anne Marie Dempsey, Carrie Elko, Mike Wade Johnson, Stevo Nystrom, Marla Seidell and Shuli "SuperShul" Suman.

PRODUCING CREDITS
"PRODUCED BY RON HOWARD"

Ron Howard's authorship extends beyond the films he's directed. In some cases, these are titles that we could potentially see Howard himself directing. The likes of Angelica Jolie in *Changeling* (2008), or Reese Witherspoon in *The Good Lie* (2014) showcase resilient women. We notice the theme of unassuming people with the pressure of the world bearing down on them, such as Andrew Garfield in *tick, tick...BOOM* (2021). The nasty details between the marriage of Lucille Ball and Desi Arnaz are not the focal point of *Lucy & Desi* (2022), rather the documentary seeks to present a poignant love story.

For most of the 1980s and 1990s, we see television endeavors which reflects the industry that Howard spent so much of his youth working in – but into the 2000s he turned his attention to different genres such as children's animation. Mirroring his directorial jump into documentaries, when we get into the 2010s, Howard begins attaching his name to a variety of documentary subjects which grew in popularity with the increase of streaming services during that same era.

Please note: not all the Imagine Entertainment productions are listed here as Howard does not have a producer credit on each of those. Additionally, the films Howard directed are omitted from this listing:

Leo and Loree (1980, Jerry Paris)
Skyward Christmas (1981, Vincnet McEveety) Made-for-TV-Movie
When Your Lover Leaves (1983, Jeff Bleckner) Made-for-TV-Movie
Maximum Security (1984-1985) TV Series
ABC Aftershool Specials (1972-1997) TV Series
Into Thin Air (1985, Roger Yong) Made for TV Movie

The Lone Star Kid (1986, Anson Williams) Made-for-TV- Movie
Take Five (1987) TV Series
No Man's Land (1987, Peter Werner)
Poison (1988) TV Series
Smart Guys (1988) TV Series
The 'Burbs (1989, Joe Dante)
Clean and Sober (1988, Glenn Gordon Carson)
Closet Land (1989, Radha Bharadwaj)
Parenthood (1990-1991) TV Series
The Chamber (1996, James Foley)
Inventing the Abbotts (1997, Pat O'Connor)
Hiller and Diller (1997-1998) TV Series
From the Earth to the Moon (1998) TV-Miniseries
Sports Night (1998-2000) TV Series
Felicity (1998-2001) TV Series
Beyond the Mat (1999, Barry W. Blaustein)
The PJs (1999-2001) TV Series
Student Affairs (1999, Adam Fields, Jordan Fields, Scott Fields) Made-for-TV-Movie
Mulholland Dr. (1999, David Lynch) Made-for-TV-Movie
Wonderland (2000) TV Series
The Beast (2001) TV Series
Silicon Follies (2001, Betty Thomas) Made-for-TV-Movie
The Snobs (2003, Pamela Fryman) Made-for-TV-Movie
The Break (2003, John Stockwell) Made-for-TV-Movie
Arrested Development (2003-2019) TV Series
The Alamo (2004, John Lee Hancock)
Curious George (2006, Matthew O'Callaghan)
Curious George (2006-2015) TV Series
The Inside (2005-2006) TV Series
Changeling (2008, Clint Eastwood)
Curious George 2: Follow That Monkey! (2009, Norton Virgien)
Curious George: A Very Monkey Christmas (2009, Scott Heming, Cathy Malkasian & Jeff McGrath) Made-for-TV-Movie
Parenthood (2010-2015) TV Series
Restless (2011, Gus Van Sant)
Cowboys & Aliens (2011, Jon Favreau)
When You Find Me (2011, Bryce Dallas Howard) Short Film
Katy Perry: Part of Me (2012, Dan Cutforth & Jan Lipsitz)
The Great Escape (2012) TV Series
Susan 313 (2012, Ken Kwapis) Short Film
Curious George Swings Into Action (2013, Scott Heming, Cathy Malkasian & Jeff McGrath) Made-for-TV-Movie

Curious George: A Halloween Boo-Fest (2013, Scott Heming, Andrei Svislotski & Jeff McGrath)
Out of the Blue (2013, Eva Longoria) Short Film
Evermore (2013, Biz Stone) Short Film
Little Duck (2013, James Murphy) Short Film
A Dream of Flying (2013, Georgina Chapman) Short Film
…and She Was My Eve (2013, Jamie Foxx) Short Film
Unsung Heroes: The Story of America's Female Patriots (2014, Frank Martin) Made-for-TV-Movie
The Good Lie (2014, Philippe Falardeau)
Curious George 3: Back to the Jungle (2015, Phil Weinstein)
WTF America (2015, Dan Mazer)
Breakthrough (2015-2016) TV Series
The Dark Tower (2017, Nikolaj Arcel)
Mars (2016-2018) TV Series
Genius (2017-present) TV Series
Once Were Brothers (2019, Daniel Roher)
Backdraft 2 (2019, Gonzalo López-Gallego) Direct-to-Video Movie
Peanuts in Space (2019, Morgan Neville & Behzad Mansoori-Dara) Short Film
Dads (2019, Bryce Dallas Howard)
Curious George: Royal Monkey (2019, Doug Murphy) Made-for-TV-Movie
D. Wade: Life Unexpected (2020, Bob Metelus)
69 Whisky (2020) TV-Series
Curious George: Go West, Go Wild (2020, Michael LaBash) Made-for-TV-Movie
On Pointe (2020) TV Miniseries
The Astronauts (2020-2021) TV Series
We Are: The Brooklyn Saints (2021) TV Miniseries
The Day Sports Stood Still (2021, Antoine Fuqua) Made-for-TV-Movie
Paper & Glue (2021, JR)
Julia (2021, Julie Cohen & Betsey West)
Curious George: Cape Ahoy (2021, Doug Murphy)
tick, tick… BOOM! (2021, Lin-Manuel Miranda)
The Lost Symbol (2021) TV Miniseries
Downfall: The Case Against Boeing (2022, Rory Kennedy)
Crime Scene (2021-present) TV-Series
Lucy and Desi (2022, Amy Poehler)
Under the Banner of Heaven (2022) TV Series
Leave No Trace (2022, Irene Taylor)
Web of Make Believe: Death, Lies and the Internet (2022) TV Series
Light & Magic (2022) TV Miniseries

Wedding Season (2022, Tom Dey)
Louis Armstrong's Black & Blues (2022, Sacha Jenkins)
The Tiny Chef Show (2022-present) TV Series
The Volcano: Rescue from Whakaari (2022, Rory Kennedy)
Personality Crisis: One Night Only (2022, Martin Scorsese & David Tedeschi) Made-for-TV-Movie
Willow (2022) TV Series
Jude Blume Forever (2023, Davina Pardo & Leah Wolchok)
Murf the Surf (2023) TV Series
Bossy Bear (2023-present) TV Series
Tetris (2023, Jon S. Baird)
Bono & The Edge: A Short Homecoming with David Letterman (2023, Morgan Neville)
Carlos (2023, Rudy Valdez)
The Beanie Bubble (2023, Kirsten Gore & Damian Kulash)
Frida (2024, Carla Gutierrez)
Choir (2023-2024) TV Series
The Truth About Jim (2024) TV Miniseries
The Dynasty: New England Patriots (2024) TV Miniseries

IMAGINE ENTERTAINMENT

Founded in November 1985, *Imagine Entertainment* was co-founded by Ron Howard. These are titles that Howard is not credited on, but were produced by *Imagine*:

Gung Ho (1986-1987) TV Series
Like Father Like Son (1987, Rod Daniel)
Ohara (1987-1988) TV Series
Knight & Day (1988) TV Series
Vibes (1988, Ken Kwapis)
The Dream Team (1989, Howard Zieff)
My Talk Show (1990-1991) TV Series
Cry Baby (1990, John Waters)
Opportunity Knocks (1990, Donald Petrie)
Problem Child (1990, Dennis Dugan)
The Doors (1991, Oliver Stone)
Problem Child 2 (1991, Brian Levant)
My Girl (1991, Howard Zieff)
Housesitter (1992, Frank Oz)
Boomerang (1992, Reginald Hudlin)
CB4 (1993, Tamra Davis)
Cop and a Half (1993, Henry Winkler)
For the Love of Money (1993, Barry Sonnenfeld)
My Girl 2 (1994, Howard Zieff)
Greedy (1994, Jonathan Lynn)
The Cowboy Way (1994, Gregg Champion)
Sgt. Bilko (1996, Jonathan Lynn)
Fear (1996, James Foley)
The Nutty Professor (1996, Tom Shadyac)
Liar Liar (1997, Thom Shadyac)
Mercury Rising (1998, Harold Becker)
Psycho (1998, Gus Van Sant)
Life (1999, Ted Demme)
Bowfinger (1999, Frank Oz)
Rat Bastard (2000) TV Series
Nutty Professor II: The Klumps (2000, Peter Segal)

24 (2001-2010) TV Series
Undercover Brother (2002, Malcolm D. Lee)
Blue Crush (2002, John Stockwell)
8 Mile (2002, Curtis Hanson)
Miss Match (2003) TV Series
The Cat in the Hat (2003, Bo Welch)
The Big House (2004) TV Series
Quintuplets (2004-2005) TV Series
Friday Night Lights (2004, Peter Berg)
Inside Deep Throat (2005, Fenton Bailey & Randy Barbato)
Flightplan (2005, Robert Schwentke)
Fun with Dick and Jane (2005, Dean Parisot)
Saved (2006) TV Series
Treasure Hunters (2006) TV Series
Shark (2006-2008) TV Series
Inside Man (2006, Spike Lee)
Friday Night Lights (2006-2011) TV Series
American Gangster (2007, Ridley Scott)
24: Redemption (2008, Jon Cassar) Made-for-TV-Movie
Lie to Me (2009-2011) TV Series
Robin Hood (2010, Ridley Scott)
Take Me Home Tonight (2011, Michael Dowse)
Friends with Benefits (2011) TV Series
The Playboy Club (2011) TV Series
Tower Heist (2011, Brett Ratner)
J. Edgar (2011, Clint Eastwood)
The Great Escape (2012) TV Series
How to Live with Your Parents (For the Rest of Your Life) (2013) TV Series
Those Who Kill (2014) TV Series
Get On Up (2014, Tate Taylor)
24: Live Another Day (2014) TV Miniseries
Gang Related (2014) TV Series
Empire (2015-2020) TV Series
Prophet's Prey (2015, Amy J. Berg)
The Bastard Executioner (2015) TV Series
Kindergarten Cop 2 (2016, Don Michael Paul) Direct-to-Video
Lowriders (2016, Ricardo de Montreuil)
24: Legacy (2016-2017) TV Series
American Made (2017, Doug Liman)
The Spy Who Dumped Me (2018, Susanna Fogel)
Inside Man 2: Most Wanted (2019, M.J. Bassett) Direct-to-Video
Undercover Brother 2 (2019, Leslie Small) Direct-to-Video

Why Women Kill (2019-2021) TV Series
Wu-Tang: An American Saga (2019-2023) TV Series
Filthy Rich (2020) TV Series
John Bronco (2020, Jake Szymanski) Short Film
Supervillain: The Making of Tekashi 6ix9ine (2021) TV Miniseries
Gossip (2021) TV Miniseries
John Bronco Rides Again (2021, Jonathan Krisel) Short Film
Swagger (2021-2023) TV Series
Coded (2021, Ryan White) Short Film
The Ms. Pat Show (2023-present) TV Series
The Super Models (2023) TV Series
The Slumber Party (2023, Veronica Rodriguez) Made-for-TV-Movie
Taiwan Crime Stories (2023) TV Series
Candy Cane Lane (2023, Reginald Hudlin)
Stormy (2024, Sarah Gibson)

ENDNOTES

1 - BEFORE THE DEBUT

1. This quote was slightly edited for easier reading.
   "Ron Howard on becoming a director – EMMYTVLEGENDS.ORG" *FoundationINTERVIEWS* YouTube channel. July 19, 2010.
2. Ron Howard & Clint Howard. *The Boys: A Memoir of Hollywood and Family*. William Morrow. 2021.
3. Beverly Gray. *Ron Howard: Form Mayberry to the Moon…and Beyond*. Rutledge Hill Press. 2003.
4. Ibid. (2).
5. "Ron Howard: Clint's addiction, 47+ years of marriage and rejected by George Lucas." Graham Bensinger YouTube channel. August 23, 2023.
6. The Nielsen Ratings for *Happy Days* were as follows: 16th place for the first season (1973-1974); did not place for the second season (1974-1975); 11th place for the third season (1975-1976); 1st place for the fourth season (1976-1977); 2nd place for the fifth season (1977-1978); tied 3rd place with *Mork & Mindy* for the sixth season (1978-1979); 17th place for the seventh season (1979-1980); tied 15th place with *Too Close for Comfort* for the eight season (1980-1981); 18th place for the ninths season (1981-1982); 28th place for the tenth season (1982-1983); did not place for the eleventh and final season.
   Wikipedia entry: Top-rated United States television programs by season.
7. Ibid. (3).
8. Leonard Maltin interview with Roger Corman.
   Roger Corman's Cult Classics Double Feature – The Ron Howard Action Pack. Eat My Dust! and *Grand Theft Auto* 2 Disc Set. DVD, 2011.
9. Ibid. (2).
10. To quote Howard from *The Boys* directly:
    "When my seven year contract was up, I didn't rule out staying on with *Happy Days* for a little longer. ABC offered me a financially generous new deal. But I had recently made the acquaintance of a remarkable NBC executive named Deanna Barkley… Deanna had been impressed by *Grand Theft Auto* and believed in me as a fledgling director. Through her, I struck up an informal relationship with NBC that lead me to produce and direct three modestly budgeted family-friendly television movies over the next three years, all made while *Happy Days* was on hiatus… But doing those films helped me further hone my chops and build my confidence as a director. So, when ABC and were in negotiations to stay on *Happy Days*, I asked them if their offer could be amended to include the opportunity to direct some TV movies and, perhaps, a feature for Paramount, our parent company. They turned down this request. The response I received was, 'We're happy to hear your ideas. But we don't

make blind deals like that.' NBC on the other hand, offered me a straight producing and directing deal for three more TV films, a series pilot, and partial financing for a feature film. No acting required. The financial guarantees were paltry compared to ABC's. Paramount's chief of TV, Gary Nardino, couldn't believe I was contemplating NBC's offer. 'Ron,' he said, 'did you do the math?' I had. But at that point, I knew where my heart lay."
Ibid. (2).

2 - AUTHORSHIP

1. "The Human Face of Depression." Documentary.
   Cinderella Man. 2-Disc Collector's Edition. DVD, 2005.
2. This quote has been slightly edited for easier reading.
   The Missing Widescreen Special Edition. DVD, 2003.
3. Daniel Schweiger. *Passion and Achievements: A 20-year Retrospective of Soundtracks from the Films of Director Ron Howard.* Milan Records. 1997.

3 - NEVER MAKING THE SAME FILM TWICE

1. Ron Howard & Clint Howard. *The Boys: A Memoir of Hollywood and Family.* William Morrow. 2021.
2. This quote has been slightly edited for easier reading.
   "Ron Howard Shares His Personal Connection to 'Rebuilding Paradise' and Tom Hanks | FULL INTERVIEW" IMDb YouTube Channel. January 24, 2020.
3. *Making a Splash.* Documentary, directed by Barbara J. Toennis. Buena Vista Home Entertainment.
   Splash 20th Anniversary. DVD, 2004.
4. Wilford Brimley favored improvisation. For the fishing scene in which he tells his grandson, Barret Oliver, that he's leaving with the aliens, Brimley offered to improv the entire scene, which he did a few times. A combination of all the different takes is what's used in the film.
   Audio-commentary with Ron Howard.
   Cocoon. DVD, 2004
5. Ibid. (4).
6. Salvatore Totino shot *The Missing*; *Cinderella Man*; *The Da Vinci Code*; *Frost/Nixon*; *Angles & Demons*; *The Dilemma*; *Made in America* and *Inferno*. The only other cinematographer Howard came close to collaborating with as much was Donald Peterman on *Splash*; *Cocoon*; *Gung Ho* and *How the Grinch Stole Christmas*.
7. "Ron Howard Interview The Beatles Eight Days A Week Documentary." Red Carpet News TV YouTube channel. August 2, 2016.
8. This is addressed in two interviews:
   "Pavarotti: Ron Howard on the 'unbelievability charismatic' subject of his new documentary." CBS Morning YouTube channel. May 28, 2019.
   "The life and legacy of opera star Luciano Pavarotti, according to Ron Howard." PBS Newshour YouTube channel. June 20, 2019.

4 - AGAINST ALL ODDS

1. Audio-commentary with Ron Howard.
   Cocoon. DVD, 2004.
2. Beverly Gray. *Ron Howard: From Mayberry to the Moon… and Beyond*. Rutledge Hill Press. 2003.
3. The idea is expressed in both Rick Stanton's and John Volanthen's books.
   Rick Stanton with Karen Dealy. *Aquanaut: A Life Beneath the Surface*. Pegasus Books. January 2022.
   John Volanthen. *Thirteen Lessons That Saved Thirteen Lives*. Aurum Press. July 2021.
4. In the film, Pattarakorn Tangsupakul gives the blessed bracelets to Colin Farrell who gives them to Viggo Mortensen. He refuses to take them, but Farrell insists, indicating that Tangsupakul is watching. Mortensen reluctantly does so. In actuality, Rick Stanton's girlfriend, Amp, gave him a package of beaded bracelets for the boys, blessed by a Buddhist monk, and he tossed it on the ground declaring he wasn't taking them. Amp insisted saying that the significance of the bracelets would mean something to the boys and lift their morale. This incident is noted in both Stanton's book, *Aquanaut* and the documentary, *The Rescue* (2021).
   The Rescue. Directed by Elizabeth Chai Vasarhelyi and Jimmy Chin. National Geographic Documentary Films, Ventureland, Storyteller Productions, Little Monster Films, & Passion Pictures.
   Ibid. (3).

5 - THE COMMON INDIVIDUAL

1. Jeremy Schapp. *Cinderella Man: James J. Braddock, Max Baer, and the Greatest Upset in Boxing History*." Houghton Mifflin Company. 2005.
2. This quote was edited for easier reading.
   "Morf to Morphing: The Dawn of Digital Filmmaking." Documentary. *Willow* Special Edition. DVD, 2001.
3. Audio-commentary with Ron Howard.
   How the Grinch Stole Christmas Grinchmas Edition. BluRay, 2015.
4. Ibid. (3).
5. Ibid. (3).
6. "Who School." Documentary.
   Ibid. (3).
7. Ibid. (3).
8. Frank Capra's most popular films that champion this concept include *Lady for a Day* (1933); *Mr. Deeds Goes to Town* (1936); *Mr. Smith Goes to Washington* (1939); *Meet John Doe* (1941); *It's A Wonderful Life* (1946) and *State of the Union* (1948).

6 - ROMANCE

1. According to Philbrick's book: "Chase chose to remain on-island for the birth of his next child, a son – Owen's wife, Peggy did not recover from the delivery. She died less than two weeks later." Owen Chase would

remarry nine months later. This part of the story was omitted from the film.
Nathanial Philbrick. *In the Heart of the Sea: The Tragedy of the Whaleship Essex*. Viking Press & Penguin Books. May 2000.
2. "A Look at Langdon." Documentary.
Inferno. DVD, 2017.
3. Jeremy Schapp. *Cinderella Man: James J. Braddock, Max Baer, and the Greatest Upset in Boxing History*." Houghton Mifflin Company. 2005.
4. Each of the three audio commentaries on the *Cinderella Man* 2 Disc Collector's Edition acknowledge that the kids being sent away was a questionable topic. Ron Howard mentions that Mae had made statements eluding to it, but was cagy regarding the subject. Akiva Goldsman said it came from an "accidental" sentence that one of the Braddock children said. Cliff Hollingsworth said that he never found evidence of it in his research and that one of the kids and a close family friend denied it.
Audio-commentary with Ron Howard.
Audio-commentary with Akiva Goldsman.
Audio-commentary with Cliff Hollingsworth.
Cinderella Man 2-Disc Collector's Edition. DVD, 2005.
5. Ibid. (4).
6. Ibid. (4).

7 - STRONG FEMININE CHARACTERS

1. Beverly Gray. *Ron Howard: From Mayberry to the Moon... and Beyond*. Rutledge Hill Press. 2003.
2. Daniel Schweiger. *Passion and Achievements: A 20-yearRetrospective of Soundtracks from the Films of Director Ron Howard*. Milan Records. 1997.
3. *How the Grinch Stole Christmas* grossed $346.5-million dollars in the U.S. box office. Even when adjusting all his directorial features for inflation, *The Grinch* still remains at the top for the U.S. box office.
4. Introduction by Thomas Eidson to 2003 republishing.
Thomas Eidson. *The Last Ride*. Originally published in 1995. Reissued as *The Missing* by Random House Trade Paperbacks. 2003.
5. Ibid. (4).
6. Audio-commentary with Ron Howard.
The Missing Extended Cut. DVD, 2006.
7. Ibid. (6).

8 - PARTNERSHIP/DUALITY: OPPOSITES ATTRACT

1. Audio-commentary with Ron Howard.
How the Grinch Stole Christmas Grinchmas Edition. BluRay, 2015.
2. "Ron Howard, J.D. Vance discuss new film "Hillbilly Elegy," relevance in current climate." CBS Mornings YouTube channel. December 1, 2020.
3. Audio-commentary with Ron Howard.
Frost/Nixon. DVD, 2009.
4. Ibid. (3).

9 - FAMILY

1. "Ron Howard: Clint's addiction, 47+ years of marriage and rejected by George Lucas." Graham Bensinger YouTube channel. August 23, 2023.
2. Audio-commentary with Ron Howard.
   Ransom 15th Anniversary Edition. BluRay, 2011.
3. Laurence F. Knapp. *Directed by Clint Eastwood: Eighteen Films Analyzed.* McFarland Publishing. 1996.
4. According to Beverly Gray's book: "Carrey's enthusiasm for the *Grinch* project clinched Howard's desire to direct it. 'I wanted a front row seat for this one,' he declared."
   Beverly Gray. *Ron Howard: From Mayberry to the Moon... and Beyond.* Rutledge Hill Press. 2003.
5. Ibid. (2).
6. Ibid. (2).
7. Ibid. (2).
8. Daniel Schweiger. *Passions and Achievements: A 20-Year Retrospective of Soundtracks from the Films of Director Ron Howard.* Milan Records. 1997.

10 - THE ENSEMBLE CAST

1. "The Making of *Frost/Nixon*." Documentary.
   Frost/Nixon. DVD, 2009.
2. Beverly Gray. *Ron Howard: From Mayberry to the Moon... and Beyond.* Rutledge Hill Press. 2003.
3. Audio-commentary with Lowell Ganz, Brian Grazer, Ron Howard and Babaloo Mandel.
   Splash DVD. 2001.
4. Ibid. (2).
5. Audio-commentary with Ron Howard.
   Cocoon DVD, 2004.
6. Ibid. (5).
7. Ron Howard & Clint Howard. *The Boys: A Memoir of Hollywood and Family.* William Morrow. 2021.
8. Steven Spielberg on the ending of *Close Encounters of the Third Kind*: "Twenty years later I look at my movie and I see a lot of naiveté, and I see my youth, and I see my blind optimism, and I see how I've changed. I see how little less optimistic the older I get only because I'm dealing with seven children in a very practical world, with practical decisions and things that have to be done 'on time.' I'm now a movie producer as well as a director, where as in 1975 or 76 I was just a director and I was more idealistic them. So I look at *Close Encounters* and I see a very sweet idealistic odyssey about a man who gives up everything in pursuit of his dreams, or his obsession. In 1997 I would never of made *Close Encounters* the way I did in 1977 because I have a family that would never leave. I would never drive my family out of house and home, and build a paper mache mountain in the den, and then furtherly then to get

into a spaceship, perhaps never return to them. I mean, that was just the privileges of youth! When I see *Close Encounters*, it's the one film I see that dates me, that I really look back and see who I was twenty years ago compared to who I am now."
Making of Close Encounters of the Third Kind. Documentary, directed by Laurent Bouzereau.
Close Encounters of the Third Kind. DVD, 2001.
9. Ibid. (5).
10. This fact was provided by Dr. Annette Bochenek of *Hometowns to Hollywood*.
11. Ibid. (2).
12. Edward Zwick introduction to *Love & Other Drugs*. Advance screening at AMC River East. Chicago, Illinois. October 5th, 2010.
13. "Caught in the Camera's Eye." Documentary.
EDtv Collector's Edition. DVD, 1999.

11 - AUTOMOTIVE, DECEPTION, MUSIC & RELIGION

1. Beverly Gray. *Ron Howard: From Mayberry to the Moon… and Beyond*. Rutledge Hill Press. 2003.
2. Alvin O. Turner. "Cherokee Outlet Opening." Oklahoma Historical Society.
3. "Ron Howard Introduction." Documentary.
Backdraft: Anniversary Edition. BluRay, 2011.
4. Daniel Schweiger. *Passions and Achievements: A 20-Year Retrospective of Soundtracks from the Films of Director Ron Howard*. Milan Records. 1997.
5. Peter Katz. "After the Accident: A Titanic Tragedy." *Plane & Pilot*. March 22nd, 2019.
6. This quote has been slightly edited for easier reading.
Classic FM. "Ron Howard's tribute to film composer James Horner." October 14th, 2016.
7. This quote has been edited for easier reading.
"James Horner Interview for 'Enemy the Gates' (*sic*) (Charlie-Rose-2001-03-01) PBS." Arquivos da Internet YouTube Channel. March 11th, 2023.
8. Considering that the 3-Disc BluRay set of *The Amazing Spider-Man* was released in early November 2012, and this quote came from a YouTube video that was uploaded approximately one month after the release of the multi-disc BluRay set, it's likely that this originated from a behind-the-scenes bonus feature on the BluRay. This quote has been taken from two bits in the featurette.
"James Horner: Scoring Spider-Man (HD)." Nick197 YouTube Channel. December 3rd, 2012.
9. David Hocquet. "Conversation with James Horner." *James Horner Film Music Association*. December 5th, 2014.
10. Ibid. (4).
11. Ron Howard brings this up a few different times over the years.

Ron Howard & Clint Howard. *The Boys: A Memoir of Hollywood and Family*. William Morrow. 2021.
"Ron Howard: Clint's addiction, 47+ years of marriage and rejected by George Lucas." Graham Bensinger YouTube channel. August 23, 2023.

12. Audio-commentary with Cliff Hollingsworth.
    Cinderella Man 2-Disc Collector's Edition. DVD, 2005.
13. This concept can be found in the book, *The Da Vinci Deception* where the authors credit it from the *Salon* periodical.
    Mark Shea, Edward Sri and Editors of the Catholic Exchange. *The Da Vinci Deception: 100 Questions About the Facts and Fiction of The Da Vinci Code*. Ascension Press. 2006.
    Laura Miller. "The Da Vinci crock." *Salon*. December 29th, 2004.
14. *The Da Vinci Code* Extended Cut 2-Dics Set. BluRay, 2009.
15. Ibid. (13).
16. "A Look at Langdon." Documentary.
    Inferno. DVD, 2017.
17. Audio-commentary with Ron Howard.
    Apollo 13. 4K Ultra HD, 2017.

12 - AUTHENTICITY

1. Ron Howard & Clint Howard. *The Boys: A Memoir of Hollywood and Family*. William Morrow. 2021.
2. This is recorded in both books.
   Beverly Gray. *Ron Howard: From Mayberry to the Moon... and Beyond*. Rutledge Hill Press. 2003.
   Ibid. (1).
3. "The Beatles Q and A from Abby Road Studios." The Beatles YouTube Channel. September 17th, 2016.
4. Although not every single reference was checked for this, it appears to have first come up in summer 2023 with Ron. With the release of *Argylle* in early 2024, in which Bryce had the leading role, she was asked directly about this incident and offers a few more details.
   "Ron Howard: Clint's addiction, 47+ years of marriage and rejected by George Lucas." Graham Bensinger YouTube channel. August 23, 2023.
   Andrea Mandell. "Bryce Dallas Howard Is 'Hyper Alert' as a Parent After Coping with Kidnapping Threats as a Child." *People*. February 2, 2024.
5. *The Orson Wells Show* was never broadcast or released in its entirety. It was a 78-minute pilot that also included Burt Reynolds. Ironically, it was shot by Gary Graver, the same cinematographer Howard had for *Grand Theft Auto* and *Through the Magic Pyramid*.
6. In the U.S. box office, *Apollo 13* is surpassed by *How the Grinch Stole Christmas*; *The Da Vinci Code* and *Solo: A Star Wars Story* (not adjusting for inflation). In the worldwide box office, those titles, plus *Angels & Demons* surpass *Apollo 13*'s standing. As of June 2024, on IMDb, the number of user votes that surpass *Apollo 13* by the hundreds of thousands include *Solo: A Star Wars Story*; *The Da Vinci Code*; *Rush* and *A Beautiful Mind*. Of all Howard's films, including the three made-for-tv

titles, *Apollo 13* has the sixth best score at 7.7 out of 10.0. The titles that rank higher are *Eight Days A Week* (7.8); *Thirteen Lives* (7.8); *Cinderella Man* (8.0); *Rush* (8.1); *A Beautiful Mind* (8.2). As of June 2024, on Rotten Tomatoes, *Apollo 13* has a critics score of 96% which is the fourth best score of Howard's directorial features. It is tied with *Eight Days A Week* (96%), and surpassed by *We Feed People* (100%), and *Jim Henson: Idea Man* (100%). *Apollo 13*'s audience score on Rotten Tomatoes is at 87% and is surpassed by *Rush* (88%), *Frost/Nixon* (88%); *Eight Days A Week* (89%); *Cinderella Man* (91%); *Jim Henson: Idea Man* (91%); *A Beautiful Mind* (93%); *Thirteen Lives* (94%) and *Pavarotti* (97%). Finally, *Apollo 13* has a PG rating by the Motion Picture Association of America, which slightly increases the film's accessibility to younger viewers.

7. A detailed account of the Apollo 1 launch pad fire, explosion and investigation can be found in the following books:
Jim Lovell & Jeffrey Kluger. *Lost Moon: Apollo 13: The Perilous Voyage of Apollo 13*. Reissued as *Apollo 13* by Pocket Books. 1995.
James R. Hansen. *First Man: The Life of Neil A. Armstrong*. Simon & Schuster Paperbacks. 2005.

8. Because *Apollo 13* has been lauded as one of the most historical accurate movies of all time, it's worth looking at the changes made to the film as an example in adaptation for narrative structure:
- Jim Lovell watched the *Apollo 11* moon landing from Mission Control, not at his house. This was changed as a way to introduce all the characters in the opening act of the film.
- The astronauts were not worried about Jack Swigert (Kevin Bacon) being able to dock, specifically because Lovell or Hayes could do it if Swigert couldn't. The film added that scene to emphasize how foreign it was for Swigert to be added to the mission so late in the game. In actuality, they didn't have time to run anymore simulations.
- The scene the night before the launch did not take place outside near the launch site. A version of that did occur, but the film set it with the rocket in the background for the sake of artistic stage direction.
- While it is true that Marilyn Lovell's wedding ring slipped off in the shower and went down the drain the morning of the launch, she did eventually retrieve it. She also stayed in a private beach house – not a motel.
- During liftoff, Gary Sinise is parked alone watching from an isolated grassy patch. No one would be allowed that close to the rocket for take-off; this change was made to emphasize Ken Mattingly's (Sinise's) lost moment.
- Using the stars as navigation was a keyway in which Lovell could have used to steer the spacecraft, however due to the oxygen leak they were unable to do so. Additionally, the science of reading the stars to navigate would have been too complicated to articulate on film, so that element of the story was dropped from the movie.
- There were actually several burns that took place, but the film only shows the last one. In that scene, the concept of Lovell (Hanks) keeping the Earth in the window was entirely made up as a way to give the

audience a clearer visual idea of what the burns consisted of. The windows would have been directed away from the Earth.

- Ken Mattingly (Gary Sinise) becomes a bit of a composite character in the second half of the film. Although he did run flight sims and was instrumental in bringing the three astronauts home, there were many others working on the dilemma of conserving amps.

- The joke about Jack Swigert giving them "the clap" was fictional; it was added just to give character development.

- The argument between the three of them never took place, however both Ron Howard and Jim Lovell admit "artistic license" for the scene as a way to show the tensions that were bubbling inside all of them. They decided to go with the scene because those stressful tensions needed to be presented to the audience in some way.

9. Examples of films that change history for the sake of improving the emotion include *Captain Phillips* (2013), in which Phillips actually spent hours tied up and beat up by the pirates — whereas in the film, this torture is condensed into about 10-minutes of horror. Richard Phillips said that although the play-by-play of his captivity was altered, the film encompassed the tension of the harrowing situation perfectly. In *Lone Survivor* (2013), Navy SEAL Marcus Luttrell spent more days in hiding that implied in the film, however the movie sped up events for the sake of suspense. Howard's *Frost/Nixon* and *Thirteen Lives* also does this: when comparing to the actual interviews between David Frost and Richard Nixon to the film, they are not an exact re-creation. However, the intensity between Michael Sheen and Frank Langella's exchanges are for the sake of conveying the emotions between the two men. *Thirteen Lives* has a brilliant simplification: on Viggo Mortensen & Colin Farrell's first dive, they find one worker stranded in a chamber. In actuality, Rick Stanton and John Volanthen found four workers and had to swim all four of them out. All four of the Thai workers had difficulty with the short dive as depicted through the one worker in the film.

10. Audio-commentary with Ron Howard.
    Apollo 13. 4K Ultra HD, 2017.
11. Daniel Schweiger. *Passion and Achievements: A 20-yearRetrospective of Soundtracks from the Films of Director Ron Howard*. Milan Records. 1997.
12. Audio-commentary with Ron Howard.
    A Beautiful Mind The Two-Disc Awards Edition. DVD, 2002.
13. Cliff Hollingsworth and Akiva Goldsman. *The Shooting Script: Cinderella Man*. Newmarket Press. 2005.
14. Ibid. (1).
15. Audio-commentary with Akiva Goldsman.
    Cinderella Man 2-Disc Collector's Edition. DVD, 2005.
16. Jeremy Schapp. *Cinderella Man: James J. Braddock, Max Baer, and the Greatest Upset in Boxing History*." Houghton Mifflin Company. 2005.
17. Ibid. (13).
18. Ibid. (16).

19. Akin to *Apollo 13*, on account of understanding cinematic accuracy, it's worth looking at the changes made to *Cinderella Man* to help understand narrative structure for historical accuracy:
    - Accounts of Jimmy Johnston's relationship with James J. Braddock are mixed between Johnston being dismissive towards him, or Johnston having a fondness for him. The displeasure Johnston (Bruce McGill) shown towards Braddock (Crowe) in the movie was increased. Johnston also became a semi-composite character in the movie; there were other boxing commissioners involved in the decision making of the other various bouts.
    - During the events in the film, the kids were much younger. They were all increased in age by approximately 3 or 4 years in the movie.
    - Braddock actually got paid $300 for the Abe Feldman fight (which would be over $7,000 in mid-2020s), but they changed it to nothing in the film to stress how little money Braddock was making at boxing at that point of his career.
    - Braddock did go to the boxing offices at Madison Square Garden when he was completely broke, although according to Jeremy Schaap's biography, *Cinderella Man*, Braddock went looking for Joe Gould. According to the book, Gould went away and came back with money from Johnston, whom expected he would never see that money returned. The scene of Braddock (Russell Crowe) with his hat-in-hand in the lounge offices seems to be artistic license.
    - The foreman was probably aware of Braddock's broken hand and Braddock didn't try to hide it. Nevertheless, Braddock still went out of his way to prove he could work with it being broken. It did in fact strengthen his other arm.
    - They don't think that Mae Braddock and Jim Gould's wife, Lucille, had a cordial relationship like the one they are shown having over tea in the film.
    - Similar to *Apollo 13*, they took little scraps of information and repackaged it in the film: when John Henry Lewis (played by Troy Ross) says "He ain't the same guy.", that line was said by Lewis after the fight, but they moved it into the boxing match for the film.
    - Braddock's mouthpiece never flew out of his mouth during his bout with Art Lasky.
    - The footage of Max Baer knocking-out Frankie Campbell doesn't exist. They recreated it for the film to emphasize the concern that there was for Braddock's life at the time. Additionally, Baer was very distraught after Campbell's death, apologized to Campbell's wife at the hospital, and was reported to have wept inconsolably. Baer was charged with manslaughter but was acquitted. A lot of the blame was shifted to the boxing commission and the referees for not stopping the fight. Baer's children said that the death of Frankie Campbell haunted their father throughout his life.
    - Max Baer was concern he would hurt Braddock prior to their Heavy Weight fight. Baer was 26 at the time and Braddock was 30; that age difference gave many a reason to be concerned.

- The punches in the final fight don't match up exactly between Baer and Braddock.
- There is no documentation of what Max Baer said to James J. Braddock in the ring during their match, however in the footage you can see Baer speaking. Additionally, Baer was known to say things in the ring to get into the heads of his opponents.
- Mae Braddock was listening to the fight on the radio in Guttenberg, New Jersey with her mother. The kids were not hiding away listening in a closet. In fact, the children were asleep and when Braddock won, and they didn't want to wake them with the celebratory excitement.
- The title/turtles confusion with the kids did happen, but Braddock said that in an interview *after* the Max Baer fight. In the film he's shown saying this in a press conference before the fight. It allows the film to circle back to the turtles in the ending montage.

INDEX

3:10 to Yuma, 89

Abbott, Bud, 134
Abortion, 111, 112, 119, 218
About Last Night... (1986 film), 178
Academy Award, 23-31, 35, 37, 121
Ace Ventura, 98
Adams, Amy, 37, 191
Affleck, Ben, 222
Allen, Woody, 14, 28, 50, 161, 181
Almodóvar, Pedro, 50
Always, 124
Ameche, Don, 23, 68, 171
American Broadcasting Corporation (ABC), 45, 245, 253, 254
American Gangster, 89, 250
American Graffiti, 39, 170
Anchorman, 50
Andy Griffith Show, The, 14, 39, 64, 139, 173, 222
Anderson, Paul Thomas, 222
Anderson, Wes, 50, 188, 213
Angels & Demons (book), 31, 205
Angels & Demons (2009 film), 13, 14, 18, 31, 51, 81, 90, 191, 194, 199, 202, 204-208, 213, 259
Annie Hall, 106
Antisemitism, 140
Any Given Sunday, 71
Apache, 128, 130, 131, 200
Apollo 1, 226, 260
Apollo 11, 260
Apollo 13 (1995 film), 26, 51, 53, 54, 58, 59, 61, 69, 72, 81-85, 98, 113, 114, 121, 162, 173, 174, 186, 187, 199, 210, 211, 218, 225-233, 241, 259-262
Appalachian, 141, 142
Argo (2012 film), 223
Arizona, 126
Armageddon, 50, 207
Aronofsky, Darren, 14 45, 46, 70
Asztalos, Owen, 37, 192
Austin, Jane, 63
Australia, 127

Aviator, The, 77
Away We Go, 70

Babylon (2022 film), 223
Backdraft, 17, 25, 44, 61, 69, 98, 106, 133, 160, 167, 174, 191-193, 195, 216, 218, 220, 258
Bacon, Kevin, 27, 31, 143, 144, 210, 225, 260
Badlands, 44, 49
Baer, Max, 238, 255, 256, 261-263
Baldwin, William, 25, 106, 133, 174, 192
Baños, Roque, 34, 188
Basso, Gabriel, 37, 56, 100, 141, 192
Bateman, Tom, 38, 86, 87
Bay, Michael, 50
Beatles, The, 34, 72-75, 102, 159, 164, 209, 254, 259
Beatles: Eight Days A Week – The Touring Years, The, (see "*Eight Days A Week – The Touring Years*")
Beautiful Mind, A, 28, 29, 56, 78, 89, 100, 121-124, 140, 141, 159, 185, 191, 215-217, 221, 239, 259-261
Bert & Ernie, 134, 222
Bettany, Paul, 29, 30, 35, 189, 203, 204, 207, 216
Bierko, Craig, 30, 237
Big Short, The, (2015 film), 50, 234
Bigelow, Kathryn, 14
Black, Shirley Temple, 173
Black Swan, 70, 78
Blanchett, Cate, 29, 70, 125-128, 130, 131, 133, 159, 200
Blaze, Billy, (character), 137, 138
Bogdanovich, Peter, 41
Boogie Nights,
Boston, 105
Boyd, Jenna, 29, 126-128, 200
Boys, The (memoir), 16, 40, 42, 46, 65, 173, 222, 253-255, 257-259
Braddock, James J., 52, 54, 89, 107, 165, 201, 234, 237-239, 255, 256, 261-263
Braddock, Jay, 107
Braddock, Mae, 52, 107, 165, 235
Broderick, Matthew, 234
Braveheart, 91, 162

Breakfast Club, The, 82
Brenan, Jack, 144
Brimley, Wilford, 23, 68, 171, 214, 254
Bringing Out the Dead, 124
British Film Institute (BFI), 18
Brown, Dan, 30, 31, 35, 51, 71, 201, 202, 208
Brühl, Daniel, 33, 100, 113, 144-147, 184
Buddhist, 209, 211, 255
Bullock, Sandra, 41
Burns, Ken, 218
Burton, Tim, 50, 194, 223

C-3P0, 134
Cameron, James, 41, 197
Camerlengo, 205-207
Campbell, Frankie, 238, 262
Candy, John, 23, 60, 67, 103
Capone, 77
Capra, Frank, 49, 218, 255
Captain Phillips, 58, 113, 261
Cardone, Vivien, 29, 216
Carrey, Jim, 28, 74, 81, 98-101, 114, 123, 124, 133, 155, 159, 161, 180, 215, 216, 257
Casablanca, 106
Catholic, 203, 259
Changing Lanes, 71
Chase, Peggy, 101, 255
Chase, Owen, 101, 255
Chazelle, Damien, 223
Chewbacca, 56
Christianity, 60, 199-201, 204, 206
Cinderella Man, 30, 44, 52-54, 59, 70, 74, 78, 82, 85, 89, 93, 105-110, 114, 133, 134, 140, 143, 146, 165, 173, 193, 199-201, 221, 226, 233-239, 254-256, 259-262
Civil War (American), 186, 234
Civil Rights Movement, 234
Clarke, Emilia, 133, 189, 191
Cleveland, 73
Close Encounters of the Third Kind, 49, 168-170, 172, 178, 257, 258
Close, Glenn, 26, 37, 177, 178, 214, 215
Coca-Cola, 94, 95

Cocoon, 23, 52, 57, 66-68, 70, 79-81, 106, 114, 120, 139, 159, 168-172, 193, 196, 199, 214, 218, 254, 255, 257
Coen Brothers, The, 14
Conversations with Filmmaker series, 18
Connelly, Jennifer, 29, 32, 38, 56, 109, 110, 112, 121-124, 217, 239
Considine, Paddy, 30, 108, 109, 236-239
Cookie Monster, 223
Coppola, Francis Ford, 14, 41, 49
Corman, Roger, 21, 41-43, 45, 196, 253
Cosby, Bill, 173
Costello, Lou, 134
Costner, Kevin, 90
Cotton Candy, 21, 45, 46, 101, 102, 114, 167
COVID, (see "Wuhan Coronavirus")
Cronenberg, David, 213
Cronyn, Hume, 23, 52, 59, 68, 171
Crowe, Russell, 29, 30, 52, 56, 59, 70, 74, 78, 89, 93, 100, 105, 107, 108, 114, 121-124, 133, 141, 143, 191, 200, 201, 215-217, 221, 226, 235-239, 262
Cruise, Tom, 26, 55, 56, 70, 100, 104-106, 127, 133, 161, 162, 186, 215
Cruz, Penélope, 50

Da Vinci Code, The, (book), 30, 140, 202
Da Vinci Code, The, (2006 film), 17, 30, 51, 60, 64, 93, 101, 140, 159, 175, 185, 191, 195, 199, 201-205, 207-209, 218, 221, 254, 259
Da Vinci, Leonardo, 203
Dances with Wolves, 186
Dante, Joe, 21, 41, 246
Davis, Warwick, 24, 90, 92, 93, 100, 238
Das Boot, 61
Days of Heaven, 49
De Niro, Robert, 25, 41
DeGeneres, Ellen, 28, 180
De Palma, Brian, 49, 194
DeWitt, Rosemarie, 30, 239

INDEX | 267

Declaration of Independence, The, 220
Depp, Johnny, 50
Dilemma, The, 32, 106, 109-113, 134, 208, 213, 221, 254
Director's Cuts series, 18
Dirty Harry Callahan (character), 63
Disney, The Walt (company), 35, 39, 40, 67, 189
Domingo, Coleman, 234
Dormer, Natalie, 183, 184
Downey Jr., Robert, 173
Don't Look Up, 50
Dunkirk, 214
Duvall, Robert, 26, 177, 214

E.T.: The Extra Terrestrial, 50, 168, 169, 178
Eat My Dust!, 41, 42, 142, 253
Eastwood, Clint, 14, 50, 63, 64, 70, 161, 183, 246, 250, 257
Easy Rider, 40
Eckhart, Aaron, 29, 126, 200
Edgerton, Joel, 38, 84-88, 233
EDtv, 27, 53, 55, 59, 69, 72, 140, 173-175, 178-181, 214, 218, 223, 258
Ed Wood (1994 film), 223
Eight Days A Week – The Touring Years, 34, 47, 70, 72-75, 82, 101, 102, 159, 164, 209, 220, 254, 259, 260
Ehrenreich, Alden, 35, 93, 100, 133, 189, 190
Elfman, Danny, 194
Elfman, Jenna, 28, 55, 179
Empire of Light, (2022 film), 223
Essex, The, 51, 59, 101, 187, 188, 256

Fabelmans, The, 223
Facebook, 179, 220
Fairley, Michelle, 34, 188
Far and Away, 16, 25, 55-57, 69, 70, 82, 85, 98, 100, 104-106, 126, 127, 133, 142, 162, 173, 185, 186, 215, 218, 222
Farrell, Colin, 38, 84, 86, 87, 108, 134, 238, 255, 261
Fight Club, 122
Fincher, David, 14, 122, 223, 243
Flags of our Fathers, 70

Flashdance, 82
Florida, 139, 218
Following, 45
Fonzie, 14, 135
Ford, Harrison, 170
Formula 1, 57, 85, 143, 164, 22
Formula 3, 152, 183
Friedkin, William, 194
Frost/Nixon, 31, 54, 57, 77, 78, 89, 114, 121, 142-146, 164, 167, 168, 194, 213, 254, 256, 257, 260
Frost, David, 54, 78, 114, 143-145, 164, 261

Gandalf, 92, 214
Ganz, Lowell, 22-25, 27, 66, 69, 169, 222, 257
Geisel, Theodor Seuss, (see "Seuss, Dr.")
Gettysburg, 186
Giamatti, Paul, 30, 133, 143, 235, 237-239
Gibson, Mel, 27, 69, 91, 125, 142, 145, 159-162, 186, 204
Gilford, Jack, 23, 172
Gilstrap, Suzy, 22, 45, 89
Girl with the Dragon Tattoo, The (2005 book), 201
Gleeson, Brendan, 34, 187, 188
Glenn, Scott, 25, 191, 192
Glory, 186, 234
Go Pro, 221
Godfather, The, 49
Golden Globe(s), 23, 25, 27-31, 33, 37, 64
Gone Girl (2012 book), 201
Gone with the Wind, 186
Good Year, A, 124
Goodfellas, 178
Goodman, Abdul, 219
Grade, Lew, 134
Grand Theft Auto, 21, 39, 42-45, 54, 58, 67, 90, 102, 142, 159, 160, 174, 185, 193, 199, 253, 259
Gravity, 167
Gray, Beverly, 16, 40, 41, 79, 113, 175, 253, 255-259
Grazer, Brian, 22, 23, 25-38, 66, 69, 73, 98, 125, 169, 222, 257
Greengrass, Paul, 51, 175
Griffith, Andy, 250

Grinch (character), 99, 100, 123, 155
Grinch, The, (see "How the Grinch Stole Christmas")
Grumman Team, 228, 230, 232
Gucci, Mauizio, 63
Gung Ho, 17, 24, 53, 57, 70, 79-83, 88-90, 97, 109, 114, 120, 121, 130, 134, 138, 139, 185, 191, 193, 194, 217, 218, 254

Hallowell, Todd, 25-33, 125, 167
Hancock, John Lee, 223, 246
Hanley, Dan, 22-31, 125, 227, 228
Hanks, Tom, 23, 27, 30, 32, 35, 51, 52, 58-60, 67, 82, 101-104, 113, 130, 133, 169, 170, 174, 203-205, 207-211, 219, 224-227, 233, 254, 260
Hannah, Daryl, 23, 67, 100, 103, 104, 130, 133, 169, 170, 174
Happy Days, 14, 41, 43, 45, 46, 64, 135, 185, 219, 222, 253
Harris, Ed, 27, 29, 122, 216, 217, 227-229
Harris, Harry, 54, 85
Harrison, George, 34
Hawks, Howard, 49
Henson, Brian, 38, 223
Henson, Jane, 221
Henson, Jim, 38, 55, 134, 161, 164, 221, 222
Hemsworth, Chris, 33, 34, 60, 89, 101, 134, 144-147, 183, 188
Hereafter (2010 film), 63
Hesketh, Lord, 184
Hidden Life, A, 214
Hill, Mike, 22-31, 125, 227
Hillbilly Elegy (2016 book), 36, 140, 220
Hillbilly Elegy (2020 film), 15, 36, 53, 54, 56, 57, 100, 113, 138-142, 191, 195, 209, 214, 215, 220, 256
Hirshenson, Janet, 24-32, 125
Hitchcock, Alfred, 63, 190, 191
Hobbit, The, (films), 92, 214
Hook, 50
Horner, James, 23, 24, 27-29, 85, 91, 98, 99, 123, 125, 162, 194-198, 233, 258

Hopkins, Anthony, 28, 133
How the Grinch Stole Christmas (1957 book), 98, 101, 124
How the Grinch Stole Christmas (1966 animated short), 124, 158
How the Grinch Stole Christmas (2000 film), 28, 74, 81, 90, 98-100, 108, 114, 123, 133, 155-159, 161, 168, 215, 216, 241, 254-256, 259
Howard, Bryce Dallas, 160, 169, 222, 224, 246, 247, 259
Howard, Clint, 16, 21, 22, 27, 28, 40, 70, 167, 180, 220, 224, 253, 257-259
Howard, Jean Speegle, 171, 173, 224
Howard, Rance, 21, 22, 42, 70, 199, 211, 224
Hugo, 223
Hulce, Tom, 25, 115, 116, 130
Hunger Games, The (2008 book), 201
Hunt, James, 54, 143, 147-153
Hurley, Elizabeth, 28, 180

In the Heart of the Sea (2000 book), 33, 101, 256
In the Heart of the Sea (2015 film), 33, 51, 60, 65, 83, 84, 134, 140, 186-188, 209, 221
Indian (ethnicity), 113, 141
Indiana Jones, (film franchise), 91, 170
Inferno (2013 book), 35, 208
Inferno (2016 film), 17, 18, 35, 51, 53, 78, 101, 102, 191, 199, 202, 204, 207-209, 221, 254, 256, 259
Inglorious Basterds, 214
Instagram, 179
Interstellar, 50
Invictus (2009 film), 63
Irishman, The, 178
Irwin, Bill, 28, 108, 155, 159
Istanbul, 78

James, Kevin, 32, 109, 110, 112, 134
Jaws, 5, 49, 79, 168, 170
Jay Z, 71-73, 75, 220
Jersey Boys (2014 film), 63
Jenkins, Jane, 22, 24-32, 125

INDEX | 269

Jesus of Nazareth, 203-205, 209
Jim Henson: Idea Man, 18, 38, 55, 134, 161, 164, 220-225, 260
John the Apostle, 203
Jones, Felicity, 35, 191, 208, 209
Jones, Tommy Lee, 29, 125, 126, 128-131, 133, 200, 203, 233

Keaton, Michael, 22, 24, 26, 51, 53, 59, 67, 80-83, 89, 93, 94, 97, 98, 100, 109, 120, 130, 134-139, 176-178, 184, 191, 214, 224, 238
Kermit the Frog, 223
Kidman, Nicole, 26, 55, 56, 104-106, 127, 133
Kilmer, Val, 19, 24, 29, 91, 92, 238
King, Leslie, 21, 167
King, Rodney, 174-176
King, Stephen, 63
Kozak, Harley, 25, 116
Kranz, Gene, 228-232
Kubrick, Stanley, 51

L.A. Confidential, 89
L.A. Riots, 176
La Casa Pacifica, 147
La La Land, 106
Landau, Martin, 28, 59, 214
Langella, Frank, 31, 77, 89, 144-147, 261
Langdon, Robert, (character), 17, 71, 82, 102, 201, 205-208, 256, 259
Lara, Alexandra Maria, 33, 113, 145
Las Vegas, 43, 44, 102
Last Picture Show, The, 40
Last Ride, The, (1995 book), 199, 256
Last Waltz, The, 72
Lauda, Niki, 54, 143, 145, 147-153, 269
Lee, Spike, 14, 45, 46, 175, 250
Lennon, John, 34, 159, 209
Leone, Sergio, 194
Letters from Iwo Jima, 63, 70
Les Misérables (2012 film), 89
Lincoln (2012 film), 61
Lohan, Lindsay, 173
Lord of the Rings, The, (films), 91, 92, 214

Lord of the Rings, The, (books), 92, 214
Long, Shelley, 22, 114, 136-138
Los Angeles, 43, 139, 174, 176, 196
Love & Other Drugs, 178, 258
Lovely Bones, The, (2002 book), 201
Lovell, Jim, 26, 54, 113, 227, 228, 260, 261
Lucas, George, 24, 35, 91, 170, 189, 218, 253, 257, 259

Made in America, 32, 47, 70-75, 78, 140, 216-218, 254
Malick, Terrence, 14, 44, 49, 51, 188, 194, 195, 204, 213, 214
Mandel, Babaloo, 22-25, 27, 66, 69, 169, 222, 257, 259
Manhattan, 185, 218
Mank, 223
Mantle, Anthony Dod, 33, 34, 65, 221
Martin, George, 73
Martin, Steve, 25, 61, 69, 78, 110-112, 115, 116, 119, 120, 176, 177, 185, 217
Mary Magdalene, 203, 204
Mask, The, 98
McCartney, Paul, 34, 35, 73, 159
McConaughey, Matthew, 28, 53, 55, 59, 179, 180
McGill, Bruce, 30, 238, 262
McGregor, Ewan, 32, 90, 191, 205
McKay, Adam, 50
McKay, Christian, 33, 184
McKellen, Ian, 30, 191, 203
Mean Streets, 49, 178
Melville, Herman, 187
Memento, 50, 78, 122
Memphis, 73
Mendes, Sam, 70, 194, 223
Minority Report, 179
Miss Piggy, 222
Missouri, 218
Missing, The (2003 film), 29, 47, 55, 57, 70, 83, 84, 124-131, 133, 140, 159, 173, 175, 199, 203, 224, 233, 254, 256
Momsen, Taylor, 28, 99, 100, 124, 155, 159
Moranis, Rick, 25, 115, 116
Morricone, Ennio, 194

Mortensen, Viggo, 38, 84, 85, 87, 88, 134, 238, 255, 261
Mr. Smith Goes to Washington, 99, 255
Muren, Dennis, 92
Muppet Show, The, 134
Music Man, The, 39
My Dinner with Andre, 167

National Broadcasting Corporation (NBC), 45, 46, 79, 253, 254
NASA, 226
Nasar, Sylvia, 29, 216
Nash, Alicia, 234
Nash, John Forbes, 54, 89, 140, 164, 217
Native American, 127, 130, 196, 200
Nazi, 234
Neeson, Liam, 234
Nevada, 126, 185
New Mexico,
New York City, 67, 93, 103, 125, 169, 176, 218
New York Times, The, 89, 97
Newman, Randy, 25, 26, 120, 177, 195, 196
Newman, Thomas, 24, 30, 193, 194, 195
Nicholson, Jack, 41
Night Shift, 22, 24, 51, 52, 57, 66, 67, 78, 81, 100, 102, 114, 134-138, 191, 218, 232, 238
Nightcrawler, 78
Nixon, Richard M., 77, 78, 143-147, 213, 261
Nixon (1995 film), 77
Nobel Prize, 164, 223
Nolan, Christopher, 14, 45, 46, 50, 122, 190, 191, 214
Nomadland, 79

Ohio, 139, 141
Once Upon A Time...in Hollywood, 223
OnlyFans, 179
Oklahoma, 104-106, 185, 219, 258
Oklahoma Land Run of 1893, 106, 185, 186, 258
Opus Dei, 203
Oppenheimer, 50, 214
Other Guys, The, 50
Oscars (see "Academy Awards")

Oz, Frank, 38, 224, 225, 249

Panic of 1893, 185
Paper, The, 26, 55, 69, 72, 93, 97, 98, 109, 140, 173-178, 191, 195, 214-216
Parenthood, 16, 17, 24, 44, 57, 61, 69, 78, 110-120, 130, 139, 176, 177, 185, 195, 214, 217, 218, 220, 222
Pavarotti, Luciano, 36, 53, 55, 74, 75, 115, 254
Pavarotti, 15, 36, 47, 53, 55, 70, 72, 74, 75, 115, 254, 260
Paxton, Bill, 27, 53, 210, 225
Pearl Harbor, (2001 film), 50
Pearl Jam, 71
Pennsylvania, 80, 218
Perfect Days, 79
Philadelphia, 71, 74, 140, 220
Philbrick, Nathaniel, 33, 101, 255, 256
Pi, 45
Pinto, Freida, 37, 56, 113, 141, 142
Pirates of the Caribbean (franchise), 91
Plimpton, Martha, 25, 116
Pollack, Sydney, 50
Princess Bride, The, 90, 91

Quaid, Randy, 178, 194
Quinlan, Kathleen, 27, 113, 114, 226, 227

R2-D2, 134
Ransom, 27, 44, 47, 69, 90, 98, 125, 142, 145, 159-163, 173, 174, 186, 191, 204, 208, 218, 222, 224, 257
Rebuilding Paradise, 36, 57, 78, 163, 164, 168, 173, 175, 186, 195, 209, 224, 254
Reeves, Keanu, 25, 116
Reiner, Rob, 28, 179-181
Reservoir Dogs, 44
Revolutionary Road (2008 film), 70
Riley, Charlotte, 34, 101
Robards, Jason, 25, 26, 115, 116, 214
Robin Hood: Prices of Thieves, 90
Rockefeller Center, 103
Rockwell, Sam, 31, 143
Rocky IV, 82
Rogers, Mimi, 24, 114, 139, 184

INDEX | 271

Rotten Tomatoes, 50, 260
Rush, 33, 53, 57, 58, 65, 82, 85, 89,
    100, 103, 113, 120, 142-
    153, 164, 183-185, 201,
    207, 221, 259, 260
Russell, Kurt, 25, 133, 192
Russo, Rene, 27, 160, 161
Rustin, 234
Rustin, Byron, 234
Ryder, Winona, 32, 109, 110, 112

San Francisco, 73, 179
San Fernando Valley, 174
Saving Mr. Banks, 223
Schaaf, Ernie, 238
Schindler's List, 234
Schindler, Oskar, 234
Scott, Ridley, 14, 124, 250
Scorsese, Martin, 16, 41, 49, 72, 124,
    178, 183, 204, 223, 248
sex, lies, and videotape, 45
Sesame Street, 164, 223, 224
Seuss, Dr., 28, 101, 158
Shatner, William, 41
Shaw, Helen, 25, 116-119
Shaw, Col. Robert Gould, 234
She's Gotta Have It, 45
Sheen, Michael, 31, 54, 78, 143-147
Shine A Light, 72
Shutter Island, 217
Shyamalan, M. Night, 14, 190, 191
Sinise, Gary, 27, 90, 142, 160, 186,
    191, 208, 226, 228, 260,
    261
Sixth Sense, The, 122
Skyward, 21, 45, 46, 79, 89, 101,
    102, 114, 142
Smith, Charles Martin, 21, 167
Smith Family, The, 39
Snyder, Zack, 51
Solo, Han (character), 56, 189, 190
Solo: A Star Wars Story, 15, 35, 44,
    53, 54, 56, 59, 93, 100,
    133, 159, 186-191, 209,
    259
Soloist, The, 217
Spielberg, Steven, 5, 14, 16, 44, 49,
    50, 124, 168-170, 172,
    178, 183, 218, 221-223,
    257
Splash, 23, 52, 54, 59, 60, 66-68, 70,
    79-81, 100, 102-104, 130,
    133, 134, 168-170, 172,

174, 185, 195, 213, 217,
218, 224, 254, 257
St. Louis, 218
Stanton, Rick, 54, 85, 255, 261
Stapleton, Maureen, 23, 114, 171
Star Wars (franchise), 15, 35, 56, 91,
    170, 186-191, 209, 214, 259
*Star Wars Episode V: The Empire
    Strikes Back*, 190
Starr, Ringo, 34, 73, 74
Steenburgen, Mary, 25, 110-112,
    116, 119, 120, 185
Stewart, Jimmy, 99
Sting, The, 79
Stone, Oliver, 77, 218, 249
Sugarland Express, The, 44, 170
Sunset Boulevard, (1950 film), 223
Sutherland, Donald, 192

Tambor, Jeffrey, 28, 90, 99, 100,
    155, 159, 216
Tampa Bay, 52, 218
Tarantino, Quentin, 14, 44, 188, 214,
    223
Tandy, Jessica, 23, 52, 171
Tautou, Audrey, 30, 93, 101, 159,
    203, 207
Taxi Driver, 49
Taylor, Lili, 27, 160, 208
Terminal, The, 58
Thin Red Line, The, 214
Thirteen Lives, 37, 51, 54, 83-90,
    108, 134, 175, 209-211,
    221, 226, 233, 236, 238,
    255, 259-261
Through the Magic Pyramid, 22, 45,
    46, 199, 259
Time Crystal, The, (see "*Through the
    Magic Pyramid*")
Titanic, 186
Titanic, (1997 film), 186, 197
Tham Luang, 209, 210
Tolkien, J.R.R., 91
Tom & Jerry, 134
Tomei, Marisa,
Top Gun, 82
Tora! Tora! Tora!, 61
Totino, Salvatore, 29-33, 35, 70, 71,
    126, 127, 236, 254
Touchstone Pictures, 23, 27, 67
Truman Show, The, 179, 180
Tut and Tuttle, (see, "*Through the
    Magic Pyramid*")

Twitch, 179
Twilight, (book), 201

Unhinged, 89
Utah, 126

Vance, J.D., 36, 37, 54, 141, 192, 209, 222, 256
Vance, Usha, 141
Vaughn, Vince, 32, 109-112, 134
Verdon, Gwen, 23, 171
Vice, 50
Volanthen, John, 54, 87, 255, 261

Wahlberg, Donnie, 27, 160
Walker, Benjamin, 34, 60, 134, 188
Waller-Bridge, Phoebe, 35, 189, 190
Walsh, T.J., 25, 192
War of the Worlds, (2005 film), 50
Watanabe, Gedde, 24, 80-82, 130, 134, 139
Waters, John, 213, 249
We Feed People, 37, 54, 55, 57, 78, 115, 163-165, 185, 232, 260
West, Kanye, 33, 220
Weinstein, Harvey, 140
Welcome to Marwen, 124
Wells, Orson, 224, 259
What's Up Doc?, 43

Where the Crawdads Sing (book), 201
Whishaw, Ben, 34, 187
Whoville, 74, 99, 100, 108, 155, 168
Wiest, Dianne, 25, 116
Wild Country, The, (1970 film), 39
Wilde, Olivia, 33, 145
Wilder, Billy, 223
Williams, John, 26, 85, 127, 185
Willow, 17, 19, 24, 69, 90-93, 100, 220, 238, 255
Winkler, Henry, 22, 51, 66, 67, 78, 114, 135-138, 232, 249
Wood, Evan Rachel, 29, 83, 126-128
World Central Kitchen, 163-165, 232
World Health Organization, (WHO), 208
Wrestler, The, 70
Wuhan Coronavirus, 208

Yale University, 100, 141
Yoda, 214
YouTube, 46, 179, 253, 254, 256-259

Zanuck, Richard D., 23, 79, 170
Zellweger, Renée, 30, 52, 105, 107, 108, 115, 200, 236, 239
Zemeckis, Robert, 124
Zimmer, Hans, 25, 30-33, 35-37, 194-196
Zurer, Ayelet, 32, 207

ABOUT THE AUTHOR

Michael Jolls has directed and/or produced over a hundred various projects with credits including *6 Rules* (2011); *Cathedral of the North Shore* (2013); *The Great Chicago Filmmaker* (2015); the *#SelfieGuy* series (2015-2017); *Sell Me This Pen* (2018); *A Sad State of Affairs* (2020); *The Marian Stained Glass Windows* miniseries (2022); and *Holy Ground* (2023). Jolls also worked on the *Uncle Colt & Cletus* series (2012-2014) and was featured in the *War Movie* miniseries (2023).

Jolls is the author of *The Films of Steven Spielberg* (2018) and *Make Hollywood Great Again: Cinema in the Era of President Trump* (2020), as well as co-author of the book, *Rev. William Netstraeter: A Life in Three Parts* (2019) with his brother, Daniel. He also worked as assistant editor on *David Fincher: Interviews* (2014) by Dr. Laurence Knapp for the University Press of Mississippi's *Conversations with Filmmakers* series.

www.ingramcontent.com/pod-product-compliance
Lightning Source LLC
Chambersburg PA
CBHW020633220526
45464CB00001B/127